OXFORD CLASSICAL MONOGRAPHS

*Published under the supervision of a Committee of the Faculty of
Classics in the University of Oxford*

The aim of the Oxford Classical Monograph series (which replaces the Oxford Classical and Philosophical Monographs) is to publish books based on the best theses on Greek and Latin literature, ancient history, and ancient philosophy examined by the Faculty Board of Classics.

Plato's *Symposium*: The Ethics of Desire

FRISBEE C. C. SHEFFIELD

OXFORD
UNIVERSITY PRESS

For my parents, David and Victoria

Acknowledgements

It gives me great pleasure to recall some of my intellectual debts. I would like to thank Christopher Rowe for a wonderful introduction to Plato. Thomas Johansen encouraged my interests from the start, and his support has been invaluable.

The book has its origins in a D.Phil. thesis completed in Oxford, and I wish to thank Catherine Atherton, Dominic Scott, and David Wiggins for supervising various stages of the thesis, and M. M. McCabe and Lesley Brown for an extremely helpful examiners' report. I would also like to thank the then Humanities Research Board of the British Academy for their financial assistance during this time. Most of the book was written while I was a Research Fellow at Girton College, Cambridge. I am extremely grateful to the College, and to Dorothy Thompson in particular, for providing such a supportive and stimulating environment in which to complete this research. During this time I have also benefited enormously from the Cambridge Faculty of Classics and wish to thank Nick Denyer, Malcom Schofield, David Sedley, and Robert Wardy in particular for their support and advice at various stages of my research.

I have tried out numerous ideas at various institutions and seminars and would like to thank Robert Adams, Tad Brennan and Gabriel Richardson Lear for discussions whilst at Yale in 2003, and the graduate students who attended my seminar on the *Symposium* there. Scott LaBarge provided helpful comments on material for Chapter 5 at the Arizona Colloquium on Plato's Ethics in 2003. Alexander Nehamas has been very generous with his time and insights on visits to Princeton, as have James Lesher and William Prior, who read the entire manuscript. Dominic Scott has been a wonderful sparring partner and support throughout the writing of this book. And I am extremely grateful to Myles Burnyeat, who has overseen the transformation of the thesis into a book and provided useful advice and inspiration along the way.

I would also like to thank Diskin Clay for an inspired introduction to Leonardo da Vinci's *Ginevra de Benci* at the National Gallery in Washington, the back panel of which forms the cover of this book. I am also very grateful to Oxford University Press, particularly Enid Barker and Kathleen McLaughlin, for help with the production of this book.

I am also very grateful to Carolyn Brennan, Marina Grana and Alessandra Nerdrum for many enjoyable discussions of various issues in this book. Their insights about eros have informed this book and my life. I am particularly grateful to Arif Ahmed, from whom I am learning much about the nature of a loving and flourishing life, and whose support has encouraged the completion of this book. Finally, my family have given me a very real sense of the importance of loving relationships, and I am forever indebted to them for this, especially my parents, to whom this book is dedicated.

Chapter 4 draws on material previously published as 'Psychic Pregnancy and Platonic Epistemology', *Oxford Studies in Ancient Philosophy*, (ed.) David Sedley, 2001: 1–35, by permission of Oxford University Press. Chapter 6 draws on material previously published as 'Alcibiades' Speech: A Satyric Drama', *Greece and Rome*, October, vol. 48 n.2, 2001: 193–209, copyright 2001, The Classical Association, extracts reproduced with permission.

Contents

Introduction

In the *Symposium* Plato invites us to imagine the following scene: A pair of lovers are locked in an embrace and Hephaestus stands over them with his mending tools asking: 'What is it that you human beings really want from each other?' The lovers are puzzled, and he asks them again: 'Is this your heart's desire, for the two of you to become parts of the same whole, and never to separate, day or night? If that is your desire, I'd like to weld you together and join you into something whole, so that the two of you are made into one. Look at your love and see if this is what you desire: wouldn't this be all that you want?' No one, apparently, would think that mere sex is the reason each lover takes such deep joy in being with the other. The soul of each lover apparently longs for something else, but cannot say what it is. The beloved holds out the promise of something beyond itself, but that something lovers are unable to name.[1]

Hephaestus' question is a pressing one. What is it that the perception of a beloved person or thing arouses? Why do we love whatever or whomever we love? What is it that we *really* want? According to the above account of desire (given by the character Aristophanes), the copulating lovers would welcome Hephaestus' offer. They would think they had found what they wanted: to fuse with their beloved, so that one emerged from two. According to this story, this is because we used to be complete wholes, but were torn apart by the gods; love is the name for our pursuit of this original state of unity. Socrates will disagree with Aristophanes' answer to this question. A lover does not seek the half or the whole, the philosopher explains, unless it turns

---

[1] Adapted from the Nehamas and Woodruff (1989) translation of 192d–e.

out to be good. After all, people are willing to cut off their own arms
and legs if they are diseased. It is only by the possession of good
things that we are made happy and we all want *that*. But as Socrates
explains elsewhere, although we all desire the good things that will
make us happy, we are as perplexed as the copulating lovers in the
story when it comes to specifying what this good is (cf. *Republic*
505d11 with *Symp.* 192c5). Plato was clearly struck by the idea that
the real aim of our desires is unknown to us—that we do not know
what we *really* want—and the *Symposium* is an attempt—or rather, a
series of attempts—to answer that question.

One might be surprised that a rationalist philosopher such as Plato
was interested in the nature of *erōs*. And it is, specifically, erotic love,
or better, passionate desire (*erōs*), that interests him in the *Symposium*.[2] One might think that Aristophanes was onto something when
he had the copulating lovers perplexed at Hephaestus' questions
regarding the grounds, and the aim, of their *erōs*. One might think
that *erōs* is inexplicable, that it does not involve reasons. If so, then
one might also think that *erōs* cannot be the subject of philosophical
analysis at all. In our post-Freudian climate we typically view the
relationship between our desires and reason with suspicion. So what
characterization of desire did Plato operate with in the *Symposium*
such that he not only attempted to analyse human desire, but
characterized philosophy as the highest form of it? Further, even if
one thinks that desire does involve reasons and that one could, in
principle, answer the question Hephaestus poses, why would the
nature of desire be of concern to a philosopher? And why are erotic

---

[2] The Greeks of Plato's day categorized different kinds of love: *erōs* quite commonly referred to erotic love, wheareas *philia* was most commonly used for the love
for friends or family. There is some degree of slippage between the two terms. As
Dover (1978) 43 and 49 notes, although *erōs* and its cognates frequently denote sexual
activity, *philia* can refer to sexual activity where the context is a loving and affectionate one, as opposed to a purely sexual encounter which would call for the use of
erōs. Ludwig (2002), 8 warns against the dangers of sexual reductionism in our
construal of *erōs*. He argues persuasively that it referred to intense desire (whether
bodily or spiritual) and has a wider semantic range than the purely sexual. Eros, he
argues, 'occurs in cases in which the desire, whether sexual or not, becomes obses-
sional and the subject of desire becomes willing to devote nearly all his or her life,
time, or resources to achieving the goal'. See Ludwig (2002) 13. It will be useful to
bear this in mind when considering the range of things considered as objects of *erōs* in
this text.

relationships celebrated as a potentially positive vehicle for education? This is an idea which is, at the very least, surprising and often downright shocking to us today.

The purpose of this study will be to address these questions and in a way, it is hoped, that will remove certain obstacles that have hindered appreciation of this text as a substantive work in Platonic ethics. For in some respects the *Symposium* has been seen as anomalous. It is not just that the dialogue is concerned with personal desire, a topic that does not typically receive much attention from modern philosophers, but it is set at a dinner party (not an obviously philosophical setting), and there are so few arguments and so many extended and literary speeches.[3] These features are often used to promote the study of this text most widely in literature departments and a recent edition of the text boasts that 'this is the most literary of all Plato's works and one that students of classics are likely to want to read whether or not they are studying Plato's philosophy'.[4] Even those scholars who have read the *Symposium* together with the *Phaedo* and the *Republic* as hallmarks of Platonism have had difficulties in avoiding a highly selective approach to the text. Although both its topic and its form may be surprising to us, this study argues that these features are intimately related to standard Platonic preoccupations: with the nature of the good life, with virtue and with how it is acquired and transmitted. If so, then the *Symposium* deserves to be taken more seriously by those interested in Plato's philosophy.[5]

This study argues that the apparently anomalous features of the *Symposium* are insufficient grounds for marginalizing this text in debates about ancient ethics. First, for Plato, as we shall see, our desires embody our values and beliefs about what is worth having or

[3] See Taylor (1926) 209, Stokes (1986) 115, Frede (1993) 399–400, Rowe (1998*a*) 239, and Wardy (2002) 1–2 on the particular challenges posed by the form of the *Symposium*.

[4] Dover (1980), who argues that there is 'so much unjustified and implausible assertion and so little rigorous argument' in the work, see Dover (1980) 6.

[5] The *Symposium* has just begun to receive more systematic philosophical attention from the work of Price (1989), Kahn (1996), and Rowe (1998*a*, *b*), for example. But there is still relatively little material on 'the structure and purpose of the dialogue as a whole' (Rowe 1996*b*) 239), and considerable debate about whether the philosophical material is located throughout the dialogue or just in Socrates' speech. If the latter, then how are we to read the work as a whole? For a recent and novel treatment of these issues, see Wardy (2002).

doing. Insofar as they do so they are an important part of our ethical lives. What and whom one desires determine the choices that one makes and the kind of person one turns out to be. Our desires shape our lives in important respects and affect our chances of happiness. Analysing our desires, then, is a way of reflecting on the kind of people that we will become and on our chances for living a worth-while and happy life. This kind of reflection is ethical reflection about which it is quite natural for a philosopher to be concerned. If one is concerned to change people's lives for the better, then one way to do that is by encouraging them to reflect upon their desires and to consider the kinds of things it would be good for them to value and desire. This, of course, assumes that desires are the sorts of things that are amenable to such reflection and redirection, and we shall be examining why Plato held such a view, and in what direction he thought our desires could best be shaped. First and foremost, then, this book will be concerned with Plato's ethics of desire.

Second, both the *Symposium* and the *Republic* suggest that Plato thought that our desires are, in large part, shaped by our culture and education and develop in specific cultural contexts. Two important contexts for the development of male desire, in particular, were the sorts of pederastic erotic relationships with which all the speakers in this work are concerned, and the institution of the Greek symposium in which such relationships typically took place.[6] Symposia were not just the place for the satisfaction of every desire—for food, drink, sex, beautiful sights and sounds, and the cultural riches provided in the after-dinner entertainment—but also a place where the men and young boys who were traditionally present would learn how to regulate their desires in the appropriate manner.[7] The heady mix of

[6] By pederastic relationships I am referring to the kind of relationship in which an elder male *erastēs* sought sexual favours from a younger male *erōmenos* (typically a youth on the verge of manhood) in return for providing social, political, and moral training. Such relationships were not uncommon among members of the Athenian elite during the 5th and 4th cent. For further reading on this topic see the references in n. 10 below. Symposia were dinner parties for aristocratic circles, established in Greek society from around the 7th cent. See O. Murray (1990*a*) 3–11. See Aristophanes, *Wasps* 1208–17 for the characterization of symposia as an aristocratic activity.

[7] Symposia were a forum for the display not only of material wealth (for which, see Vickers (1990) 106–7 and Boardman (1990) 126, but also of cultural wealth and prestige (on which see Burnyeat (1999) 13–15 and Calame (1999) 93–101).

drink, beautiful young boys, flute girls and music was seen as a productive testing ground for the development of virtue, since it aroused the very desires that could threaten the social order and provided an appropriate context for their regulation.[8] In Greek literature *erōs* was, at best, perceived as an ambiguous force which could bring blessings if properly regulated and controlled.[9] The symposium and pederasty appear to have been two regulative institutions which met a need to control *erōs* and ensure that it could lead to positive social benefits.[10] At best, in his association with an older man the younger partner would receive a fitting education. The educative dimension to the symposium was an important feature of the after-dinner entertainment. Lover and beloved would recline together on the same couch, with the lover singing *skolia*, or reciting poems to his beloved. There was an educative dimension to these practices insofar as the young boys who were traditionally present would learn of the great deeds of their predecessors and be inspired to emulate them, and the older male educators, who would recite such poetry and speeches, would reinforce those values for themselves. The symposium was a place where one learnt how to value and desire the right sorts of things and in the appropriate manner. It was a place where virtue was supposedly reinforced and passed on to the young, a place where men were both displayed and made.[11]

---

[8] In the *Laws* 1 and 2 Plato explores the symposium as a forum for the development of virtue in much the same way as the battlefield was an appropriate testing ground for the development of courage. For a discussion of this text, see Tecusan (1990) 238–63.

[9] On the ambiguous nature of *erōs*, see Thornton (1997) and Calame (1999). On the ambiguous nature of *erōs* in Plato, see *Rep.* 3. 403 compared to 9. 572e, 573a–b, *Phdr.* 266a.

[10] On the symposium as a forum for the regulation of *erōs*, see Pellizer (1990) 178–80, and Tecusan (1990) 238–63. That pederasty was an important social institution in Classical Athens is now a commonplace of Classical scholarship; cf. Dover (1978); Foucault (1985); Calame (1999) 89–110.

[11] On the educative function of the symposium, see Bremmer (1990) 135–49; Calame (1999) 93–101; Burnyeat (1999) 13–15; Wohl (1999) 376. The evidence for the presence of young boys beyond the Archaic period and into the Classical period is not decisive, but the educative dimension to the symposium remained important. That Plato was aware of the educational power of the symposium can be seen from the way in which Socrates introduces the topic of poetry in the *Republic* after he has introduced symposia; see Burnyeat (1999) 13.

All the speakers at Agathon's symposium can be seen as drawing on such practices by praising the benefits that an erotic relationship of this sort could bring: whether it is the fostering of heroic virtue on the battlefield, as it is in Phaedrus' speech, or cultivating the virtues of the politicians (however ironically that is intended) in Aristophanes' speech, or acquiring wisdom for Pausanias' ideal lovers. Much sympotic literature, prior to Plato's *Symposium*, was concerned to reflect upon the practices of the symposium by exhorting their listeners to drink in moderation, love in the right manner, and praise and thereby desire the right sorts of things.[12] So both the setting of this dialogue at a symposium, and the focus on the erotic relationships that typically took place at such an event, is a natural way in which to explore the ethics of desire in such a culture, since the context itself was one which attempted to make *erōs* work towards certain cultural norms.

Third, the kind of praise speeches (encomia) that occupy Plato's *Symposium* were an important way in which young people were educated and virtue was transmitted and so, too, not a peculiar medium for a philosopher concerned with the nature and transmission of virtue. The encomium was an exercise of epideictic oratory, designed, in part, to present the speaker as someone in possession of socially valuable knowledge, who could provide uplifting examples for the listeners and encourage them to adopt the practices and behaviour praised.[13] To praise something is to say in what respects

---

[12] A good examples is Xenophanes (fr. 1, trans. Gerber), who exhorts symposiasts to 'Praise the man who, when he has taken drink, brings noble deeds to light, in order that there may be memory and a striving for virtue'. Cf. Hunter (2004) 6, who argues that 'from an early date the literature of the symposium frequently involves a meta-discourse upon the conduct of the symposium itself; the overriding interest in their own procedures which characterises many members of modern clubs and societies found an ancient counterpart in sympotic reflections upon symposia, and Plato's *Symposium* is to be seen within an evolving fourth century tradition of prose *sympotika*, which look back to the sympotic poetry of the archaic period'. Cf. Xenophon's *Symposium*, Plato's *Protagoras* 347c–e and *Laws* 1 and 2 with Tecusan (1990) 238–63.

[13] Thus Aristotle writes: 'To praise a man is in one respect akin to urging a course of action. The suggestions which would be made in the latter case become encomia when differently expressed ... Consequently, whenever you want to praise anyone, think what you would urge people to do; and when you want to urge the doing of anything, think what you would praise a man for having done.' *Rhetoric* 1. 1367[b]36–1368[a]8; trans. W. Rhys Roberts.

the thing praised is *kalon*, beautiful or fine, and, on that basis, desirable and worth pursuing. There is an intimate relationship between the praiseworthy, the beautiful, and the excellent life advocated, for example, by one's elder lover in a sympotic context.[14] The praise speech was an important way in which desires were moulded in particular ways. Now, if one is concerned to improve people's lives by encouraging reflection upon their desires and consideration of the kinds of things it would be good for them to value and desire, then a good way to do so will be by examining the sorts of things one should praise as *kalon* and thereby advocate as objects of desire. For if education is concerned to produce good and flourishing individuals, then one way to ensure that result is to encourage the appreciation of those things that are truly valuable and worth pursuing in the context of a human life, an appreciation which was typically fostered by the encomium.

In both its form and its content, then, the *Symposium* is intimately related to Plato's larger ethical concerns with the nature of the good life. Erotic relationships, of the sort that all the speakers are concerned with, and which typically took place at symposia, were an important way in which virtue was transmitted. In this study the examination of the accounts of different erotic relationships, then, will be at the same time an examination of the different accounts of education and virtue. Seen in this light, the *Symposium* is thematically related to the *Protagoras*, the *Meno*, and the *Republic*, and it belongs amongst the canon of dialogues concerned with moral education. The *Symposium* offers us a distinctive take on moral education—one where *erōs*, although an incidental theme in such dialogues, is now central. But this should not blind us to the presence of much familiar territory. In those dialogues the discussions of education, the nature of virtue, epistemology, and moral psychology are interconnected themes. We might, then, expect the same from the *Symposium* and this study is an attempt to show that it delivers.

[14] For which see Nightingale (1993) 114 with (1995) 103–4; cf. Kennedy (1963) 167–73; Cole (1991) 71–94.

1

Erōs and the Good Life

1. LEARNING FROM LOVERS

The *Symposium* is itself presented as an act of *erōs*. The dialogue opens with a group of Socratic devotees whose affection for Socrates has led them to remember and pass down the narrative we are about to hear. It begins with Apollodorus, an intimate companion of Socrates, claiming, in response to a request by an anonymous friend, that he is not unrehearsed in narrating the speeches at Agathon's symposium. This conversation recalls another between Apollodorus and Glaucon, which took place two days before. Glaucon had already been given a report of this banquet by another person who heard it, in turn, from Phoenix, and that account was unclear (172b4–5). He wants to hear the account again, this time from Apollodorus, because Apollodorus is a devoted friend and follower of Socrates, one whom Glaucon accordingly expects to have been present (172b5 ff.). Apollodorus is surprised at Glaucon's supposition that the event was a recent one (172c1): in fact, the party at Agathon's took place a long time ago, when Apollodorus was just a boy. Agathon has since been out of town for many years, and Apollodorus has only been a follower of Socrates for three years (172c6). As it turns out, Apollodorus heard the account from Aristodemus, another lover and follower of Socrates, who was himself present at the party (173b22–3). Apollodorus assures Glaucon that he did check some of the details with Socrates himself (173b5). Glaucon, evidently impressed with Apollodorus' Boswellian devotion, urges Apollodorus to relate the account as they walk into town (b7). The result of this conversation, so Apollodorus proudly repeats to the anonymous friends (henceforth Anon.), is that he is 'not unrehearsed'. The convolutions of the prologue highlight the fact that Apollodorus and others have ensured that this account has been preserved over a long period of time because, as devoted followers and friends of Socrates, they have made it their business to be attentive to Socrates' words and deeds (172c4–6). This chain of reception of which we are now a part is inspired by *erōs*. And Socrates makes his first appearance in this dialogue as an object of that *erōs*, a man whose appearance of happiness has inspired a slew of followers eager for the same benefits (cf. 173d6).[1]

Loving Socrates has inspired both Aristodemus and Apollodorus towards an appreciation of the philosophical life, to which they are recent converts (172c6). Apollodorus begins to explain the connection between the two:

Apoll. In fact, quite apart from thinking I benefit from it, I myself get an amazing amount of pleasure from any talking I do, or hear others doing, about philosophy; other sorts of talking, especially your rich businessmen's talk, bores me and I pity you who are my friends because you think you are achieving something when you're achieving nothing. Maybe you in your turn think I am in a wretched state, and I think what you think is true; however, I don't just think you are, I *know* you are.

Anon. You're always the same Apollodorus, you're always insulting yourself and everyone else. You seem to me to suppose that simply everyone is in a miserable state except Socrates, starting with yourself. Where on earth you got that nickname of yours—'Softy'—I've no idea; when you talk you're always as you are now, savaging yourself and everybody else except Socrates (173c3–d10).[2]

---

[1] Halperin (1992) 93–129 describes this as 'the erotics of narrativity'. Cf. Henderson (2000) 288. Seeing the prologue as a chain of reception inspired by *erōs* helps to explain the predominance of indirect discourse in the text. Prior to Halperin's article much of the debate over the significance of the prologue's recycled narrative centred on the question of the dialogue's historicity. Bury (1932) xvii–xix argued that Apollodorus' verification of the account suggests a degree of historical truth, whilst the inadequacy of Phoinix's account may be a way of discrediting a rival and distorted account of the original occasion (perhaps an account by Polycrates). But as Rowe (1998*a*) 142 has argued, this assumes the dialogue's historicity from the outset. Moreover, as the narrative unfolds, a couple of blatant anachronisms (182b6–7, 193a2–3), and the mention of the army of lovers in Phaedrus' speech (178e–179b)—referring to events which took place after the dramatic date of the dialogue—make it very difficult to read this text as if it were concerned with historical veracity. On these anachronisms see Dover (1980) 10.

[2] Reading *malakos* 'softy', instead of *manikos* 'mad' at d7–8 with Rowe (1998*a*), who argues that this makes better sense of the surprise caused by his 'savaging

The contrast between the happiness of the philosopher, and the materially abundant, and yet somehow impoverished, life of those who do not value wisdom, is in effect a promissory note for the advocacy of the philosophical life in Socrates' speech. And it is this promise of genuine happiness that philosophy holds out to its devotees that is illustrated by the appeal of both Socrates and his characteristic conversations to all those who are eager to hear them. Socrates appears to Apollodorus to be living a worthwhile and happy life. As such his philosophical conversations are pursued with the hope that they will effect a similar transformation in those who practise them. This stands in contrast to the materialistic goals of Apollodorus' interlocutor; a valuation of wealth, he believes, will lead only to unhappiness.[3] Apollodorus pities such types for being unaware of their deficiency: they are satisfied that they are achieving something when, according to Apollodorus, they are achieving nothing. Apollodorus himself used to wander around in a similarly self-satisfied state (173a1–2), but having come upon Socrates he is now, at least, aware of his wretchedness and values philosophical conversation instead (cf. 173c3–4). Although he appears to his friend to be wretched (173d1), he refuses to admit that he knows that he is in a bad way, because he is confident that he is on the right path and will, eventually achieve happiness, as he thinks Socrates has (d6). By contrast, Apollodorus claims he knows the others to be in a bad way since, we infer, they are not even aware of their deficiency, and so do not practise the philosophical life (173d1–3). Apollodorus' harsh words to his anonymous friend urge him to reflect on the kind of person that he will turn out to be as a result of his desires—an unsatisfied and wretched one, apparently—and on his chances for living a worthwhile and happy life. What Apollodorus' own chances are remains to be seen.

The salient point for now is that the context for Apollodorus' conversion to a life of such promise is an attraction towards Socrates. It is Socrates who has made Apollodorus realize something that he lacks and strives to become, and it is through an association with him that Apollodorus has learnt to transform his desires in what he

everyone else except Socrates'. Unless otherwise indicated, all translations of the *Symposium* are from C. J. Rowe (1998a).

[3] The contrast with material riches is one that Socrates draws in the *Apology* in his description of the philosophical life (29d–e, 30a7–b4, 38a1–6).

perceives to be a more fruitful direction. Apollodorus' autobiograph-ical explanation for his practice of philosophical conversation high-lights the transformative potential of erotic relationships that will become a central feature of the dialogue. Socrates' appearance of happiness has aroused both an erotic attachment *and* educational benefits. These are intimately related: it is because Apollodorus perceives Socrates as an exponent of the happy life that he is drawn to him and encouraged to try to embody that value in his own life by adopting Socrates' characteristic philosophical lifestyle. Socrates has this effect on many others in the dialogue: Aristodemus and Alcibi-ades, in particular, as we shall see. These Socratic intimates also perceive something valuable about Socrates and this basis for their attraction makes them realize something they themselves lack and strive to achieve. The reason why we can learn from lovers, the prologue suggests, is that our attraction to them urges us toward something valuable that we desire to realize in our own lives— happiness, however that is construed—and in associating with them we hope to transform our lives in new and beneficial directions.

The positive benefits that such relationships can bring will be a central feature of all the speeches at Agathon's symposium. The sorts of relationships with which all the speakers are concerned were an important way in which desires were educated to ensure that *erōs* could lead to positive social benefits. As we shall see when we turn to the speeches themselves, in his association with an older man the younger partner was supposed to learn about the sorts of things that are worth pursuing (wisdom for Apollodorus), and the manner in which one should pursue them (by philosophical practice). An important context for associating with one's lover and receiving this sort of education was the symposium. The symposium was both a context for *erōs* and for education. And when Socrates enters the narration with 'one of his greatest lovers' (173b3–4), this is where he is leading him. By taking Aristodemus to this banquet, Socrates makes his first appearance in the dialogue as both a lover and educator.

Apollodorus recounts how the two men proceeded to the sympo-sium and in so doing invites us to reflect upon Socrates' role as lover and guide. Apparently, Socrates encouraged Aristodemus to come along to Agathon's symposium (since he was not officially invited,

174b1).[4] Aristodemus had expressed fears about going uninvited to the symposium, but then agreed to do 'whatever Socrates commands' (174b2) as long as he makes a defence on his behalf. Socrates says that they will deliberate together about what to say (174d2–3) and the two men started their journey. But Socrates stopped, wrapped in thought, and urged Aristodemus to go on ahead independently (174d4–e1). He left Aristodemus to approach the reputedly wise and beautiful Agathon alone, while he was left behind (174d6). Although Aristodemus seems to want to resign authority to Socrates—he wants to be guided there and provided with something to say on arrival (174d1)—Socrates resists. He will deliberate *together* with him en route, and guide him in the right direction, but at a certain point Aristodemus must go it alone. Socrates, it appears, may have encouraged Apollodorus and Aristodemus to revise their conceptions of happiness (*eudaimonia*) and to pursue the life of philosophy, but we are left to wonder just how far he will take them and in what capacity. If Aristodemus is attending this symposium with Socrates as part of his moral education, then we are invited to consider just what role his relationship with Socrates plays in achieving that end.[5]

On arrival at the symposium we are invited to reflect upon similar themes. The beautiful host Agathon flirtatiously invites Socrates to recline beside him so that he can enjoy the benefits of Socrates' wisdom. This request draws on the sympotic practice of the beloved reclining next to his lover and receiving his wisdom.[6] But Socrates rejects his advances as follows:

---

[4] The figure of the ἄκλητος seems to have been a commonplace in the description of feasts; see *Odyssey* 13. 430, 17. 382; Archilochus fr. 78 D; Xen. *Symp.* 1. 13; cf. Fehr (1990) 185–96.

[5] It may also be significant that both men present themselves very differently in their approach towards the beautiful and wise Agathon. Aristodemus is deficient and needy, concerned that a φαῦλος, as he puts it, should go uninvited to the feast of the σοφός (174c7). But Socrates appears as a lover of Agathon, dressed up beautifully so as to approach this beauty (174a9; cf. Alcibiades' jealousy at Socrates' attention to Agathon at 213c). This may be taken to provoke reflection upon the nature of a lover: How do we approach the objects of our attraction? As deficient and needy, like Aristodemus? Or beautiful, like Socrates? Cf. Lowenstam (1985). See Ch. 2 for a discussion of the nature of a lover.

[6] There will be various attempts to negotiate the seating plan in this dialogue. For example, both Alcibiades and Socrates wish to sit next to Agathon, the most beautiful man at the party and recently crowned σοφός. Cf. Henderson (2000) 299.

It would be a good thing, Agathon, if wisdom were the kind of thing that flowed from what is fuller into what is emptier in our case, if only we touch each other, like the water in cups which flows from the fuller into the emptier through the thread of wool (175d4–e2).

The mention of the wine cup (*kulix*) is particularly appropriate given its role at symposia, and roots this model of the transmission of knowledge in a sympotic context where lovers would transmit their wisdom to their chosen beloved as they pass the wine cup. Socrates, in effect, condemns the model in his response to Agathon. Wisdom is not to be transferred from the resourceful into the resourceless in this active–passive manner. How a love relationship is to foster and inculcate wisdom will be a central concern of Socrates' speech.[7]

The interaction between Socrates and his devotees introduces some of the dialogue's central themes. What we want out of our love relationships is ultimately the happiness that Apollodorus believes Socrates can provide. One is drawn to a lover of a particular sort because they embody something perceived to be of value and, in associating with them, one is inspired to engage in the sorts of pursuits that one believes will deliver happiness. To his followers, associating with Socrates has encouraged the pursuit of wisdom and leading the philosophical life somehow promises to deliver the happiness they seek. We shall need to know more about the connection between happiness and the desire for wisdom, and just how an association with a lover is supposed to lead to that end. For although the relationship between Socrates and his followers emphasizes the transformative potential of erotic relationships we are also invited to wonder whether, in fact, any of these men have been improved by Socrates and, if not, what went wrong. The self-conscious way in which Apollodorus and Aristodemus imitate Socrates in their style (173b2), self-deprecating habits (173d9), and devotion to philosophical conversation (173c2–6) raises questions about whether this is a productive way to learn from one's lovers. Should Apollodorus be making an 'ascent' to town to talk about Socrates and his peers? Should Aristodemus be following Socrates, 'as usual' (223d10) and

---

[7] See Luc Brisson (1999), who argues that Plato's *Symposium* is centrally concerned with criticizing the dominant model of education in his time.

adopting his habits of dress (173b2)? Will such practices provide the wisdom and happiness they seek? What is wrong with Agathon's approach to Socrates? If such men desire the wisdom and beauty they see in Socrates, and which promises to deliver *eudaimonia*, how do they go about getting it? How, if at all, can Socrates provide it? Exactly what role do our lovers play in a happy life?[8]

The beginning of the *Symposium* not only raises some of the central questions of the dialogue, but it focuses in particular on Socrates as a lover-cum-educator. In many dialogues where Plato is concerned with moral education, he is often just as concerned with Socrates as a teacher and a role model. The charge of his having corrupted the youth is never far from view, and many dialogues appear to defend Socrates from this charge. These are also key themes in this text and ones we shall return to more explicitly when we examine the description of Alcibiades' notorious relationship with Socrates. But the substance of this defence, and the answer to many of the above questions, is to be found in the accounts of *erōs* provided by the speakers at this symposium. Once we have an account of the nature and aims of *erōs*, and its role in a flourishing life, we will be in a better position to determine how an erotic relationship can lead to positive benefits and to assess Socratic *erōs*, in particular.

---

[8] For Apollodorus' 'ascent' from Phaleron to town, see 172a. For an informative discussion of road imagery in the *Symposium*, see Osborne (1994) 86–90. Halperin (1992) 93–129 argues that Apollodorus engages in the wrong sort of practice. Instead of engaging actively in philosophy, he simply repeats what others have said. Support for this might be drawn from the predominance of μελετάω in the prologue, a common rhetorical term for memorization (cf. *Phdr.* 228b). But one might object that Apollodorus does say that he takes pleasure in making λόγοι himself, or in hearing them (cf. 173c3–4). And it is not particularly unSocratic to remember philosophical λόγοι. In the *Timaeus* Socrates rehearses a *Republic*-style conversation (*Ti.* 17b–19b). Further, at least Apollodorus has the right desires and is devoted consistently to the philosophical life; he is 'always the same', says Glaucon (173d4). Compare Alcibiades, who is inconsistent in his attachment to the philosophical life, and does not take pleasure in philosophical discussion; he flees from Socrates and blocks up his ears (216a5–8). There are further reasons for suspecting that Apollodorus has a misguided conception of philosophical practice, however. As Nussbaum (1986) 168 argues: 'Socrates' pupils, inspired by personal love, tend not to follow his advice. Instead of ascending to an equal regard for all instances of value they, like Alcibiades, remain lovers of the particulars of personal history.' For further discussion of their misguided attachment to Socrates, see below, Ch. 6, s. 3.

2. THE SPEECHES OF PHAEDRUS, PAUSANIAS, ERYXIMACHUS, AND ARISTOPHANES

All the speakers at this symposium will be concerned with *erōs* as a guide towards the attainment of good things and happiness, and in so doing they begin to answer many of the questions posed by the prologue. For the expressed agenda of this symposium is to offer an encomium to *erōs* (personified as a god, Eros); in other words, it is to show that *erōs* is good and does good things.[9] There is a self-referential dimension to the exploration of the beneficial effects of *erōs* at a symposium since the context itself was one that attempted to make *erōs* work towards certain cultural norms. The framing question of this section will be to explore how, for each speaker, *erōs* performs this beneficial role. The speeches will be as much about presenting the speakers as the best candidates for the title of σοφός—a contest which will become explicit in the case of Agathon and Socrates (175e7–10)—as it will be about *erōs*.[10] The two are related. For if (at best) erotic relationships were typically educational relationships, designed to lead to the acquisition of virtue and happiness, then presenting oneself as knowledgeable about the benefits of *erōs* will inevitably involve presenting oneself as wise about virtue and how one should achieve it.[11]

---

[9] When Phaedrus requests that *erōs* form the topic of conversation he does so because it has not received proper praise (177b1). Eros was, of course, the subject of much poetry and prose, so the emphasis here must be on showing that *erōs* is a good thing and does good things, a task which would by no means be obvious to a contemporary readership. (see above, Introduction). Neither the ode to Eros (the god) in the *Antigone* (781–801), nor the ode in Euripides' *Hippolytus* (525–64) could be seen as praising Eros for his beneficial effects. This is the gap Phaedrus proposes to fill. The later *Rhetorica ad Alexandrum* describes the encomiastic procedure as follows (35): The speakers must praise the external blessings of the subject, for example, his wealth, beauty, and good birth. Then the subject's virtue proper must be discussed, which was traditionally divided into the traditional four Greek virtues. After praising the subject's ancestry, the speaker must turn to the achievements (ἔργα) of his subject. On this procedure, see Dover (1980) 12.

[10] For the competition between Socrates and Agathon, see Bacon (1959) 415–30.

[11] Or, as Socrates puts it later, a lover will discuss 'virtue, and the sorts of thing the good man must be concerned with, and the activities such a man should involve himself in' and so on (209c1–2).

Although Socrates' extended critique of their accounts will show that, from a certain perspective, there is something amiss in his predecessors' speeches, the various accounts of *erōs* nonetheless introduce certain central features of the role of *erōs* in moral education. Or so I shall argue. The participants are, after all, the καλοὶ κἀγαθοί of the day, representatives of a wide variety of Greek wisdom, and it is expected that they will say some interesting things about *erōs* and its role in the good life, and that their accounts will deliver reputable opinions on the topic, backed up by the authority of ancient tradition or current expertise.[12] But we shall also see that their speeches bring to light puzzles and inconsistencies that stand in need of resolution by the next speaker(s). Reading the speeches in this way will form part of an argument for the claim that the speeches have an important philosophical role in the dialogue, a claim to be substantiated later, when we come to examine the relationship between Socrates and his peers. The previous speeches contain some plausible and often insightful views that raise significant issues and questions, and in so doing the speeches serve as useful starting points for further inquiry.[13] This approach will have implications for our reading of the whole dialogue. If this is a plausible account of the role of the speeches, then they will form an integral part of an overall understanding of *erōs*. They will not, as is often supposed, be extraneous to a philosophical account. Let us see how they do so.

[12] Along with Bury (1932) lvii, I agree that there is little evidence for the view proposed by Sydenham and endorsed by Schleimacher and Ruckert that Plato is presenting historical people behind these speakers. They seem rather to be 'five intellectual types', as Bury puts it, that reflect the intellectual currents at work in the 5th and 4th cent. See also Rowe (1998*a*) 9. In other Platonic dialogues, some of those present are linked to famous wise men. Phaedrus is linked to Hippias in the *Protagoras* (315c) and to Lysias in the *Phaedrus* (228a). Pausanias is linked to Prodicus in the *Protagoras* (315d), Eryximachus' speech links him to Hippocrates, as we shall see; Aristophanes needs no introduction, and Agathon is linked to Gorgias (*Symp.* 198c). One might read the speeches not just as a loose collection of representative samples of Greek wisdom, but as displaying a temporal movement from the epic wisdom of Phaedrus' speech to the later rhetorical wisdom of Agathon.

[13] One might compare Aristotle's use of *endoxa* in these respects (for the description of *endoxa* in Aristotle see *Topics* 2, 100^{b}22 ff.; and for his use of *endoxa* see *Nicomachean Ethics* 1145^{b}1–2 with *Eudemian Ethics* 1.1, 1216^{b}26–35). For the differences between Plato's procedure here and Aristotle's endoxic method, see below (Ch. 7, s. 1).

Phaedrus' speech (178a6–180b8) is a literary collage packed with allusions to the great poets. He begins with Hesiod and follows encomiastic procedure in his celebration of the birth of Eros (178b4; *Theogony* 116–17, 120), and he continues with Acousilaus (178b8), Parmenides (178b9 ff.), and Homer (179b1). Although he is clearly concerned to display his knowledge of the great poets, an approach which lends itself more to bold statement than considered reflection, his speech is nonetheless a thought-provoking account of how *erōs* can lead to virtue.[14] His central claim is that there is no greater good than a lover, or a beloved, because *erōs* has the most power when it comes to the acquisition of virtue and happiness (178c3–d1; 179a8; 180b6–8). This power is apparently due to the fact that *erōs* can instil a feeling of shame at shameful things and a love of honour in the case of fine ones (178d1–2). Without this attraction towards the *kalon* and aversion to the shameful, he continues, it is impossible for any individual or city to perform good actions (178d3). And this sense of the *kalon* required for virtue, Phaedrus claims, is best cultivated through an erotic relationship. Indeed, an army of lovers would be invincible, for in the presence of one's lover or beloved one is ashamed to pursue anything shameful and aroused to the performance of noble deeds (179a5). As examples of this phenomenon he cites Achilles' heroic exploits on the battlefield and Alcestis' act of self-sacrifice for her husband (179b5–180a4). Such virtuous behaviour, he concludes, was motivated by *erōs*.

According to this account there is some connection between an erotic relationship, an appreciation of the *kalon*, and a striving for virtue. The idea that lovers somehow bring out the best in us is a promising suggestion, not only because this seems to be true (if they are worth being with at all), but also because this would go some way towards explaining the role of *erōs* in moral education. Phaedrus' claims are that in the presence of either lover or beloved one is inspired to pursue the *kalon*, and that this pursuit issues in virtuous actions. The relationship between a love relationship, *erōs* for beauty,

---

[14] An example of this unconsidered reflection is his citation of Parmenides to support the claim that Eros is the oldest god, which is followed by an assertion that 'because he is very old he is also the cause of very great goods for us as human beings' (178c1–3). He never explains the connection between Eros' age and his beneficial power.

and virtue, will be central in this dialogue and crucial to an exploration of the benefits of *erōs*. For if it is the case that *erōs* can instil a love of the *kalon*, and it is the case that this is necessary for virtue, then it will have been shown that *erōs* has positive potential. But we need to know *how* a love relationship can instil an appreciation of the *kalon* and what beautiful things lead to virtue, rather than, say, idle staring or sex. Is it the case that a lover or beloved is seen as beautiful in some way and that an appreciation of this beauty arouses us to pursue beauty more widely, for example, in the pursuit of fine actions? But why, one might ask, does the perception of beauty issue in the performance of noble deeds, rather than sex? According to Phaedrus such relationships foster a love of honour, and it is the realization of this aim in our erotic pursuits that motivates such action. But, again, we will want to know what this appreciation of the *kalon* involves such that it arouses this aim and why it is that *erōs* aims at honour, rather than sex or wisdom, for example. Surely our desires can manifest themselves in the pursuit of these goals, too. If so, then we need to know just what sort of *erōs* can lead to this end in particular, and why it does so.

Pausanias' speech (180c3–185c3) builds on Phaedrus' idea that *erōs* can lead to the acquisition of virtue (cf. 185b1–c1) and in so doing he begins to address some of the above. He begins by criticizing Phaedrus for ignoring an important distinction necessary for the praise of *erōs*: 'it is more correct to preface what one says by first saying what sort of *erōs* one should praise' (180d1). Pausanias says that he will remedy this error and 'indicate the *erōs* one should praise, and then praise him in a way worthy of the god' (d1–3). Eros, he explains, has a twofold nature; it is not all *erōs* that issues in the benefits Phaedrus claimed, but only *erōs* of the right sort. This is the heavenly as opposed to the vulgar *erōs*, which privileges the soul over the body. Attraction to a beautiful soul will be concerned to encourage the development of the soul and its characteristic virtues (184c3–4) rather than seeking the sort of physical expression found in 'vulgar *erōs*'. Perhaps rather surprisingly, then, Pausanias goes on to describe this relationship as an exchange of sexual gratification for wisdom: if he finds a lover of the right sort, a young boy should yield himself to an older man for the sake of an education (185b4–5). The benefit of *erōs* for the soul is that it is more stable than that of the body; the bloom of the body fades and desire based on this attraction is therefore bound to be inconstant (183e1–6). But love for the 'right sort of character', by contrast, can remain as an object of love for life, 'attached as [it] is to something permanent' (184a). So, if we want to find a fulfilling and secure match, and one that will issue in the benefits Phaedrus praised, we need to turn our attention towards the soul. This is the type of correct pederasty that is apparently encouraged by the laws of many city–states, which privileges those who make virtue their central concern (185c3).

Since lover and beloved aim at the production of virtue, *erōs* is, again, seen as important to moral education. But are we any clearer about how this works? Although Pausanias fails to clarify just what the connection is between *erōs* for the soul, virtue, and wisdom, we can perhaps extrapolate as follows. If Phaedrus is right that *erōs* can lead to the attainment of virtue, and that this has something to do with appreciating the *kalon*, then one must surely have a lover who can guide one towards the appreciation of the right sorts of beautiful things. For if one is concerned only with the beauty of the body, then it is unclear how that can lead to an appreciation of the sort of beauty required (somehow?) for virtue. Pausanias suggests that cultivating wisdom is intimately related to virtue (184d1–2) and goes on to claim that the best relationship occurs when the lover is able to help the man become wiser and better, and the young man is eager to be improved by his lover (184d–e). If virtue is intimately connected to wisdom (a relationship that remains to be clarified), then one can see why *erōs* must be focused on the areas responsible for its realization: the soul. *Erōs* of this sort, we may suppose, will not issue in idle staring or sex because *erōs* of this sort is attracted towards the beauty of soul and so, we might suppose, will encourage an appreciation of the beautiful psychic qualities that attracted one in the first instance. If we take it that there is an intimate connection between attraction towards the beauty of soul and virtue (as Pausanias' focus on the soul suggests), then perhaps it is the case that if a lover falls for a beautiful soul, then what he is really attracted to is the potential of that soul *for virtue*. If so, then perhaps the very act of someone loving us for some perceived psychic beauty will foster the development of those attractive features. And this would go some way towards explaining why a relationship of this sort can have such positive potential. For a lover will want to encourage the development of those beneficial qualities which attracted him in the first place, and a beloved will desire to be worthy of the love that attracts the lover and, consequently, to make himself (his soul?) as attractive as possible. A good relationship, we may agree, is often one in which your partner sees the best in you and in so doing encourages you to develop those good characteristics. If someone is attracted to us because of physical qualities, then that relationship is one that might encourage the development of those qualities (by going to the gym, for example). But if someone is attracted to our souls, then they might encourage the development of psychic qualities, intelligence and so on (by taking degrees and writing books). This is why, perhaps, lovers can be powerful forces for self-improvement. In order to be convinced of this we will need to know more about the relationship between attraction to the beauty of soul and the cultivation of wisdom, and just what role a relationship is supposed to play in the acquisition of this end. Is this end best served by a pattern of exchange between lover and beloved?[15] We shall need to read on.

The next speaker agrees with Phaedrus that the proper outcome of such a relationship is virtue (188d4–9), and with Pausanias that this requires education (187d3–4). Eryximachus begins by claiming that although 'Pausanias started well on his theme, [he] failed to finish it off satisfactorily'; his task, as he puts it, is 'to try to round off what has been said' (185e6–186a2). He begins from the duality of *erōs* noted by Pausanias and expands this distinction so that it applies not only to the human sphere, but in the universe at large (186a2–b2). The heavenly *erōs* Pausanias praised manifests itself by bringing together opposite tendencies and creating harmonious relations between them (187c2 ff.). In order to instil this harmony in the human soul we need a suitable education, and a good practitioner to serve as our lover (187d2–3). This is the sort of lover to which Pausanias referred, under the auspices of the heavenly muse (e1) and this lover is here identified with various forms of expertise. An expert lover is one with moderation and justice who embodies this harmony and

---

[15] Socrates' rejection of Agathon's advances at the start suggests that there is something wrong with this model (175d4–e2; cf. 219a1–3).

order. He has the greatest power, apparently, 'providing us with all happiness and enabling us to associate and be friends both with each other and with the gods' (188d8–9).[16]

Eryximachus, then, agrees with Phaedrus that the aim of *erōs* is virtue. And if Pausanias is right that it is only *erōs* for the soul that can produce this, and if (as Pausanias also claimed) the development of the soul's characteristic virtues requires wisdom, then the correct lover must have an expertise. According to Eryximachus it is even more important than Pausanias suggested that we have this science of *erōs*. According to his synoptic account of *erōs*, there are even larger ramifications to vulgar *erōs* than Pausanias envisaged. What is not so clear is why this expertise should be associated with the medical art (186c5–6), or music, prophecy, and astronomy (187c2–3), in particular. All of them apparently promote heavenly, harmonious, *erōs*. But the connection between the harmonious order promoted by these *technai* and the development of the virtues he mentions is not so clear (188d5). Is the suggestion that the virtues are, or require, a kind of harmony? And, if so, a harmony of what? Eryximachus claims that the proper realization of this *erōs* is 'moderation and justice, towards the good, both among us and among the gods... providing us with happiness and enabling us to associate and be friends both with one another and with the gods' (188d5–9). So *erōs* involves the promotion of a harmonious order between men and gods, and this somehow issues in, or is, *erōs*' characteristic virtue. If so, then the positive potential of *erōs* must be brought about by an expertise able to promote this harmony. Although Eryximachus explains that the medical art produces a harmonious effect on opposite powers in the body, we need an account of the sort of expertise

---

[16] Eryximachus describes the medical art, in particular, as concerned with the reconciliation of opposite powers, drawing on the Empedoclean harmony of opposites. See Bury (1932) xxix; Rowe (1998*a*) 148; Dover (1980) 113. However, the numerous cultural authorities Eryximachus draws on mark him out as an exponent of a wide range of technical knowledge (e.g. Heraclitus at 187a3–4 and the Hippocratic medical writers (for which, see Edelstein (1945)). Given the quite exceptional (and rather confusing) breadth of his discussion, one is tempted to speculate that Plato is presenting Eryximachus as a polymath in the style of Hippias, with whom he is associated in the *Protagoras* (315c–e). For Hippias as a polymath, see *Hip. Mi.* 363e ff., *Prt.* 315c, 318e.

that can achieve this in the area of the human soul. He suggests that musical education promotes correct *erōs* in the soul, but it is not clear what this expertise is here, nor how it achieves happiness and harmonious relations with the gods. Until we know what 'knowledge of *ta erōtika*' involves (188d2) we shall not know how to bring about the positive benefits the speakers thus far claim for *erōs*.

It is difficult not to read much of Aristophanes' speech as a parody of Eryximachus'.[17] (He has also been hiccuping throughout Eryximachus' speech, 185c7–8.) It locates itself, not surprisingly, as comic, true to the muse he invokes (189b6–7). Although his focus throughout is the Eryximachean notion of 'the healing power' of *erōs* (189d1, 193d5), this healing *erōs* is not discussed through appeals to experts, but in a fantastic tale of the origin of our sexual orientation.[18] Fantastic though it may be, however, Aristophanes' speech 'fills in', as he puts it, an important gap in the accounts thus far. In order to appreciate why *erōs* has such 'healing' and beneficial effects for human beings we need an account of human nature and its needs. Apparently human beings were originally whole, but they became too powerful, made an ascent to the divine, and were punished by being divided in two to lessen their strength (190b–e). Since our natural state is whole, we are forever seeking our other half to make us complete again. This is the cause of our desire to love one another (191d). When a person meets his other half they are struck by a sense of belonging to one another and desire never to be separated. No one, he explains, would think that mere sex is the reason each desires the other; the soul of each person longs for something else, but cannot say what it is (192d). This something that they long for is their own self—fully realized and complete in another. For the human race to find happiness, then, we must each find the partner naturally suited to us (193c5).[19]

---

[17] On which, see Bury (1932) xxx–1 and Dover (1980) 113.

[18] On the origins of the story see Dover (1966).

[19] Since Empedocles also discussed double beings (B57–62, 336–8 KR), it is likely that this part of his tale continues the parody of Eryximachus' favoured authorities. As Bury has noted, there was a Hippocratic treatise which offered a theory of the origin of the sexes. See περὶ διαίτης 28 ff. with Bury (1932) xxxii. But by offering his own fantastic version of the origin of the sexes, Aristophanes seems to be playing with the Hippocratic authorities Eryximachus employed in his speech.

According to this account, then, the power of *erōs* derives from its use to us as needy creatures. Human beings are incomplete and need to strive towards a state of self-realization and happiness. This state of fulfilment, it is claimed, does not consist in honour or virtue, but in the *oikeion*, what is akin to ourselves. And this is what is found in another. A state of unification with our other half is where our happiness resides. We desire what we lack and have not yet become and the erotic expertise discussed by Eryximachus must therefore involve the ability to discern what these deficiencies are—what it is that we are lacking—and how they should best be remedied by finding the appropriate partner.

The idea that we need first to clarify what our needs are and then to ascertain whether or not the objects of our attraction can meet them sounds intuitively plausible. What is not so compelling is the account of what this need boils down to and the manner in which another person can meet it. Why, as Socrates will ask him later, do we desire what is akin to ourselves when we are willing to amputate our own limbs if they are diseased (cf. 205d10–11)? Our attachment to our own selves is one that seems to be grounded in the recognition that there is something good about that self. If we discover that is not the case we seek medical or psychotherapeutic attention to rid ourselves of objectionable baggage. If so, then it cannot be the *oikeion* as such that attracts, but something else that we desire—*something good*. And if that is the case, then the correct erotician must be able to determine what this good is that we need and how we can best go about getting *that*. Further, if it is good things that will bring us happiness, how can fusion with another individual provide that? The romantic individualism of this account has led to immense popularity down the ages. The idea that there is another person out there who can make us complete and happy resonates with many of our modern conceptions of romantic love. But the account invites us to wonder whether we really want to be joined together with the objects of our love, never to leave them even for a moment, and to live and die in their arms, as Hephaestus promises? It would surely have to be an all-consuming and enduring passion to sustain that state. If what we lack and desire are the good things that we believe will make us happy—healthy limbs and peaceful souls, for example—then is this best served by constant unification with another person? What would their lives bring to ours, and ours to theirs in such a state? We tend to view such intense unification as a 'honeymoon *period*' because it is viewed as a state which is not sustainable—alone—for human happiness. We might think it preferable to lead a life with another, but not solely in and through that other. Seeing other persons as the repository of all that can make us happy is, perhaps, a heavy burden for any individual to carry. But if we reject the comedian's reductio of our erotic myopia, then what exactly is the role of individuals in the pursuit of the good and happy life?

3. INTERMISSION (193D6–194E3)

After Aristophanes' speech, we are told of some flirtatious banter between Socrates and Agathon. This puzzling exchange can be read as a reflection upon some of the themes that have arisen so far. Socrates claims that he is afraid to deliver his speech after the fine array produced already, and he reminds the symposiasts of Agathon's recent bold display in the theatre, which they are honouring on this particular occasion. Agathon responds by saying that he is more afraid of delivering a performance in front of this small but intelligent group (194b6–8), a remark which Socrates uses to encourage this particular lover to reflect on the role of shame in our aspiration towards the *kalon*. Would Agathon feel shame, he asks, if he were doing something shameful only in front of a few intelligent people, or in front of ordinary people, too (c9–10)? Sensing the onset of a characteristically Socratic elenchus, Phaedrus interrupts this discussion and pleads for them both to continue with the encomiastic format (d4–5).

Had this discussion continued, Socrates might have returned to Phaedrus' discussion of the role of shame in our aspiration towards the *kalon* and the production of virtue. Agathon admits that he would feel shame towards those he deems wise, if he were doing something shameful (194c5–8). The perception of some value in a particular group motivates him towards the production of a suitably *kalos logos* in this instance. (Whether he actually achieves this is a further matter.) If Agathon perceives no value in his audience, by contrast, he appears to feel no qualms about failing to deliver such a *logos*. This episode suggests that if virtue is really to be achieved it must be generated in the presence of those who are (perceived to be) of real value (i.e. wise). Such partners will encourage shame about the right sorts of things, namely a lack of genuine wisdom in this case, and a striving toward what is truly *kalon*. The type of conversation that Socrates is prevented from pursuing in this sympotic context is particularly suited to inducing the sort of shame necessary for the production of wisdom and virtue, as Alcibiades will explain later (216b–c).[20] Sympotic conversation, by contrast, is both motivated by, and fosters, desire for a different goal.[21] Whether this is an expression of a truly beneficial *erōs* and is productive of genuine wisdom and virtue remains to be seen.

4. AGATHON'S SPEECH (194E4–198A1)

The interlude is a fitting preamble to Agathon's speech, for which he will receive the largest applause and yet he will be shown to care more for pleasing the crowd than for wisdom. His speech is packed with mythological allusions (195b7, c2–3, d2, 196, a, c, e, 197b), it is self-consciously stylized (194e4, 197c3), and embellished with the rhetorical flourishes of his day.[22] Much of the speech is constructed in equal units and parallel clauses, and he clearly draws on his playwriting skills in his ample use of poetic rhythms.[23] The most conspicuous part of the speech is a display of Gorgianic rhetoric, as Socrates will confirm (197c–e with 198c1–3).[24] But Agathon's account also returns to the themes laid down by his predecessors. The previous speakers

[20] When Phaedrus interrupts this conversation and pleads for them both to continue with encomia, Socratic conversation is repeatedly contrasted with the speech-making appropriate to this symposium (διαλέγεσθαι 194d4, 5, e3).

[21] Cf. Nightingale (1993) and (1995) 110–32.

[22] For which see Bury (1932) xxxvi and Dover (1980) 124.

[23] Rowe (1998*a*) 161; Dover (1980) 124.

[24] See Dover (1980) 123–4 for an analysis of the Gorgianic features of this speech with Denniston (1952) 10–12.

have discussed the benefits to human beings for which *erōs* is responsible, but, according to Agathon, they have failed to explain the sort of nature that is responsible for those benefits (194e5–8). This is the central point of Agathon's speech.

'There is one correct method for any praise of any subject [he explains], namely to describe in speech what sort of character whoever is the subject of the speech has in virtue of which he is actually responsible for what' (195b7). According to Agathon, *erōs* can cause the benefits previously praised because lovers are beautiful themselves (195a7), and so drawn towards beauty in others (196b2–3). This attraction of like to like issues in the production of good things: 'from the love of the beautiful all good things come about for both gods and men' (197b8–9). Whilst 'agreeing with Phaedrus on many other things' (195b6), he rejects the idea that Eros is an ancient god on the grounds that he flees old age and is always with the young and, given the principle of like to like, Eros must himself be young. Further, Eros is also delicate, graceful, supple of form and in every way supremely beautiful. And then there is Eros' virtue (196b5–6): as well as justice (195bc), Eros shares most fully in moderation (196c5), courage (d1), and wisdom (d5). Agathon then, 'takes his turn in honouring his own expertise as Eryximachus honoured his' (196e1–2) and identifies this wisdom with poetic expertise. Because Eros is so bountiful himself he can induce others to wisdom and virtue ('for the sorts of things one either doesn't have or doesn't know, one can't give to another or teach anyone else', 196e5–6). Indeed, 'everyone who is touched by *erōs* turns into a poet' (196e1–2), or becomes productive in some creative endeavour.

According to this account, then, the reason why *erōs* can have such positive benefits is that it is an aspiration towards beauty, and good things (such as virtue, now construed as poetic wisdom) arise from *erōs* for beautiful things. This draws on the theme, introduced by Phaedrus, that there is some relationship between *erōs* for beauty and virtue. But we are none the wiser about the details. Why does *erōs* for beauty issue in the *creation* of good things, rather than straightforward *possession*? It is surely possible to think of beautiful things that one desires to possess, rather than to create. Why, then, is *erōs* creative? Since Agathon characterizes lovers as already in possession of almost all the good things that one can imagine: health, beauty, grace, moderation, justice, courage, wisdom, and so on, it is not clear why they should engage in erotic endeavours at all. Why not just sit back and enjoy their state of abundance? This account is certainly at odds with the Aristophanic model of a lover's needy nature; at least that picture could explain the origin of erotic pursuits. If we do not know why erōs issues in such productive activity, then we will not know the end this activity is supposed to serve, nor what activity best leads to this end. Like his predecessors, then, Agathon's speech raises some significant issues and questions.

5. THE STATUS AND ROLE OF THE ACCOUNTS

Each speaker thus far has attempted to praise the role of erōs in our attainment of good things and happiness. Taken together, their ethical reflections upon the role of erōs in the good life present some significant ideas, albeit ones that need further clarification. Although each speaker criticizes his predecessor in some way, we have also seen that they incorporate elements of the previous speeches and supplement certain features of their accounts. This is explicit at numerous points. Eryximachus claimed that Pausanias failed to bring his speech to a close (186a), and is concerned that he, too, may 'have left out many things in my praise of erōs, but that was certainly not my intention. If I have left anything out, it is up to you Aristophanes to fill in the gaps' (188e). After Aristophanes, there is a concern that Agathon and Socrates might be at a loss for things to say because of 'the many and various things that have already been said' (193e5–7). But Agathon rises to the challenge and hopes to deliver a complete and unbeatable performance: 'let me leave nothing out', he says at the start (196d5). This manner of supplementing and building on one's predecessors lends itself to reading the speeches as one 'intertextual web', a characteristic feature of sympotic discourse.[25] The accounts of each are incomplete, but taken together

---

[25] See Stehle (1997) 222, from whom I take the phrase. Commenting on sympotic discourse more generally, Stehle argues that: 'All of the forms that this might take, the singing in turn, the new turn on the known song, are designed to keep the discourse collective, while at the same time highlighting each person's contribution. The

they can be see as parts of an overall picture of the role of *erōs* in the good life. Phaedrus explains that the aim of *erōs* is virtue. Pausanias adds that it is *erōs* for the soul that can achieve the virtue he praised. Eryximachus adds that the correct application of *erōs* must be governed by knowledge. Aristophanes 'fills in' with an account of human nature and its deficiencies which attempts to explain why *erōs* has such beneficial effects. And Agathon attempts to explain these beneficial effects as creative expressions that result from an encounter with the *kalon*, towards which *erōs* is essentially directed.[26]

But we have seen that in addition to their incompleteness, there are many puzzles and inconsistencies that remain for those who would like a clear and consistent account of the role of *erōs* in the good life.[27] Among the most pressing puzzles are the following. Phaedrus presents the idea that *erōs* can lead to the acquisition of virtue by instilling a sense of shame and a striving towards the *kalon*. But he leaves us wondering just what the connection is between an erotic relationship, an appreciation of the *kalon*, and a striving for virtue. Pausanias agrees that *erōs* can lead to virtue, but goes on to argue that it is only *erōs* which privileges the soul over the body and,

participants must constantly respond to one another, but the full forms . . . require the work of more than one contributor. One could say that ideally the symposium should create one intertextual web.' As Rowe (1998a) 8 argues, the responsiveness in this case takes the form of competitiveness, a prominent feature of encomia in the 5th and 4th cents (on which, see Nightingale (1995) 117).

[26] Compare Rowe (1998a) 8, who argues that: 'The capping effect of the first five speeches means that they already, in a sense, represent a single whole, culminating first in the speech of Agathon . . . and then in Socrates' contribution . . . But we should be wary of supposing that there is, or is meant to be, any sense of a gradually developing picture of *eros* . . . with each speaker fitting new and better pieces to the jigsaw. Socrates, after all, prefaces his account with a general criticism of the others, and proceeds immediately to reduce Agathon's speech—which everyone else thought brilliant—to rubble. It is in any case hard to construct a joint account that might emerge from the sequence from Phaedrus to Agathon. All five are essentially individual contributions, with each attempting to go one better than the one before in an apparently haphazard way.' The view I am developing here implies that the relationship is not quite so haphazard.

[27] And this, of course, will not be everyone. There are many merits to the speeches thus far and other criteria they can be measured by which may not involve clarity and consistency (e.g. literary finesse, humour, etc.). I am concerned here with what relationship, if any, they have to a *philosophical* account of *erōs* and that will be one in which clarity and consistency are important criteria. See the discussion of Socrates' critique of his peers below, Ch. 7.

as a consequence, is concerned to encourage the development of the soul and its characteristic virtues that can lead to that end. But we were left wondering about the relationship between wisdom and virtue and how a love relationship is supposed to foster that end. Eryximachus argues that the correct application of *erōs* must be governed by knowledge. But it is not clear what knowledge of *ta erōtika* consists in. Aristophanes' account of human nature and its deficiencies leaves us wondering why we should desire the *oikeion*, and whether there is anything particularly productive about being welded together with another person. And Agathon invites us to consider why *erōs* for the *kalon* is *productive* of good things and whether (and, if so, why) it is a state of plenitude that motivates this beneficial and productive *erōs*.

Various significant issues and questions relating to the role of *erōs* in the good life emerge from reflection upon this 'web', which raises some of the difficulties and problems in need of resolution by the next speaker, Socrates.[28] Indeed it highlights where the agreements and the disagreements are on the subject of *erōs*. The previous speakers seem to agree that *erōs* has some relationship to *eudaimonia* (180b7, 188d8, 193d5, 194e6, 195a5) and that this has something to do with pursuing beauty (178d1–2, 196e4–5), and virtue (179d1–2, 184d7, 185b5, 188d4–9, 196d4–e6). The disagreements lie in their accounts of the nature of this virtue and happiness. In one account virtue is heroism on the battlefield and related to, or identified with, honour (Phaedrus). In another, wisdom is somehow central to virtue (Pausanias). For Eryximachus the virtues are those of the doctor or seer who can promote a harmonious order (188d). Aristophanic *erōs* pursues the *oikeion*, though he also highlights the virtues of the politician that result from that pursuit (192a7–8), and Agathon identifies virtue with poetic skill (196d5, e1). At numerous points it is suggested that *erōs*' beneficial effects are related to wisdom (182b7–c2, 184d1, 187c4–5, 184e1, 196d5–6), but this is variously construed as medical expertise and poetic skill (186c5, 196e1–2). The accounts leave it unclear why *erōs* should manifest itself in such virtue and just what such virtue is supposed to be. Further

---

[28] This is not to make the further claim that the speakers themselves should be taken to be suggesting these specific puzzles.

disagreements are to be found in the accounts of the aims thought to constitute, or lead to, *eudaimonia* (honour, the *oikeion*, some kind of wisdom?).

The 'intertextual web' created by the speakers raises some of the difficulties and problems in need of resolution by the next speaker, in way that is suggestive of a significant philosophical role. But although Socrates criticizes and responds to his predecessors as the others have done, he does so in such a way that many have wondered whether and, if so, how his account fits into their intertextual web at all. He claims that all the speakers (note the 'you' plural):

attribute the greatest and most beautiful characteristics possible to the thing in question, whether they are true of it or not, and if they are false, well, that is of no importance. It seems that what was proposed was that each of us should appear to be offering an encomium to Eros, not that we should actually offer him one. It is for that reason, I imagine, that you rake up everything you can think of saying and attribute it to *erōs* (198d7–e6).

Since Socrates says that he will speak differently from his predecessors (199b2–5), in a way that privileges the truth, we may be tempted to see a sharp break in the text between the 'rhetorical and poetical [and] the dialectical'. If there is such a break, then does this imply that, from Socrates' perspective at least, the previous accounts are nothing more than literary frivolities, 'fanciful performances' with little to offer to our understanding of *erōs*?[29]

---

[29] See Rowe (1998*a*) 8, Jowett (Plato I) 256, Bury (1932) I. iii, and Dover (1980) 5 n. 1 on this issue. They all agree that the speeches are 'rhetorical and poetical, rather than dialectical', but there is some disagreement over how sharp a distinction is to be drawn between Socrates and his peers. For varying interpretations as to why Plato should offer us *five* such speeches if they are 'fanciful and partly facetious' performances' (Jowett), see Rotscher, who argues that the speeches are arranged in order of ascending importance, and Hug, who argues that the speeches are arranged according to aesthetic considerations (cited from Bury (1932) I. iii). See also Isenberg (1940) on the order of the speeches. Grube (1935) 96, Brentlinger (1970) 21, and Markus (1971) view Socrates' speech as the culminating stage of a dramatic structure encompassing all the speeches which in its totality expresses Plato's view, but they do not explore this in any detail. Reeve (1992) 91 also argues that the speeches 'contain some grain of what Plato takes to be the truth about love'. Cf. Wardy (2002) 2, who agrees that significant 'patterns' emerge by reading the speeches in their totality, but disagrees insofar as he 'resist[s] the temptation to hear a single voice as authoritative'. My view defended here and in Ch. 7 is that the speeches have a philosophical role to play

This question has larger ramifications. It is by now something of a commonplace to complain when reading Platonic scholarship that either the philosophical or the literary content of a particular work has been underestimated. The *Symposium* offers particularly rich pickings in this area since the diverse and entertaining speeches have given this text recognition as the most literary of all Plato's works, and yet it has also just begun to receive more systematic philosophical attention.[30] Although we may not, after all, agree with Socrates that his criteria (whatever these may be) are those that are best for delivering an insightful speech about *erōs*, if we are to read the *Symposium* as a philosophical text, then clarifying where this material is located will be important. It is difficult to dismiss the previous accounts as nothing more than literary frivolities from this perspective, since they occupy a large part of this text (twenty-seven Stephanus pages compared with nineteen for Socrates). It is hard to believe that Plato would have us wade through these accounts without good reason. Moreover, within the drama itself, the speeches remembered by Aristodemus and reported by Apollodorus were picked out as 'worthy of remembrance' (178a4); others were assigned to the scrap heap. We have also seen that they raise significant issues and contain promising suggestions which, as we shall see later, are employed in Socrates' own account, one which professes to 'speak the truth'. This suggests that they make at least some kind of contribution to a philosophical understanding of *eros,* and yet Socrates' critique does suggest that a fresh start somehow needs to be made. The relationship between Socrates and the previous speakers in the *Symposium* is a matter of some difficulty and controversy.

A careful reading of Socrates' critique of his peers does nothing to undermine the idea that they raise significant issues and questions about the topic at hand. Socrates' central claim is that his predecessors have not made the truth their priority (198e1–6). He does not say that the accounts are actually false, just that *if* they are false, then

---

insofar as they raise significant issues and questions which are resolved in Socrates' account. So there is no sharp break between Socrates and his peers (contra Rowe), and Socrates' speech is authoritative *for a philosophical account of erōs* (contra Wardy). Socrates' account may not be authoritative when assessed by other (non-philosophical) criteria, however.

[30] In the work of Price (1989), Kahn (1996), and Rowe (1998*a, b*), for example.

that seems to be of no importance to the speakers.[31] This leaves room
for the possibility that his predecessors may have hit upon the truth,
but if they did, it would have been in spite of themselves, since they
did not aim for this goal (198e2). But Socrates does imply that they
have no *knowledge* about *erōs*. They have been more concerned to
appear to be offering an encomium to Eros than with actually
offering him one (e4).[32] This concern with appearances rather than
truth motivates the attribution of all sorts of characteristics to *erōs*,
without any clarity about whether and, if so, how these characteristics actually do apply to *erōs*.

There are some substantive views about knowledge and method
behind this assessment of the previous accounts which Socrates
begins to clarify when he turns to Agathon's account next. He
approves (199c) Agathon's methodological rule (195a) and the distinction it implies (201e): one should first display the character *erōs*
has and then go on to explain what it does. Socrates' approach shows
that he believes that questions concerning the nature of the subject
are prior to questions about the effects of the subject. For as he makes
more explicit elsewhere, it is only when one has correctly identified
the nature of one's subject matter that one can go on to make

---

[31] It is difficult to determine what is involved in the characterization of their
speeches as 'fictitious' or 'false'. Janaway (1995) notes that in the *Republic* the young
guardians should be educated first in the *pseudeis logoi* and later in true discourse
(376e11–377a2). So, he argues that *pseudeis* 'must merely be a way of classifying
discourses, not in itself a reason for objecting to them'. He cites Guthrie (1975) 457,
on the neutral use of *pseudos* in this passage, who suggests that 'fiction', 'fictitious',
'invented' convey the sense of the term. The implication that their speeches are
fictitious can be taken to refer, in part, to their ample use of mythology and poetry,
in accordance with sympotic tradition. For poetic and literary references in the
Symposium, see 174b (*Il.* 10. 222–6); 177a (Eur. *Melanippe*); 178b (Hes. *Th.* 116–20,
Parmenides B13 with B12); 179b (the Alcestis story); 179d (the Orpheus myth); 180a
(Homeric and Aeschylean versions of the Achilles and Patroclus story compared);
182c (for the story of Harmodius and Aristogeiton); 183e (*Il.* 2. 71); 187a (Heraclitus
B51); 190c (*Il.* 5. 385, *Od.* 12. 308); 195c (references to Hesiod and Parmenides); 195d
(*Il.* 19. 92–3); 196d (Soph. fr. 235; *Od.* 8. 266–366); 196e (Eur. fr. 663); 198c (*Od.* 11.
633–5); 199a (Eur. *Hipp.* 612); 208c (line of unknown origin); 208e (references to
Alcestis and the legendary king Kodrus of Athens); 214b (*Il.* 11. 514); 215b (the myth
of Marsyas); 219a (*Il.* 6. 232–6); 220c (*Od.* 4. 242, 272); 221b (Aristophanes, *Clouds*
362); 221c (references to Achilles and Brasidas); 222c (*Il.* 17. 32).

[32] The speakers seem more concerned with 'the probable', rather than 'the necessary', as Socrates implies later (200a9; cf. 201a8).

inferences about the kind of benefits that such a character can bestow and how it can bestow them.[33] Since the other speakers have not identified erōs' nature, they cannot know what it is about such a nature that leads to the virtue they praise as its proper outcome. We can imagine Socrates saying (as he does more explicitly elsewhere): 'When I do not know what erōs is, I shall hardly know whether or not it happens to lead to benefits, or whether or not the one having it is happy' (cf., for example, *Laches* 190b7–c2). Without such knowledge accounts of erōs' benefits are speculations based on personal experience and contemporary culture. That is, perhaps, why we are offered such diverse views about the nature of erōs and its relationship to virtue. The speakers have not begun by identifying the nature of erōs first and so they have no firm basis on which to infer anything about its beneficial effects. When Phaedrus attempts to settle a dispute about the status of the lover and beloved he merely cites the conflicting accounts of Aeschylus and Homer (180–1; cf. 178b, 178c for further reliance on tradition and agreement). As Socrates makes plain elsewhere, the poets could be used in support of almost anything since there is no way of determining what they mean (*Prot.* 347e). The 'many and various things said' on the subject (193e6–7), we infer, manifest the inconsistencies which have not been generated by the appropriate procedure.[34] Since they do not adopt a method which prioritizes the correct identification of the subject under discussion, they do not know what erōs is; consequently, they cannot know what it is about *such a nature* that leads to the acquisition of virtue.[35]

In order to have knowledge about erōs one must be able to identify the nature of the thing under discussion and go on to make

---

[33] This manner of investigating a subject is familiar Socratic procedure; see, for example, *Meno* 71a5–b7, *Rep.* 354c1–3.

[34] On the association between inconsistency, polymathy, and *poikilia*, see Theognis 213–8; Pindar, *Olympians* 1. 28–9; Xen. *Mem.* 4.4.6–7 with Blondell (2002) 61.

[35] Perhaps the importance of the proper order and the absence of such order in the previous accounts is that 'other cause' responsible for Aristophanes' attack of hiccups (185c7–8). This other cause may be the kind of disorder which Eryximachus explains as a manifestation of wayward erōs. The speeches thus far both express and foster disorderly erōs, one indication of which is Aristophanes' hiccups. For an alternative explanation of the hiccups in terms of a surfeit of speeches, see Brentlinger (1970) 13.

inferences about this nature and its beneficial effects on that basis.[36] So to imply that Agathon and others do not have knowledge of *erōs*, is to imply that they cannot provide a clear and consistent account of *erōs* because they do not have a viable definition of *erōs* on which to ground their views about his proper functioning, and from which to infer his benefits. And this is not to say (or imply) that they have no plausible beliefs about *erōs*. Many of the things said by the previous speakers will be included in an account professing to 'speak the truth'. For example, the claim that *erōs* desires what it lacks (191a5–6); that *erōs* is of beauty (197b8); that *erōs* for the soul is more valuable than *erōs* for the body (184a1); that good things arise from the love of beautiful things (197b8–9); that *erōs* aims at virtue (178c5–6, 179a8, 180b7–8, 188d5–6), the good (188d5), and happiness (180b7, 188d8); that *erōs* must be governed by knowledge (188d1–2; cf. 184d1–e1), or at the very least, that it has some intimate relationship to *phronēsis* (182b7–c2, 184d1), *epistēmē* (187c4–5), *sophia* (196d5–6), and that *erōs* brings together the human and the divine (188d8–9). The accounts may have hit upon the truth in these areas, as their later inclusion in an account professing 'to speak the truth' will strongly suggest. The previous speakers may believe many fine things about *erōs* (and some false ones, as we shall see), but they do not know why these opinions are true. To know why these things are true of *erōs*, one must have a definition of *erōs* which these statements involve. And to acquire this one must adopt a method designed to lead to that end. Nothing so far, then, rules out the possibility of continuity between a philosophical account and those with no concern for the truth. The previous speakers may be like 'untrained soldiers in a battle, who rush about and often strike good blows, but without science'.[37]

Significantly, when Socrates demonstrates what a philosophical procedure of this kind must at least involve he does so by engaging directly with the views of his host. Socrates begins by subjecting Agathon to an elenchus (199c3 ff.) designed to scrutinize Agathon's

---

[36] This procedure might suggest parallels with other dialogues in which the priority of definition is discussed (for which see Benson (1990) 19–65 and Prior (1998) 97–113). Of course, those who believe that Socrates was not committed to this principle will not find such parallels illuminating.

[37] Aristotle, *Metaphysics* 985ᵃ. I thank Jim Lesher for this reference.

proposed characterization of *erōs* personified as a beautiful god, Eros. Agathon's speech may well have been picked out for elenctic scrutiny because Agathon is the most conceited of the symposiasts.[38] But Agathon's speech may also have been selected because his speech, at least, attempts to clarify the nature of the subject before making inferences about its beneficial effects. If one must begin an investigation, as Socrates suggests, with an identification of the subject matter, then examining Agathon's speech will be the best place to start.[39] Although this testing ends with Agathon's frank admission that he did not know any of the things which he said then, as he puts it (210b10), it also shows that Agathon' speech contains some promising insights which, when properly developed, lead to some plausible views. Let us see how it does so. Agathon had claimed that Eros' nature is beautiful and that Eros pursues beauty (197b). On reflection, he is also shown to believe that Eros lacks what he desires (200e1–5). Even those who apparently desire what they already have, such as a healthy man who desires health, really desire something they lack, namely the possession of that thing in the future (200d4–6, 200d9–10). These opinions are inconsistent. For if Eros desires beauty and lacks what he desires, then Eros cannot possess beauty. Either Eros does not, in fact, pursue beauty, or Eros lacks the beauty he desires (either now or in the future). Both Agathon and Socrates preserve the view that Eros pursues beauty, which leads to the preliminary conclusion that Eros' nature is such that he lacks the beauty he desires (202d1–3). Agathon evidently did not propose a viable account of Eros' nature (as a beautiful god) on which to base his account of its beneficial effects.

---

[38] As Socrates explains elsewhere (*Apol.* 21c5–7), the aim of the elenchus is to investigate such types in order to show that they are not wise if they are not and to learn from them if they are (*Apol.* 21c7–8, 22b5, 23b6–7). Typically such types are politicians (*Apol.* 21c3–22a) poets (*Apol.* 22a8–c8), and craftsmen (*Apol.* 22c4–e5), many of whose areas of expertise are celebrated here. But among this particular group Agathon is the most celebrated. If Socrates can show that the 'most wise' Agathon, who is being honoured by the speakers for his theatrical victory at this very banquet, is not in fact knowledgeable about important matters, then he is also casting aspersions on his peers.

[39] Agathon's speech is, in this respect, an improvement (199c). One might compare here the similar difference between Lysias' speech and Socrates' first speech in the *Phaedrus*: although Socrates' first speech is misguided, it is nonetheless methodologically sounder than that of Lysias.

But this is not to say that Agathon's speech is nonsense. Socrates goes on to show that Agathon is right that Eros has some relationship both to beauty and to divinity; he is muddled about the precise nature of those relationships. This is a muddle to which Socrates himself, apparently, was subject, before he met the mysterious Diotima (201e3–7). Indeed Socrates presents his own account as a repeat performance of this meeting because he used to say very similar things to Agathon. Agathon (and the young Socrates) was on the right track when he claimed that Eros is of beauty, and that good things arise from *erōs* for beautiful things (197b8) as we shall see; he was wrong to infer that because good things arise from the desire for beautiful things that Eros must himself be in possession of those things. For if Eros desires what he lacks, then Eros cannot be beautiful and good. Agathon had not thought through the implications of his beliefs and, consequently, he had misunderstood the precise nature of the relationship between *erōs* and beauty.

Agathon's mistake here allows Socrates/Diotima to home in on something valuable—because it is partially right (*erōs* does have an intimate relationship to beauty, 197b, which Socrates develops at 201a)—and to clarify the precise nature of *erōs'* relationship to beauty. Socrates emphasizes the importance of the points agreed to during the elenchus of Agathon and continues the discussion—*on the basis of the things agreed between them*—in much the same way in which he and Diotima proceeded (201e2–7). He goes on to play the roles of both the Agathon who now realizes that he lacks wisdom about these things (201b11–12), and Diotima, who was 'wise in these things and much else' (201d3). In so doing Socrates shows the productive effects of clarifying the puzzling relationship between *erōs* and beauty that emerged from Agathon's speech. He explains how his initial reaction to the notion that Eros lacks the good and beautiful things he desires was to assume that whatever is not good and beautiful must be the opposite (201e8–9, 202b1–2). But he came to realize (perhaps through similar elenctic scrutiny) that there is a realm of intermediates between the opposites good and bad, beautiful and ugly (202a1–e1), and wisdom and ignorance (202a5–9). Socrates readily agrees that there is such a state as correct belief—believing truths without being able to account for them, but is still puzzled about Eros' status. In particular, he has difficulty with the belief that Eros is a great god and that the gods possess all good things, such as wisdom (as Agathon and Phaedrus had also held), and at the same time that Eros has an intermediate status in relation to these things. Diotima points out to Socrates that he himself does not believe that Eros is a god (202c1–4). She guides Socrates to see that, given that he has agreed that Eros lacks what he desires (202d1–3, which repeats Agathon's agreement at 201a–b), and that the gods possess good things (202c6–8), Eros cannot be a god (202d5). Eros' status in relation to the mortal and the immortal is analogous to his status in relation to wisdom and ignorance: he is a great spirit in between the two realms 'and everything spiritual is in between god and mortal' (202d13–e1). So, the clarification of the nature of *erōs*' relationship to beauty leads to the claim that Eros cannot be a god but an intermediate being.

When a viable account of *erōs*' nature is reached Socrates' expression refers back to Agathon's encomium (204c with 197b). Agathon had, in fact, confused the lover with the beloved in his account of *erōs*' nature. The way in which Socrates returns to Agathon's speech after he has formulated his own corrective account of *erōs*' nature suggests that there is no sharp break between their accounts of *erōs*' nature. Indeed, Socrates seems concerned to emphasize a degree of continuity between himself and Agathon by showing how the clarification and development of the view that *erōs* has an intimate relationship to beauty—a promising view—leads to a plausible and consistent set of conclusions. It would seem that Agathon's speech, at the very least, addresses some of the right sort of issues and questions that an explanatory account of *erōs*' nature needs to clarify. And that is perfectly compatible with Socrates' earlier critique.[40]

---

[40] To say, then (with Rowe 1998*a*: 8) that Agathon's speech is 'reduced to rubble' is perhaps too strong. For a more positive assessment compare Stokes (1986) 146: 'In the talks as recorded Socrates takes over the part of Agathon and Diotima that of Socrates. The *Socrates* of the story has accepted exactly the same propositions (201e) as the Agathon of the *Symposium*; and Diotima, although she has naturally not heard Agathon's encomium and the ensuing discussion, bases her arguments on Agathon's admissions and implications, or (occasionally) corrects them.' He argues that 'every question Socrates has asked has been explanatory of Agathon's original encomium. In each question Socrates either extracts from Agathon a relatively clear inference or he asks for a resolution of a difficulty or ambiguity', see Stokes (1986) 130, 114.

If this is the case for the other accounts, too, then we will have good reason not to ignore them as extraneous to a philosophical understanding. We shall be able to clarify their role more precisely after examining Socrates' speech. For we should like to know whether, for example, the previous accounts have more than pragmatic utility in directing our attention towards possibly promising theories. If they play a role in a developing understanding of *erōs*, then how substantive is this role? My reading of the speeches so far has tried to tease out a number of issues and questions that we would expect a clear and consistent account of *erōs* to resolve. We will need to see whether this is, in fact, the case, that is, whether there is evidence of the sort of engagement with puzzling issues that emerged from Agathon's account. Socrates will not submit all the accounts to the same procedure as Agathon's, however. We are given a sample of what a philosophical inquiry must involve in the elenchus of Agathon, and we are told that numerous elenchi have been involved in his account. But we have not witnessed such processes and will have to struggle through many of the puzzles alone. If we achieve any greater clarity about the topic, though, we should not forget how we arrived: by struggling through some salient views about *erōs*, realizing where the gaps are and where the problems lie, before being guided towards the revisionary world of philosophical *erōs*. If so, then marginalizing the previous accounts of *erōs* would inhibit a proper understanding of the topic.

If Socrates is to do any better than his predecessors we would like to see how following his criteria for truthful speech-making provides answers to the puzzles that emerged from the previous accounts. We need him to explain why a striving for the *kalon* issues in the virtue Phaedrus praised. We also need to know what relationship holds between *erōs* for the soul, wisdom, and virtue (Pausanias), and how knowledge of *ta erōtika* can lead to this end (Eryximachus). Further, what is it that *erōs* really lacks and desires (Aristophanes)? If it is the beautiful, then how and why does *erōs* for the *kalon* produce the good things and beneficial effects these accounts have claimed for *erōs* (Agathon)? If we cannot answer these questions then we will not have understood how *erōs* can lead to the virtue they praise as its proper outcome. In order to do that we need to clarify what 'virtue [consists in] and the sorts of thing the good man must be concerned with, and the activities such a man should involve himself in' and so on (cf. 209c1–2). If Socrates is to take this task upon himself, then we should expect his methodological procedure to deliver substantive views on *eros'* nature, its aims, the role of the *kalon* and virtue, and an account of *eros'* proper activity and functioning. Let us see how his account fares.

2

Socrates' Speech: The Nature of *Erōs*

Socrates' account resolves many of the issues from the previous speeches. His account of how *erōs* leads to the acquisition of virtue is complicated and the following few chapters take it in stages. As we have been led to expect, we start with the nature of *erōs* and only then does Socrates go on to make inferences about the kind of benefits that *erōs* can bestow and how it can bestow them. In the first part of this chapter we will be examining his account of *erōs* as an intermediate psychological state. In our desire for beauty, he explains, we are confronted with the beauty and goodness that our mortal natures lack, and yet we awaken a more than human ability to transcend that nature and to strive towards a divine state of possession. In a sense, then, Aristophanes was right that we desire what we lack. This point, as we have seen, was provided with argumentative support during the elenchus of Agathon. But if *erōs* is only a state of lack, then it is difficult to see how *erōs* can lead to the productive effects claimed for it. If *erōs* is to be a beneficial state, then it must be resourceful, too. Socrates will argue that the nature of *erōs* is, in fact, intermediate between a state of lack and resource, and it is a dynamic interaction between the two sides of its nature that issues in the productive effects previously claimed for *erōs*.

Socrates will also claim (in partial agreement with Agathon) that *erōs* by nature pursues the beautiful and good things it lacks. This account of *erōs'* nature explains, in part, how *erōs* can work for our benefit: *erōs* can work for our good because it is its very nature to aspire towards the good and the beautiful. The 'vulgar *erōs*' that concerned Pausanias is not a proper expression of *erōs'* nature. Since, according to this account, it is *eros'* nature to strive towards the good, for *erōs* to find its proper expression one needs to ensure that it is able to identify correctly the good it seeks. In this chapter we will also be examining the beginnings of an account of how such a process is possible. Socrates argues that *erōs* is cognitively informed and thereby explains how it is amenable to education and redirection towards truly productive ends. Further, *erōs* is not just amenable to philosophical education, but best expressed in such activity. Pausanias was onto something when he claimed that there was an intimate relationship between *erōs* and wisdom; for *erōs* desires beauty, and wisdom is one of the most beautiful things, so *erōs* is, in the highest degree, a lover of wisdom. Socrates goes on to sketch the outlines of an account of how *eros'* nature manifests itself in this pursuit. In doing so, he lays the foundation for his account of the education of desire towards its proper object.

1. *ERŌS* AS INTERMEDIATE

In Socrates' examination of Agathon we saw that the clarification of the nature of *erōs* as a desire for beauty and for what one lacks leads to the claim that *erōs* personified is not a god, but an intermediary being. For if lovers were in a divine state of possession, they would not desire the things of which there is no need. One does not typically expect such demotion of status in an encomium.[1] But although demoted from divine status, Eros as an intermediary being is still of great benefit to human beings. Socrates explains that its power is:

that of interpreting and conveying things from men to gods and from gods to men—men's petitions and sacrifices, the gods' commands and returns for sacrifices; being in the middle between both, it fills in the space between them, so that the whole is bound close together. It is through this that the

---

[1] Contrast Isocrates, who in his *Bsiris* , often taken to be one of the first attempts to lay down rules for the encomiastic genre, writes that: 'it is necessary for those who wish to eulogize a person to represent him as possessing a greater number of good qualities than he actually possesses' (4); cf. Nightingale (1995) 103. See also Aristotle, *Rhetoric* 1368^{a}22–3, 26–9; *Rhetorica ad Alexandrum* 1425^{b}36–40, where this procedure is called 'amplification'.

whole expertise of the seer works its effects, and that of priests, and of those concerned with sacrifices, rites, spells and the whole realm of the seer and of magic. God does not mix with man, through this it is that all intercourse and conversation of gods with men takes place, whether awake or asleep; and the person who is wise about such things is a demonic man, while the one who is wise in anything else, in relation to one or other sort of expertise or manual craft, is vulgar. These spirits, then, are many and of all sorts, and one of them is Eros (202e3–203a8).

The characterization of Eros' relationship to the divine, and the idea that various forms of expertise express that relationship, picks up on Eryximachus' account of an *erōs* which issues in a relationship with the gods by means of various *technai* (188d1–2). Much of Socrates' account will be concerned with the erotic *technē* that leads to this flourishing intermediate state. The highest mysteries of the ascent will provide an account of the *ta erōtika* mentioned by Eryximachus and describe the 'rites' *erōs* engages in as part of its divine communication. Happiness, Socrates will argue, consists in a godlike life of contemplation of the divine form (211d1–3). And one who completes the ascent will successfully communicate with the divine and win the friendship of the gods (212a5). But that is to get ahead of ourselves. How Eros' intermediate nature enables him to 'bind the whole together with itself' and bring such benefit is first addressed in the aetiological story which follows this description of *erōs* (203b1–204c6).

The story begins as follows:

When Aphrodite was born, the gods held a feast; and among them was Poros [Resource], son of Metis [Wisdom, Craftiness]. Their dinner over, Penia [Lack] came begging, as one might expect with festivities going on, and placed herself around the doors. Well, Poros had got drunk with nectar (wine, you see, did not yet exist), and gone out into Zeus' garden; now, weighed down with drink, he was sleeping. So Penia plotted, because of her own resourcelessness, to have a baby from Poros, and she lay down beside him and conceived Eros (203b2–c1; trans. Rowe with modifications).

Eros was conceived as a result of the lack both experienced and personified by his mother, who schemed to relieve her lack by conceiving a child from Poros. Poros appears available to supplement Penia's lack (203b7–8). As the offspring of this couple, Eros has a nature which oscillates between the characteristics of his parents. From his mother, Eros has need as his constant companion

(203d3), but 'in virtue of his father, Eros is a schemer after the beautiful and the good, always weaving plans... resourceful in his pursuit of *phronēsis*, and a lover of wisdom throughout his life' (203d4–7). His nature is neither that of a mortal nor that of an immortal; rather he lives and flourishes when he finds resources due to his father's nature (203e2), and then dies because the resources are always slipping away from him (203e3–4), though he has the ability to 'come back to life again' thanks to the nature of his father (203e3).

Eros' heritage from Penia and Poros describes the sense in which Eros is 'in between' the mortal and the divine realms. The description of Penia, who was not invited to dine with the gods but instead came begging at the feast, places her outside the divine realm. Poros, by contrast, who is implicitly described as a god (203b2–3), joins the feast of the other gods and lies in a stupor in the garden of Zeus (203b5–7). When Eros is described as 'in between' the mortal and the immortal, then, we are to understand that status as deriving from his mortal and divine parents, Penia and Poros, who have given him this complex nature. The lack of good and beautiful things, inherited from his mother, is characteristic of the mortal. But the resources inherited from his divine father enable Eros to scheme 'after the beautiful and the good' (203d4) and replenish that lack. It is because of Poros that Eros εὐπορεῖ (cf. ὅταν εὐπορήσῃ, 203e1–3). From the description of Eros' fluctuation between the qualitites of his parents we can see that he at least temporarily manifests the divine properties of his father, but then those of his mortal mother; and so on forever. The acquisition (τὸ ποριζόμενον) does not remain long enough for it to be said that he 'is rich' (πλουτεῖ), but neither does his state of deprivation last long enough for it to be said that he is poor (ἀπορεῖ). Eros' fluctuation between a state of lack and possession gives lovers an intermediate nature. Agathon and the others, Socrates explains, had in fact, described the *object of love* in their accounts of *erōs*, but the nature of a *lover* is a needy, yet productive, state of aspiration, of the sort just described (204c6).[2]

---

[2] On the notion of the intermediate more generally in Plato, see D. Frede (1993) 404–7. It is helpful that the passage specifies the way in which *erōs* is intermediate. The intermediacy could be a neutral state in between two extremes, so that a thing is neither the one extreme nor the other. It could also indicate that something partakes

This 'rather long story' makes good the promise to speak the truth about Eros, understood in terms of answering the questions: What is Eros and then what is it like (201e1)? In answer to the first question we are told that Eros is an intermediate being (202a–203a); in answer to the second, that he is a complex mixture of the needy and the resourceful (203b1–204c6). Before exploring this part of the account it will be necessary to broach interpretative issues arising from the integration of this story into the mainstream of Socrates' account. It will already be apparent that there is a fusion of Eros the spirit or god and *erōs* the psychological state.[3] At several points in the story this seems deliberate (e.g. 204b3). Correspondingly, the story of Eros fades into the rest of the analysis without any indication of a shift in status, and, as we shall see, the story refigures many of the salient points established during the elenchus of Agathon, and prefigures many of Socrates' later points. Since Socrates claims that this story illuminates the nature of a lover (cf. 204c2–6, esp. 5–6 τὸ δέ γε ἐρῶν ἄλλην ἰδέαν τοιαύτην ἔχον, οἵαν ἐγὼ διῆλθον) and corrects the mistakes of Agathon's account (204c2–3), we are invited to analyse just how it does so. This feature of the account, in addition to the parallel between Socrates and Eros, expressed, above all, in Alcibiades' encomium of Socrates (215a4–5), very strongly supports integrating this section of the account into the rest of the account of *erōs* rather than isolating it as a mythical digression.[4]

---

of both extremes either simultaneously or sequentially. For the clearest statement of this latter view see *Grg.* 467e3–5, where Socrates asks, 'Now is there anything that is not either good, or bad, or what is between these, neither good nor bad?', which is later elaborated to mean 'Such things as sometimes partake of the good, sometimes of the bad, and sometimes of neither' (468a1). For further discussion of the notion of the intermediate, cf. *Ly.* 216c, *Prt.* 351d, *Grg.* 467d–468c. However, our passage suggests that Eros is intermediate between the mortal and the immortal in a *dynamic* sense, which is to say that he fluctuates between the characteristics of his mortal and divine parents so that at one time he is poor, at another he is rich.

[3] For the logical problems involved in this fusion, see Castagnoli (2001).

[4] On the parallels between Socrates and the description of Eros in the story, see Osborne (1994) 86–117 and Rowe (1998*a*) 176. The story has received little detailed attention in recent times, with the notable exception of Stokes (1986) 150–1, who integrates the story into his account of Socrates' dialectical response to Agathon's speech. Ancient Platonists saw it as central, however. See Dillon's (1969) study of Plotinus' reading of the story, for example.

But the integration of the story does raise interpretative concerns. First, since it is a story (cf. μακρότερον διηγήσασθαι, 203b1), should we subject it to the kind of analytical scrutiny that other parts of the account invite, for example, the elenchus of Agathon? Second, if it can be subjected to such scrutiny, then why does Socrates offer us a story at all, rather than a straightforward description? In answer to the second question, one may begin by appealing to the encomiastic format, a standard feature of which was to praise one's subject through their parentage. Since *makrologia* and *diēgēsis* are rhetorical terms, and Socrates introduces this section of the account by calling it 'a rather long story' (203b1), we might infer that he is appealing to the rhetorical sensibilities of his audience.[5] But if so, the first question becomes even more pressing: if Socrates is performing 'out of philosophical character', so to speak, are we justified in subjecting this section of the account to philosophical scrutiny? Behind this question is an assumption we might wish to question, namely that a distinction between a story (such as the one about Eros' parentage) and an argument (such as the elenchus of Agathon) implies a contrast between a narrative mode for which aesthetic appreciation is the appropriate response, and another for which philosophical analysis is the correct response. The distinction between myth and argument, and the assumptions behind such a distinction, are a large issue.[6] As Annas has argued with reference to the application of the distinction to Plato, the criticism of stories in the educational discussion of *Republic* 2 and 3 focuses, in the main, on their content, a focus which leaves room for the inclusion of stories that have the right (philosophical) content—and thereby allow for philosophical scrutiny.[7] The fact that Socrates envisages stories with the right (philosophical) content suggests, at the very least, that the distinction between stories and argument should not be taken to imply that stories, as such, have no philosophical substance, and should therefore receive no philosophical analysis. Socrates' criticisms of the

---

[5] Cf. *Prt.* 334c–335c, where *makrologia* is characteristic of the continuous exposition of the sophists, and *Phdr.* 266e1 for *diēgēsis* as a technical rhetorical term. *Makrologia* is associated with Gorgias (by Aristotle, *Rhetoric* 1418^{a}36); cf. Kennedy (1963) 63.

[6] See the discussions of Murray and Rowe in Buxton (1999).

[7] Annas (1982) 119–39.

earlier speeches in the *Symposium* similarly suggest that the salient distinction for him in this text is between those speeches that show no concern for the truth, but only for rhetorical effectiveness, and those that may share a similar form, but privilege the truth. Since he was dismissive of the kind of encomia given by the other speakers— encomia, he complains, where the truth about *erōs* was ignored (198b1–199b5)—we seem justified in supposing that the stories which Socrates tells about Eros the 'great spirit' are figurations of truths about *erōs*. If Socrates is to make good his aim to speak the truth about the subject, then his arrangement of words and phrases and his choice of praise must, ultimately, serve that aim. Since the story does make good the promise to speak the truth about *erōs*, understood in terms of answering the questions 'what is *erōs*' and 'what is it like?' (201e1), we may suppose that the format may be more palatable to Agathon's dinner guests, but the content, since it carries out this distinctive philosophical agenda, is very much Socrates' own.

2. *ERŌS* AND ACTION

So far Socrates has provided an account of the nature of *erōs* as a deficient, yet productive, state. Agathon was right to claim that *erōs* aspires towards beauty, but wrong to think that desiring agents are in possession of those things towards which they aspire. For if they desire what they lack, then they cannot be in the state of abundant possession Agathon claimed for them (203c7 with 195c6–196a1, esp. 197d7 reflected in Socrates' language here); if they were, they would be like the slumbering and inactive Poros and fail to engage in the creative endeavours Agathon praised. Socrates goes on to explain that this intermediate state is productive. Though *erōs* lacks what it desires, it strives towards the possession of the good and beautiful things it lacks and in so doing it moves us towards the beneficial ends praised by his peers as the proper outcome of *erōs*.

Socrates' account of *erōs*' intermediate nature amounts to an analysis of *erōs* into two functional aspects, one of which is responsible for what we would, strictly speaking, term 'desire', the other of which is responsible for deliberation, by which I mean that it is responsible for scheming and finding the means to satisfy the desire. It is the dynamic between these two aspects of *erōs* that issues in something productive. Let us take another look at the story to see how these aspects function in the experience of desire. Since 'one does not desire what one does not think one needs' (204a6–7), Penia (embodiment of perceived need) is logically prior to Poros (embodiment of resource of any kind). Penia's priority in this respect is illustrated by the point that it is Penia who initiates the interaction with the drunken, slumbering Poros. The experience of a lack is the origin of desire: So, (1) when *s* experiences a lack, then *s* desires *x*. This builds on the point established in the elenchus of Agathon that desire is always based on a perceived lack (200e2–5). It was also made explicit earlier that lack and desire is always *of* something (199d1–2): (2) it is desire for a determinate *x*. The *x* which is the object of the desire is identified by Penia. Hence, when *s* desires *x*, *s* specifies an object *x* which appears to be such as will satisfy the experience of lack. What it is about *x* that makes it appropriate to desire it is that (3) it is characterized as *kalon* or *agathon* in some respect and desired under that description (cf. 201a8–10, b6–7, c4–5, 202d1–3, and later at 206a11–12). This point is brought out in the story by Penia's attraction to Poros who, as noted, lies asleep in the garden of those happy beings who possess good and beautiful things (cf. 202c6–11 with 203b2–7). What is required for the presence of desire is that *x* should appear *kalon*, but there are many things that appear such: for example, honour, money, or wisdom (205d1–5; cf. 208c3). We shall learn later that there are many things that are only *kalon* in a qualified sense (211d ff.), but the salient point at this stage is that *x appears* to be *kalon* in some way, and is therefore desirable. (This is importantly different from the claim that *x* appears *kalon* because it is desired. The claim here is rather that *x* is desired because it is, and/or seems, *kalon*.)

Penia and Poros are not clearly separated in the description of Eros' nature, but the story suggests that the characteristics inherited from Penia are those responsible for (1), (2), and (3). But because she is without resources (203b8), she is unable on her own to remedy the experience of lack, and so needs Poros, whose characteristic features are responsible for the ability to find the means to remedy a perceived lack and pursue the object set by Penia:

He is a schemer after the beautiful and the good, courageous, impetuous and intense, a clever hunter, always weaving new devices, both passionate for wisdom and resourceful in looking for it, philosophising through all his life, a clever magician, sorcerer and sophist (203d4–8).

Although Poros is characterized as the deliberator, Penia is also described as 'scheming (ἐπιβουλεύουσα) because of her lack, to have a child from Poros' (203b7). So we might also say that although Penia perceives a lack of resources, she still has some resources to recognize what she lacks, and to give her some sense of what is required to remedy that lack. If she had absolutely no grasp, then she would never get anywhere at all; and if she had sufficient resources, then there would be no need for Poros.[8] Nonetheless, it is Poros who deliberates about the means to attain the object specified by Penia; he is able to find the means to attain Penia's goal and to provide something (τὸ ποριζόμενον, 203e2–3).

The literal sense of this seems to be that when *s* desires *x*, *s* has the ability to deliberate and find the means to attain *x*. It is clear from this story that what Penia lacks and Poros provides are good and beautiful things (cf. 203d4–5). Desiring agents, then, who are by nature schemers after good and beautiful things, 'come back to life again' as such persons, that is, as persons who are able to scheme after, and to provide, good things. This confirms the point made during the elenchus of Agathon that *erōs* is of good and beautiful things (201a5), a point made more explicit after the end of this story (204d–e). There is a connection (which is figured by the intercourse of Penia and Poros) between the first three stages and the resulting provision (4): the experience of need motivates the deliberation which attempts to find the means to remedy the lack of the desired

---

[8] The initial scenario between Penia and Poros is one in which Penia is quite an active partner. Poros is lying in the garden of Zeus inebriated after a bout of nectar-drinking. He lies inactive and sluggish. Penia takes the opportunity to have sex with Poros during his drunken slumber. It is this active arousal of Penia that motivates Poros into activity. Penia's active role here is signified in the first word used to describe her, προσαιτήσουσα (203b4). This word appears twice in Plato's *Phaedrus*, where it is used of the *erastēs* 233e2–e7, that is, of the active partner in the male homoerotic relationship. Similarly, Penia waits around the doors (203b5) in the manner of an *erastēs* courting his *erōmenos*. Penia's lack is not such as to prevent her from taking some steps towards a resolution. See below for the implications of this characterization of Penia.

end and generates a provision designed to meet it. So, the result of *s*'s desire for some specifed *kalon x* is that *s* deliberates about how to attain this *kalon* thing, the result of which is a provision designed to satisfy that lack.

At this point we do not know what this provision is or how one should go about getting it. Socrates later uses the verb εὐπορεῖν and cognates to describe various actions and productions of desiring agents as they attempt to procure a chosen good. The examples of such things range from 'securing the throne' (208d4–5) and 'dying on behalf of one's husband' (208d2–3) to 'creating poems' and 'making laws' (209d ff.). Since there is a range of objects, or states of affairs, which appear *kalon* or *agathon*, there is, correspondingly, a diverse range of objects, or states of affairs, which may be desired and pursued. Even if one has identified something *kalon* or *agathon*, one still has to specify which of several courses of action (such as 'securing the throne', 'law-making', or 'philosophy') issues in its possession. When Socrates describes the various ways in which people attempt to satisfy a desire for honour, for example, by generating heroic actions such as 'throne-securing', he describes them as 'providing themselves (ποριζόμενοι) for all time to come with immortality and memory and *eudaimonia*' (208e4–5). When describing the attempt of the educative pederast to procure honour Socrates says that 'he is full of resource (εὐπορεῖ) with things to say about virtue' (209b8). The use of εὐπορειν and cognates relates these various activities to the work of Poros, who was described in the story as deliberating about the beautiful and the good and generating τὸ ποριζόμενον (203e4). The way in which the language of this story is drawn on later in the speech suggests that Socrates is providing an account of *erōs* analysed into two component parts, or functional aspects, which explain the mechanisms that lead to particular actions and productions.[9] It also provides further support for the claim that the story of Eros' birth is an integral part of Socrates' account.

---

[9] When applied to a textual example (e.g. 208d5, 209d5), we might schematize the account of *erōs* as follows: (1) Kodrus perceives continued honour as *kalon* (due to Penia); (2) Kodrus lacks honour [either now or in the future] (Penia, again); (3) Kodrus deliberates to secure the throne for his sons (Poros as *epiboulos*); (4) Kodrus provides honour for himself (the resulting provision). Or, (1) Lycurgus perceives honour as *kalon*; (2) Lycurgus lacks honour; (3) Lycurgus persuades the populace to accept the implementation of his good laws; (4) Lycurgus procures honour for himself.

The above account may seem similar in some respects to theories of intentional action that identify two separate components—the agent's desire for a certain goal, and a belief that a certain action will lead to the desired goal. But behind such theories is an assumption that Socrates does not share: that reason and desire are distinct sorts of things, where belief alone cannot motivate action and motivation is fundamentally non-rational.[10] Such views operate with the notion that an action is started by (non-rational) desire that employs reason only to the extent that an agent needs to find the means to satisfy that desire. The desire, as such, is not grounded in reasoning activity. Socrates' account of *erōs* may appear superficially similar in that it is a two-part analysis, where one aspect is responsible for desire as such (the realization of lack and initial motivational impetus), and the other is responsible for deliberating, or scheming, to find the means to satisfy that desire.[11] But the account is importantly different from such theories. First, both aspects of *erōs* involve cognitive processes: (*a*) *x* appears to the desiring agent to be *kalon* in some way and is desired because it is characterized as *kalon* (it does not appear *kalon* or *agathon* because you desire it),[12] and (*b*), *y* is thought to be an appropriate way to procure *x*. Second, the deliberating aspect of *erōs* also involves desire and has a motivational input of its own (cf. 203d4–7). So there is no clear demarcation between desire and reason.[13]

From the notion that reason and desire are fused in the experience of *erōs*, one might conclude that *erōs* is not best conceived merely as a form of desire. This might seem to be a consequence of analysing *erōs* into two component parts, one of which is responsible for desire as such and the other of which is a deliberating principle that attempts

---

[10] On the difference between Plato and modern theorists of intentional action, see e.g. Cooper (1999) 121 and Kahn (1987) 77–81. Kahn contrasts such a Platonic position with Hobbes's claim that: 'the thoughts are to the desires as scouts and spies, to range abroad and find the way to the thing desired' (*Leviathan* 1.8). Cf. also Hume's claim that reason is the slave to passion (*Treatise* ii, 3.3).

[11] In the words of Hobbes, Poros might be said to act as 'a scout and spy who ranges abroad to the thing desired'.

[12] As it does on a Hobbesian view: 'But whatsoever is the object of any man's appetite or desire, that is it, which he for his part calleth good', *Leviathan* 1.6; see Kahn (1987) 78.

[13] To say that reasoning is involved in *erōs* is not, of course, to say that it always involves reasoning correctly.

to find the way to satisfy that desire. If we are to conceive of *erōs* as 'desire', then we need to incorporate a deliberative component of *erōs* into that notion ('*erōs* is a schemer...', 203d4). One way to think about *erōs* is along Aristotelian lines. Aristotle's notion of *prohairēsis* incorporates both desire and reasoning about how to get what is desired (*NE* 6. 2, 1139ª20): 'The origin of action is *prohairēsis*, and the origin of *prohairēsis* is desire together with reason that aims at some goal' (1139ª31). Aristotle also refers to *prohairēsis* as 'deliberative desire' (3. 2, 1113ª11; cf. 6. 2, 1139ᵇ5).[14] *Prohairēsis* is, then, desire combined with thought, it is a want that emerges together with reasoning. There is a structural analogy with the *Symposium* in the sense that *erōs* has two components, where one aspect is responsible for what we might term desire (the aspect derived from Penia), and this is combined with a further aspect that schemes to get what it wants (Poros). The mistake here would be to identify *erōs* with the Penia aspect alone. The experience of lack is more primitive than *erōs*, or rather (contra Aristophanes), *erōs* is not just an experience of lack, and a yearning. The story of Eros' dual parentage indicates that the picture of *erōs* here is a combination of the two components outlined, what we might term rational, or deliberative desire.[15]

---

[14] I thank Lubomira Radoilska for these references.

[15] This raises questions about the scope of *erōs*. Socrates may be leading us towards the heights of the philosophical ascent, but he will later include animals in his discussion of *erōs* (207a7–c1), creatures excluded from *logismos* (207b7). I take it that *logismos* refers to reasoning activity. For other passages where Plato excludes animals from *logismos*, or *logos* cf. *Rep.* 441a–b, *Laws* 963e. For a discussion of the implications of this exclusion, see Sorabji (1993) 7–16. So how might this cognitively informed drive function in animals? Since they experience *erōs*, we must take it that the two functional aspects of 'lack' and 'resource' are involved. Animals must, then, be able to perceive a thing as *kalon*, perceive a lack of this *kalon* thing, and take steps to remedy their lack of it. But since they do not have *logismos*, they cannot have rational understanding of the *kalon* (which many human lovers also do not have, as we shall see). So it must be the case that experiences of 'lack' and 'resource' are not cognitively informed in the same way in animals. They have some cognitive endowment perhaps—sufficient for them to perceive a thing as *kalon* and to take steps to procure that desired thing—but this will be a lower-grade cognitive function. Socrates has already explained that cognitive states are more complex than the simple poles of knowledge and ignorance; there is the state of belief—*doxa*—for example (202a5–9). Socrates does not specify just what cognitive endowment animals do have, but some cognition, such as *doxa* perhaps, must inform their erotic experiences. In the *Timaeus* animals are said to have *doxa* (77a–c).

There are further implications to be drawn from this account of *erōs*. The characterization of *erōs* as involving the perception of an object or state of affairs as *kalon* or *agathon* in some way is crucial to the later characterization of philosophy as an attempt to direct and inform *erōs*. As we shall see in the discussion of the 'ascent' to the form of beauty, philosophical practice of the sort Socrates advocates will attempt to ensure that desiring agents both desire the right kind of thing(s), and that they exhibit the right responses to those desires and scheme more successfully after good and beautiful things. These cognitive elements of *erōs* raise the possibility of misjudgement, which will be central to Socrates' account of a hierarchy of beautiful objects, some of which are 'more valuable' than others. One might try to convince a Humean subject that some desired objects conflict with, or frustrate, other desires, but no rational choice between *desiderata*, as such, would be possible. Reasoning would only be involved in realizing one's preferences, and not choosing between preferences. On Socrates' account, however, *erōs* responds to value perceived to be in the object. Value, for Socrates is an objective matter. Some cognitive activity is involved in choosing objects according to which object is perceived to be most *kalon* and on that basis most desirable. It is this crucial difference which allows philosophical practice to play the central role of directing our desire towards objects deemed to be of greater value.

If we are persuaded that *erōs* functions in this way, then we are also allowing for the possibility that we can be mistaken in our choice of what ends to pursue and in our manner of pursuit. Put differently, if we desire things because they are beautiful and it is not just our desiring these things that makes it so, then we might have some investment in discovering what sorts of things really are valuable and desirable. Such a view is, to some extent, implied by (though not explicit in) the previous accounts of *erōs*, and the erotic-cum-sympotic context at large. For why would we need to learn from lovers about the sorts of things that are good for us to value and pursue if it is only our believing them to be so that makes them worthy of pursuit? The praise of certain things as *kalon*, which was common to the educative context of the symposium, is surely driven by the assumption that it is only in the pursuit of certain kinds of beauty that one can live an excellent and happy life. One needs to educate *erōs* so that it learns to value the right sorts of things, that is, those things that lead to ends which are, in fact, good. Left to its own devices *erōs* will be unable to recognize what is truly valuable and so will be unable to play a role in a worthwhile and fulfilling life, the kind of role which justified the erotic practices of the symposium.

Socrates' account of the nature of *erōs* provides the leverage for his subsequent account of the philosophical education of *erōs*. In particular, it provides the leverage for his subsequent account of a hierarchy of beautiful things, some of which are deemed more valuable than others. For, if there were no evaluative judgements involved in our erotic experience, philosophical practice would have no role to play in directing and informing our desires towards certain objects rather than others. We need to bear this in mind later in the account; for there are certain implications of this view of *erōs* that some have found objectionable. If *erōs* is grounded in the perception of valuable properties possessed by the desired object, then we might not expect *erōs* to be directed towards a particular beautiful object with any degree of exclusivity. If there are other things that exhibit the same property then what grounds, on this account, would a rational agent have for not pursuing that object with equal vigour? This account of desire not only raises the possibility of misjudgement, but also the possibility of promiscuity. Further, if there are some beautiful objects that are more valuable than others, then it would seem that *erōs* will, on perceiving that fact, move away from less valuable objects towards those that are truly beautiful. Desiring agents, it would seem, will be sensitive to error, promiscuity, and hierarchy. Socrates will be exploiting all these features of *erōs* in his attempt to direct it towards a truly valuable object.

3. *ERŌS* AND THE GOOD

A further implication of this account of *erōs* is one that will become prominent shortly: all *erōs* is directed towards good and beautiful things. As Socrates puts it later, all *erōs* is for the good (205e7). The moral psychology that is emerging from Socrates' account indicates that all *erōs* is rational in the sense that it is based upon judgements about the value of the object of attraction. No one experiences *erōs* for anything unless it is perceived to be good or beautiful in some way. This needs to be construed carefully for a variety of reasons. First, Socrates includes animals in his account, creatures explicitly included from *logismos* (207b7). If *logismos* refers to reasoning activity of some sort, then it would seem that this is not required for *erōs*. Since they experience *erōs*, they must be able to perceive a thing as *kalon* or *agathon* in some respect and be able to take steps to remedy their lack of it. Some lower-grade cognitive function must be sufficient then.[16] Second, there are numerous cases where we seem to desire something bad. In such cases, Socrates would claim that even in cases where I seem to be desiring something bad I have, in fact, just made a mistake, for I intended to pursue a good thing and was just mistaken about its real nature. The focus on intended, rather than actual objects of desire is clear from the subsequent account. As we shall see later, there are many things desiring agents pursue as good (e.g. fame) that are, in fact, images of the true good (wisdom; cf. 208c3 with 210e5–6, 212a3–5). It is not that in desiring these things they know them to be an image; rather, as we shall see, they just fail to identify correctly the good they seek. What motivates *erōs* in such cases—and indeed in all cases—is the perception of some good or beautiful feature of the object or state of affairs in question.[17] But we should bear in mind that Socrates' claim is that all *erōs* is directed towards the good, and not that all desire is so directed. It may well be the case that *erōs* is a specific form of desire, and not reducible to the category of desire as such. If so, then we can draw no general conclusions about desire as such from this account. All we are entitled to infer is that the kind of phenomenon that concerns Socrates here is that kind of desire based on considerations about the good, and not that all desire is so grounded.[18]

---

[16] See n. 15 and Appendix for further discussion.

[17] Compare *Meno* 77b–78b; with the discussion of the counter-examples to the claim that we all desire the good in Nakhnikian (1994) and Scott (2006).

[18] It is, of course, true that the terminology used to describe desire is not drawn exclusively from ἐρᾶν and cognate words, but also from ἐπιθυμεῖν and βούλεσθαι. For the use of ἐπιθυμία see 200a2; for βούλησις see 205a2: κτήσει γάρ ἀγαθῶν οἱ εὐδαίμονες εὐδαίμονες, καὶ οὐκέτι προσδεῖ ἐρέσθαι ἵνα τί δὲ βούλεται εὐδαίμων εἶναι ὁ βουλόμενος; cf. ταύτην δὴ τὴν βούλησιν, 205a5; καὶ πάντας τἀγαθὰ βούλεσθαι αὐτοῖς εἶναι ἀεί, a6–7. Earlier, during the elenchus of Agathon, Socrates had also used the

The intimate relationship between *erōs* and the good is an important part of the answer to why *erōs* can lead to the benefits previously praised for *erōs*. For it is not the case that *desiring* what is good is a difficult achievement on this account: we all have the right desires. The achievement is to ensure that *erōs* does not make mistakes about what things are really *kalon* and *agathon* and such as to satisfy desire. In Socrates' account of the good things and virtue *erōs* can deliver, there is no need to struggle against a 'vulgar *erōs*' of the sort mentioned by Pausanias. The struggle, if there is to be one, will be between our beliefs about what sorts of things really are good and beautiful and such as to satisfy us. And this will not be a struggle against a 'blind drive'; *erōs* is 'heavenly' by nature and directed towards good and beautiful things.

4. ERŌS AND WISDOM

Socrates has already gone some way towards explaining how *erōs* can work for our good: it is, by its nature, an aspiration towards the good and the beautiful. Further, I have argued that the analysis of *erōs* is devised with the needs of the later analysis of philosophical practice in mind. Describing *erōs* as cognitively informed explains how it can be amenable to education and directed towards a genuinely valuable end. Now, Socrates concludes his account of *eros*' nature with an account of Eros as a philosopher (204b2–4). This account of philosophical *erōs* further prepares the ground for his later claim that *erōs* is best expressed in philosophical activity (210e5–6 with 211d1–3).

---

verbs ἐπιθυμεῖν, βούλεσθαι, and ἐρᾶν interchangeably: ὁ ρως ἔρως ἐστὶν οὐδενὸς ἢ τινός, 199e6–7. Three lines later he switches to ἐπιθυμία : ὁ ρως ἐκείνου οὗ ἔστιν ἔρως, ἐπιθυμεῖ αὐτοῦ ἢ οὔ, 200a2–3; cf. also 200a5, 6, 9. A few lines further on Socrates uses βούλησις, βούλομαι (200b4, b9, c4), but ἐπιθυμεῖν is reintroduced and used interchangeably at c5 and 6–7; d1; cf. also 3–4; 5. Compare similar slippage amongst the terms for desire at *Meno* 78a5 ff. *Gorgias* 466b–468e, though the *Charmides* shows a clear terminological distinction at 167e. But just because all *erōs* is a kind of desire, that does not entail that each and every desire is a kind of *erōs* and directed towards the good and the beautiful. Later in the account we will have good reason to limit the scope of *erōs* to a quite specific phenomenon. For *erōs* involves pregnancies and beautiful media, as we shall see. For a full discussion of this issue see Appendix.

In order to determine why *erōs* should manifest itself in such activity, we need first to clarify the relationship between the pursuit of beauty that characterizes all desiring agents and the pursuit of wisdom characteristic of the philosopher, in particular.

We have learned amongst other things that Eros is 'a schemer after the beautiful and the good...desirous of wisdom and resourceful, and a lover of wisdom throughout his life' (203d4–7). Although these lines suggest that there is some relationship between scheming after the beautiful and the good and desiring wisdom (one already intimated by Pausanias), the relationship between the two is not made explicit until the end of the story. We now learn that the fluctuation between a state of lack and possession that places Eros in between the mortal and divine realms also places Eros in between wisdom and ignorance (203e5) in a way characteristic of the philosopher. Socrates provides an explicit argument for the claim that Eros must be a philosopher (ἀναγκαῖον Ἔρωτα φιλόσοφον εἶναι, 204b2–4), on the grounds that Eros is concerned with beauty (b3), and wisdom is amongst the most beautiful things (b2–3). So it is inferred that one important object of Eros' pursuit must be wisdom. Philosophizing throughout his life is a way (a very good way, as we shall see) of Eros' 'scheming after the beautiful'.

The claim that Eros pursues wisdom commits us to saying that philosophy is one important activity of *erōs* but not necessarily that it is the only one.[19] For just as there may be other beautiful objects besides wisdom (we are told only that wisdom is amongst the most beautiful things: ἔστιν γὰρ δὴ τν καλλίστων ἡ σοφία, 204b2–3), there may also be forms of *erōs* other than philosophical *erōs*.[20] But the argument does rely on a particularly strong relationship between beauty and *erōs*. For if the claim were only that if something is desired, then it is beautiful, it would not necessarily follow that Eros pursues wisdom. The claim is also needed that if something is perceived to be beautiful, then it is desired (where the perception of

---

[19] The fact that Eros is a philosopher is not a necessary truth, then, but a claim that follows necessarily from the premises of the argument.

[20] I take it that τῶν καλλίστων is a partitive genitive rather than an objective genitive, so that wisdom 'is amongst the most beautiful things', rather than 'of the most beautiful things'. The argument relies on the partitive genitive, since it is this sense that relates *erōs* for beauty and wisdom.

beauty is sufficient, and not just necessary, for *erōs*). The argument would run as follows: If *x* is perceived to be beautiful, then Eros desires it; wisdom is perceived to be beautiful; therefore Eros desires wisdom. It also seems to be the case that wisdom is desired not because it is just an instance of beauty, but because it is one of the most beautiful things. The superlative may suggest that there is a correlation between the degree of (perceived) beauty in an object and the degree or intensity of *erōs* experienced for that object. If so, then there may be a further implicit assumption at work here. The argument would be that: Eros is concerned with the beautiful (204b3); the more beautiful the object, the more Eros desires that object (implicit); wisdom is one of *the most* beautiful things (b2–3); therefore Eros is, in the highest degree, a lover of wisdom. This argument would make sense of the use of the superlative here, but also, and crucially, it would prepare the way for the ascent to the form of beauty—the most beautiful of all beautiful things—which is revealed as the ultimate object of *erōs* for all desiring agents. At such a time, we realize that all *erōs* culminates in *erōs* for the form of beauty, since the form of beauty is the only truly (unqualifiedly, immutably) beautiful thing. The exposition has not yet reached the point where these matters become clear, however. Until then, all such premises remain implicit, and the aims of other lovers are not excluded, aims which will later be exposed explicitly as shadowy imitations of *erōs* for the one true beauty, just as the objects of their *erōs* are only likenesses of the form (cf. 212a3–7).

Having established what will turn out to be a crucial connection between *erōs*' characteristic pursuit of beauty and wisdom, Socrates goes on to explain those aspects of *erōs* that are relevant to the pursuit of wisdom. Since Eros is both deficient and resourceful in relation to the beautiful things he lacks and desires, and wisdom is amongst the beautiful things he desires, then Eros has an intermediate position in relation to wisdom and ignorance (203e3–5). The argument for this claim runs as follows: Eros 'philosophises throughout his life' (203d7). Those who philosophize are in between ignorance and wisdom, unlike either the gods who already are wise (204a1–2) or the ignorant who are not even aware that they lack wisdom (a3–7). Nobody who already has wisdom philosophizes (204a1–2), for they do not desire that which they do not lack (204a6–7, with 202d1–3).

Nor do the ignorant philosophize, for they are unaware of a lack of wisdom and therefore do not strive to remedy that lack (204a4–6). Eros philosophizes throughout his life (203d7). Thus Eros is between wisdom and ignorance.

Socrates goes on to describe how this state of cognitive intermediacy functions in Eros' nature.

As a philosopher, [he is] necessarily between wisdom and ignorance. What makes him like this is again his birth: he has a father who is wise and resourceful, a mother who is not wise and resource-less (204b4–6).

As we can see from this passage, in the aetiological story, Poros is linked to *euporia* (εὐπορία) linguistically and conceptually (204b6, 203d7) and Penia is likewise connected with *aporia* (ἀπορία) (203b9, 204b7). From the description of Eros' fluctuation between the characteristics of his parents in the first passage, we infer that Eros at least temporarily manifests the characteristic of his mother—*aporia*—but then that of his divine father—*euporia*—and then again, that of his mortal mother—*aporia*—and so on. So Eros' nature is not, strictly speaking, either deprived or wealthy, but fluctuates between both *aporia* and *euporia*. This fluctuation is responsible for his epistemic intermediacy (204b4–6). Since a defining characteristic of Eros' intermediate status is not just a lack of wisdom, but an awareness of that lack, those who pursue wisdom are not just those who are lacking in wisdom, but those who are aware that they have this particular deficiency.

Although the characterization of the philosophical character as one who is aware of a lack of wisdom suggests a particularly Socratic construal of *eros'* philosophical nature, one cannot simply assume this at this point. Nor should we want to make such an assumption at this early stage in the speech. If Socrates is offering a general account of *erōs* personified as a philosopher, it should be an account that applies to everyone who values *sophia* as one of the *kallista* and one need not be a Socrates to meet this criterion.[21] The audience to

---

[21] The lovers of sights and sounds in *Republic* 5 might also fit such a description. Such types seek out 'beautiful sounds and colours and shapes and all the artefacts made from these' (476b)—and can therefore be described as lovers of the beautiful. But they are excluded from the ranks of the philosophers because they cannot see the form; they confuse likeness with reality (476c).

whom Socrates is delivering his speech at this symposium represent the cultural and political elite of Athens at the time, and could all be said to value *sophia* as one of the *kallista*.[22] This, after all, is what they are all doing at this symposium—celebrating, and perpetuating, their respective claims to wisdom in a given area. They present themselves as knowledgeable in a certain area, such as law-making (Pausanias), the medical art (Eryximachus), and literary skill (Agathon). As such they might all lay claim to *sophia* in the broad sense in which Homer, for example, would be taken as a source of *sophia* (e.g. by the eponymous protagonist of the *Ion*). Before such types can be excluded from the ranks of the true philosopher, we need an account of what wisdom is, how a deficiency in this area is perceived, and how one remedies that deficiency. We shall not be offered that until the description of the 'ascent' to the form of beauty.[23]

Since we know that the account will lead to a stricter philosophical sense, however, let us see what we can make of the Socratic resonances to this depiction of *erōs'* philosophical nature. The strong association of *aporia*, at least, with the procedures of the Platonic Socrates is clear to any reader of the Socratic dialogues, where the

[22] Many of the symposiasts refer to wisdom in their speeches. Pausanias, for example, refers specifically to philosophy and yet it will become increasingly clear that the kind of activity he envisages is far from Socrates' conception (cf. 182b7–c2, 184d1). He believes, for example, that *sophia* is the kind of thing that can, and should, be exchanged for sexual favours from a beloved (cf. 184c3, d2). This is the kind of exchange that Socrates refuses twice in the dialogue (cf. 175d3–e2, 218d7–219a4). Eryximachus uses *epistēmē* to indicate medical expertise (187c4–5), and Agathon refers to *sophia* where the context makes clear that he is referring to some kind of literary expertise related to poetry (196d5–6).

[23] Pericles' statement in his funeral oration that Athenians 'philosophize without softness' suggests that many Athenians were engaged in an activity which they characterized as philosophy (Thucydides 2.40.1; see also the description of Solon as 'philosophizing in his travels' around Egypt in Herodotus 1.30). Nehamas, (1999) 110, argues that: 'In the fourth century B.C. the terms "dialectic", and "sophistry" do not seem to have had a widely agreed upon application. On the contrary, different authors seem to have fought with one another with the purpose of appropriating the term "philosophy", each for his own practice and educational scheme.' See also Nightingale (1995) 14–15. Plato, she argues, 'appropriated the term for a discipline that was constructed in opposition to the many varieties of "wisdom" recognised by Plato's predecessors and contemporaries'. For the broad sense of *philosophia* in Plato, see, for example, *Phaedo* 60–1. There is also a more common (non-philosophical) use of *aporia* and *euporia* as a contrasting pair: see Aristophanes, *Wlth* , esp. 469, 576, and Aristotle, *Pol.* 1297ª29–36, for example.

dialectical activity is typically one in which *aporia* is a precondition of progress.[24] There is no need to take *aporia* in Plato as exclusively associated with the elenchus, but in many dialogues it is the elenchus that ensures that those searching for wisdom become aware of the limitations of their knowledge. This activity typically aims to establish whether the parties concerned are mistaken about a definition of an ethical term, and to create the awareness that a topic on which an interlocutor thought he could expound at length and with ease is, in fact, a difficult one of which he has no clear knowledge. Socrates himself was notorious for being in a state of *aporia*, and for putting others in a similar state, too.[25] This is the kind of response that Agathon experiences after the elenchus (201b11). The realization of ignorance is a defining feature of *erōs'* philosophical nature here. Unlike the ignorant, who do not take steps to remedy that which they do not think they lack (204a4–6), one who is aware of a lack of wisdom (and perceives wisdom as *kalon*) will, by contrast, be motivated to remedy that lack. Further, since one who is aware of a lack will have some sense of the thing that they are lacking (just as Penia could find her Poros in the story), we may infer that any attempts to remedy that lack will be informed by that awareness.[26]

---

[24] Aristotle in *Sophistical Refutations* 8, 169^{b}23–9 associates the establishment of ignorance with peirastic dialectic, the method he associates most strongly with the Socrates of Plato's Socratic dialogues; cf. Bolton (1993) 132, who notes that Aristotle is here echoing Socrates' description of his own practice at *Apol.* 21c7–8, 23b7, d8–9, *La.* 200a, *Charm.* 166c–d. That this is seen as characteristic of Socrates' method can be seen also in Alcibiades' speech, 216a5. Note, too, that at the start of the dialogue Socrates presents himself as aware that his wisdom (a term used to describe Socrates' state by Agathon) is 'an inferior sort of wisdom, or even a debatable one, existing as if in a dream' (175e2–4). This self-deprecating stance is characteristic of one who is aware of his deficiencies.

[25] Awareness of ignorance is a defining characteristic of Socratic philosophy as outlined in the *Apology*, one which places Socrates in between the wise and the ignorant (*Apol.* 21d2–6; see also 21b4, 22d1, 23b3). For Socrates' *aporia* see also *Prt.* 361c, *Ly.* 222c, *La.* 200e. For his role in putting others in such a state, see *Eu.* 11b, *Grg.* 522b, *Meno* 80a1–3, *Tht.* 149a.

[26] The active role given to Penia in the story may be taken to suggest that *aporia* is—to some extent—a resourceful state. Of Penia it is said that she 'schemed, because of her lack, to have a child from Poros' (203b7–8). Scheming is, strictly speaking, a characteristic of Poros (203d4–5), one which is activated in response to Penia's perceived deficiency. But this description suggests that Penia's lack is not such as to prevent her from taking some steps towards a resolution. This may be taken to suggest that the experience of *aporia* also guides the inquirer in the direction in

Although the realization of ignorance is a precondition of a philosophical character here, awareness of ignorance is not itself what
constitutes that intermediate state.[27] As the following lines go on to
make clear, it is the dynamic fluctuation between *aporia* and *euporia*
that is responsible for the cognitive intermediacy characteristic of the
philosopher. The picture that emerges then is *aporia* plus some
notion of progress—*euporia*. So if we are to determine how *erōs'*
nature operates in the pursuit of wisdom, we need to clarify this state
of *euporia*. This will prove crucial when we come to explore philosophical activity later in the ascent. Let us take another look at the
story. The cause of Eros' intermediate philosophical status is said to
be his birth: he has a father who is wise and resourceful and a mother
who is not wise and resourceless (204b5–7). The nature of the father
is here associated with wisdom. One might suspect, then, that Poros'
inheritance—*euporia*—is to be associated with some kind of wisdom. Support for such a suggestion might be drawn from the fact
that it is the nature of the father that results in a provision of some

which more fruitful answers may lie. To be aware of one's lack is to be aware of what
some of the problems are, and to realize what the problems are is already to be on the
right path. Although there are differences between Plato and Aristotle on the role of
aporia in inquiry, the notion that realizing what the problems are is the first step
towards progress is shared. For Aristotle, ἀπορίαι are themselves objects of investigation, in part, because they 'illuminate the path of progress'. In a claim which reads
like a comment on Meno's paradox of inquiry, he writes that 'those who inquire
without first stating the difficulties are like those who do not know where they have to
go; besides, one does not otherwise know even whether one has found what one is
looking for, for the end is not clear to such a person, whereas to one who has first
discussed the ἀπορίαι, it is clear' (*Metaphysics* 995ᵃ27–b2). For the differences between the Platonic and Aristotelian conceptions of ἀπορία, see Matthews (1999) 99–
107. Both Matthews (1999) 107, and M. Frede (1996) 145, argue that the idea that
ἀπορίαι are themselves targets for inquiry appears most prominently in later Plato
(and Aristotle).

   [27] The epistemic status of awareness of ignorance is a much debated question. See
McCabe (1988) 331–50, Vlastos (1985) 1–31, Lesher (1987) 275–88, and Bolton
(1993) 121–52. In light of McCabe's arguments one might characterize the philosopher in the *Symposium* as intermediate in the sense that he lacks first order knowledge
(and is to that extent resourceless), but he possesses some second-order knowledge in
terms of which he judges himself to be deficient (and is thus resourceful). But
however epistemically rich one makes *aporia* we are still left with trying to determine
the nature of *euporia*. Second-order cognitive states will play some role in determining just how one perceives a lack of wisdom and, as a consequence, what steps one
takes to remedy that ignorance, but there is little indication that *euporia* itself should
be identified with such states in this text.

sort (203e4). But wisdom is not, strictly speaking, said to belong to Eros, but to Poros, Eros' father. How Eros inherits this wisdom is a further question. Further, this provision is a result of the *euporia*, and not what the *euporia* itself consists in. The resources inherited from Poros are to be identified not with the possession of the wisdom Eros lacks and desires, but rather with an ability to scheme and find the means to procure that knowledge. From his father [Eros] 'is a schemer after the beautiful and the good, courageous, impetuous and intense, a clever hunter, always weaving new devices, both passionate for wisdom and resourceful, philosophising throughout his life, a clever magician, sorcerer and sophist' (203d4–8). In virtue of his father, Eros can find the means to procure the knowledge he realizes he lacks. He has ἐπιβουλία, good deliberative skill, which makes him resourceful at getting the knowledge he lacks. From his mother, then, Eros may lack wisdom, but he does not lack the ability to provide what he lacks: Eros *knows how to get wisdom*. So, those who desire wisdom are intermediate in the sense that they lack substantive wisdom and are aware of it (ἀπορία), but they have resources to the extent that they are clever at getting it (εὐπορία)— they can deliberate and scheme after knowledge (203d4–7).[28]

At this stage it is unclear what 'knowing how to get wisdom' consists in. But an earlier passage clarifies what this must involve. The nature of Eros' intermediate demonic status was explained with the example of the cognitive state in between wisdom and ignorance:

Don't you recognise that having correct beliefs, even without being able to give a rational account of them, is neither a matter of knowing (since how could something irrational be knowledge?), nor of ignorance (how could something that hits on what is the case be ignorance?) Correct belief is,

---

[28] Clarifying the state of *euporia* precisely has implications for our understanding of the philosophical character in this text—Socrates. For it is sometimes held that there is a tension in Plato's view of Socrates in this text. On the one hand, he appears to embody the description of *erōs* as an eager seeker after truth, and, on the other, he seems to be wise and 'know all that is necessary for a good and beautiful man to know', as Alcibiades puts it later (222a1–6). Analyzing the details of *erōs*' nature indicates that there is no tension between these two. Socrates also manifests the euporetic aspect of *erōs* in that he knows how to pursue wisdom. This is, of course, different from supposing that he has the knowledge he knows how to pursue. See further below, Ch. 6.

I imagine, something of the sort in question, between wisdom and ignorance (202a5–9).

This description of the intermediate here illustrates how a lack of knowledge might be perceived, and how, in turn, one might try to remedy that lack. *For a philosopher who has been educated by Diotima*, at any rate, being aware of a lack of knowledge must involve the awareness that one lacks a *logos* of a certain sort. Being resourceful at getting knowledge must somehow involve scheming after, and procuring, such a *logos* (202a5). At least one of the ways in which a lover of wisdom might express this *euporia* in his search for knowledge, then, is through the ability to procure *logoi*.[29]

We are also told that this resourcefulness results in something substantive—'a provision' (203e3–4). Again, at this stage, we do not know what this provision is exactly. We know only that it must result in something perceived to be 'beautiful and good' (since Eros is a schemer after the beautiful and the good, 203d5), and that it is relevant to the possession of wisdom (since wisdom is one of the most beautiful things, 204b3). Since having a *logos* is relevant to the possession of wisdom, it seems reasonable to take it that this provision is a *logos* of some sort, and that it will be *kalos* to the extent that it aids the search for wisdom (cf. 198d1–2). But it is important to notice that it is neither said nor implied that the resulting provision is knowledge nor, consequently, that Eros' fluctuation takes place from knowledge to ignorance. This would suggest that if knowledge were supplied then that, too, would 'flow away', but Eros' fluctuation is one that operates *between* knowledge and ignorance.[30] So if the search for wisdom involves scheming after, and procuring a *logos*, we must take it that the *logos* provided is, in some sense, deficient. It

---

[29] Socrates argues elsewhere that the wise person can always provide an account of his beliefs: *Grg.* 465a2–5, 500e4–501a3, *La.* 189e3–190b1. At this stage in the *Symposium*'s account we do not know what this *logos* would be or how one would get it. As we shall see later, the emphasis on the generation of *logoi* in the philosophical ascent suggests that this characterization of knowledge is in play there too. If so, then the *logos* needed seems to be a definitional one. I infer this from the fact that the lover's progress towards knowledge—progress which involves the delivery of *logoi* at every stage—is not complete until he has come to know ὃ ἔστι καλόν (211c8–9).

[30] This passage is about *erōs*, which, as the example of the gods (and the ignorant) made clear, operates in between knowledge and ignorance, i.e. when knowledge is not yet possessed.

is not the *logos* necessary (or sufficient) for knowledge—for if it were, then Eros would fluctuate from knowledge to ignorance when this thing provided 'flows away' and this is not the case: he operates between these poles. We need a more subtle understanding of the role that *logoi* play in the search for wisdom. It may well be the case that one tries to provide numerous *logoi* that are deficient in some way. Having an 'unaccounted matter' (ἄλογον πρᾶγμα), then, must be measured in terms of the kind or quality of the *logos* provided. It need not mean that one does not have any sort of *logos*, just that one does not have a *logos* of the right sort. When we reach the description of the ascent to knowledge of the form, we shall see that the pursuit of wisdom involves the provision of numerous *logoi* and the search does not cease until one has come to know ὃ ἔστι καλόν (211c8–9) and, we infer, can then provide the right sort of *logos*—a definitional one.

Socrates clarified Eros' intermediate status with the example of the intermediate cognitive state of correct belief. The terms used to describe this intermediate state between ignorance and wisdom are strikingly similar to the terms used to describe the poles of Eros' cognitive intermediacy here (cf. 202a2–3 with 204b4–5). Although Socrates does not explicitly ascribe correct belief to Eros (it is only a parallel, albeit a significant choice of one), it does fall between the two relevant extremes of wisdom and ignorance; and so one might take it that correct belief is one outcome of Eros' philosophical activity.[31] Since we are told that 'the acquisition does not remain long enough for it to be said that he is wealthy, but neither does his state of deprivation last long enough for it to be said that he is poor, [Eros] is in between wisdom and ignorance' (203e3–5), it is clear that whatever is provided is transient; it 'flows away'. One could make good sense here of the claim that the philosopher is in between wisdom and ignorance 'because the thing provided always flows away' (203e4) in the manner of the correct belief–knowledge distinction, which Socrates puts forward in an argument at the end of the *Meno*. A defining feature of correct beliefs there is that 'they are not

---

[31] Correct belief may be *one* outcome, but not necessarily the only one. In the demonstration with the slave in the *Meno*, for example, the slave provides a correct belief only at the end of a long process involving the delivery of numerous *logoi*.

willing to remain long, and escape from a man's mind' (98a1–3). In light of this characterization one could say that the thing provided 'always flows away' because it lacks the right kind of *logos* that would render it stable (cf. the role of the *aitios logismos* in 'tying down' beliefs at *Meno* 97e5–98a8).[32]

So far then, we have clarified the sense in which someone who pursues wisdom as one of the most beautiful things might employ *aporia* and *euporia*—*erōs'* characteristic nature—to serve that end. As to be expected, the description of the pursuit of wisdom relates to the general analysis of the pursuit of beauty: (1) wisdom is perceived as *kalon* or *agathon* (it is one of the most beautiful things). (2) There is a lack of wisdom experienced on the part of the desiring agent in question (ἀπορία). (3) But she is able to scheme after wisdom; she has *epiboulia* (ἐπιβούλια), deliberative skill, which allows her to be resourceful in this pursuit. (4) The pursuit of wisdom generates a *logos* which 'flows away'—perhaps because it is unstable and not supported by the right *logos*. This deficiency is experienced again and so she has another experience of *aporia*. But since she knows how to remedy that lack she schemes again; and so on. The constant attempt and ability to replenish ourselves of the good and beautiful things we lack and desire (in this case, wisdom) forms part of the explanation of how *erōs* can lead to the productive effects claimed for it. Philosophers, like all desiring agents, are those who are aware of, and able to transcend, their characteristically mortal limitations and

---

[32] The description of the thing provided always 'flowing away' does not, it might seem, sound much like positive progress, and yet the description of *erōs'* fluctuation between *aporia* and **euporia** suggests some such progress. I thank Lesley Brown for this objection. The parallel with the slave in the *Meno* may prove helpful here, too. Let us suppose that his *logos* flows away in the flux of argument because it is not tied down by an explanatory account. Now we might still count the slave as making positive progress because the very objections that render his *logos* unstable also show where the difficulties are which stand in need of resolution by further attempts. And if *euporia* is to be measured in terms of knowing how to get wisdom—*epiboulia* and so on—then this will surely count as a positive euporetic experience. Progress can be measured in terms of knowing how to proceed, rather than in terms of a given result at a given time. In answer to the further objection that if one knows how to proceed then one gets the right results (i.e. *logoi* that do not flow away), it may be said that knowing how to proceed is something that comes in degrees. One can meet one objection, only to find a more sophisticated one on the horizon. One might still like to know how *substantive* progress towards knowledge is to be made. On this issue, see below, sect. 5, and Ch. 4, sect. 2.

to strive towards a divine state of possession. This is a positive depiction of *erōs* both in a general sense and for the case of the philosophical character, as we shall see.

5. SOCRATES AND DIOTIMA

It is crucial to Socrates' overall argument that *erōs* is productive and not just an aspiration towards the beauty and wisdom it lacks. For the expressed agenda is to show that *erōs* is of great benefit; if so, then *erōs* had better be resourceful in its pursuit of desired ends. Socrates' account of what exactly this *euporia* consists in will concern us in later chapters, but for now, notice than this productive aspect of *erōs'* nature is not only described, but also exemplified, in Socrates' own behaviour at this symposium. He plays out the dynamic fluctuation between the aspects of *erōs* just described in his interaction with the mysterious figure of Diotima introduced after the elenchus of Agathon (201b ff.).[33] By embodying philosophical *erōs* in the presentation of his speech, and demonstrating its productive effects, Socrates lends further support to his account of a productive and beneficial *erōs*.

Since Socrates divides himself up, so to speak, into two roles—that of the lacking (youthful) Socrates (who is in the same state as Agathon), and the resourceful Diotima who knows how to remedy the deficiencies in Socrates' *logoi*—we can see his behaviour as embodying the complementarity of these two sides to *eros'* philosophical nature. As we have seen in the previous chapter, in contrast to the confident stance of his peers, Socrates begins his inquiry with an elenchus designed to expose weaknesses in the previous account, and to yield an awareness of the difficulties involved in giving an

---

[33] Although some scholars have tried to show that Diotima was a real person, the consensus is that she is a Platonic fiction, a view which finds support in the references to the preceding speeches. Aristophanes, for one, is not fooled by this alien voice (212c5–6). On this issue see Bury (1932) xxxix; Cornford (1971) 122; Halperin (1990*a*) 257–308; Rowe (1998*a*) 173. The use of other voices is not unique to the *Symposium*; see, for example, *Meno* 81a–b. But if Diotima is a fictional voice, then why is she introduced? I hope the following makes a contribution to that question.

account of *erōs*. Socrates reassured Agathon that he used to be in the same position as Agathon is now and was puzzled by similar issues (e5). The reason he visited Diotima, he explains, was that he was aware that he was in need (καὶ ἐγὼ αὖ ἔλεγον ὅτι οὐκ εἰδείην, 207c1, γνοὺς ὅτι διδασκάλων δέομαι, c5). This awareness motivated him to seek out the resourceful Diotima, just as the experience of need motivated Penia to find her Poros in the story. In contrast to Socrates (and Agathon), Diotima is presented as wise (201d3), and *sophistēs* (208c1), like Poros (who is 'clever' and 'able', 203d6–7, *sophistēs* 203d4). Further, Diotima's Mantinean origins and her apparent postponement of the plague suggests a connection to the seer's art which was described as part of the erotic-cum-demonic art earlier in the speech (202e3–203a7).[34] Since Diotima will reveal the rites that *erōs* engages in as part of his communication with the divine (210a–212a), practices which culminate in friendship with the gods (a6), it seems reasonable to take it that she embodies the knowledge and rewards of the erotic art. Diotima embodies the euporetic aspect of *erōs* which transcends the limitations of a mortal, deficient, nature.[35] In his role play with Diotima Socrates explains that he provided new and better *logoi*, which promised to meet these deficiencies. For example, the issue that came to light after the elenchus of Agathon was that if *erōs* lacks the things it desires, and is not, after all, beautiful and good himself, then we are left wondering whether *erōs* is ugly and bad (201e10). This puzzle prompts Socrates to

[34] In Eryximachus' speech the plague was said to be an erotic disorder (188b1–3), so perhaps her involvement with the plague is a particular sample of the erotic knowledge which she reveals in its generality.

[35] Nothing I have said so far addresses Diotima's gender. Halperin (1990*b*) esp. 129 argues that her gender 'signals Plato's departure from certain aspects of the sexual ethos of his contemporaries and thereby enables him to highlight some of the central features of his own philosophy', in particular, the creative aspects of *erōs*. By identifying Diotima with the euporetic and productive aspect of *erōs* my reading supports this claim. Later we shall see that *euporein* and cognates are related to the activity of giving birth. Desiring agents try to provide something for themselves by producing it, and a precondition of this creative activity is a state of pregnancy (for which see below, Chs. 3 and 4). With these aspects of the account in play we can see more readily why the euporetic element is characterized as female. We shall also have good reason for agreeing with Halperin that part of the force of gendering these ideas is to carve out a new educational model distinct from the pederastic relationship espoused by Pausanias, for example. See also Brisson (1999).

rethink his position and, after considering the possibility of a realm of intermediate states, he revises his *logos* accordingly (202a1–2). This, in turn, brings to light a further difficulty: if *erōs* does not possess good and beautiful things, then desiring agents cannot, after all, be divine; *erōs* is, in fact, an intermediary being, and poised between the mortal and the divine (202e1–2). Although we have not witnessed the elenchi involved in the provision of all these answers, we are given a sample of such a process in the elenchus of Agathon. This has made it clear that one needs to scrutinize beliefs, perceive argumentative deficiencies, and respond to those by providing new and more persuasive answers. The interaction between Socrates and his alter ego dramatically illustrates certain aspects of the philosophical procedure for pursuing wisdom. Diotima is part of the positive presentation of Socrates, or rather, philosophical *erōs*, in this dialogue. Socrates is not just the aporetic character familiar from the elenctic dialogues, but also a resourceful thinker. Philosophy is also a creative, euporetic activity and the familiar elenctic Socrates will also play another role.

Socrates' presentation raises a question for this text. In many of the dialogues of definition the experience of *aporia* appears as the terminus of a philosophical argument.[36] In the *Meno*, for example, which is perhaps the most explicit characterization (and defence) of the role of *aporia* in an inquiry, Meno expresses his irritation and his doubts about Socrates' procedure (80a1–3). He says he is numbed by the experience and does not know how to remedy his lack at this stage. He sees no way forward. Since Socrates goes on to show Meno how progress is possible, many scholars have seen the dialogue as part of a transition towards a more constructive presentation of the 1philosopher.[37] Socrates will show Meno that *aporia* is but one philosophical experience, a stage on the road to progress. Since the *Symposium* weds *aporia* with *euporia* in its presentation of the

<hr>

[36] The dialogues typically thought to be amongst the so-called 'elenctic dialogues', or 'dialogues of definition' are *Charmides, Crito, Euthyphro, Hippias Minor, Ion, Laches, Protagoras*; cf. Vlastos (1983) 27.

[37] See, for example, Irwin (1995) 133, Vlastos (1983) 55–6. There is some debate over the form that this takes. For some scholars, it accommodates the elenchus: cf. Irwin (1995) 133, Nehamas (1994) 221–49, and Fine (1992) 200–27. But in a later article (1991*b*: 107–32) Vlastos argues that the elenchus is dropped in the so-called middle dialogues, and is superseded by a new method.

philosophical character, and displays this coupling in the movement of Socrates' account, the association with such dialogues becomes a strong one. If we look to other dialogues that serve as parallels to the way in which *aporia* is coupled with some notion of progress, this is to be found particularly prominently in dialogues like the *Meno* and the *Phaedo*. If this is the case, then, we have at least circumstantial evidence that the *Symposium*, like these dialogues, is operating with a constructive characterization of the philosopher.[38] Exploring these parallels should confirm the constructive description of the philosopher in this text and this is not a detour from the main argument: it is crucial to persuading us of the beneficial effects of (philosophical) *erōs* required for a proper encomium.

Before one can clearly locate the *Symposium* in this constructive context, it is worth considering afresh the claim—underlying Meno's irritation—that *euporia* is not conjoined with *aporia* in the kind of discussion which we see in numerous dialogues of definition. As we have already noted, the specification of *aporia* and *euporia* as the *termini* of the philosopher's intermediacy is strongly suggestive of

---

[38] Socrates' two personae raise questions about whether 'Socrates' is to be identified with the historical Socrates, as some have supposed, and 'Diotima' with the Platonic Socrates. See, for example, Cornford (1971) 125, 129; Markus (1971) 134; Vlastos (1981) 21 n. 58. Support for a Socratic–Platonic distinction is often found in the disparaging remark Socrates reports having heard from Diotima (209e5–210a2). But Diotima raises doubts about Socrates' ability to understand certain parts of the speech because Socrates, we should recall, is playing the role of *Agathon* (201d–e). He comforts Agathon with the thought that he, too, used to make the same mistakes about *erōs*, but now, as a mature Socrates who has learnt about these things from the wise Diotima, he has come to understand 'erotic matters'. Socrates' abject ignorance belongs to the past and is rehearsed here *for the sake of his host*, who has just been refuted. It is not the mature Socrates who would not understand the erotic matters of the ascent, but the young, inexperienced Socrates who used to be in just the same state in which Agathon is now (201d8). Although aligning the inexperienced Socrates with Agathon in this way makes it unlikely that any distinction between an inexperienced and a mature Socrates marks a Socratic–Platonic distinction, one might still wonder whether the constructive figure of Diotima marks a departure from the earlier elenctic dialogues, and thereby from the historical Socrates. I wish to make it clear from the outset that my argument here does not rely on either the claim that the elenctic dialogues are earlier than the *Symposium*, or on the claim that the Socrates of the elenctic dialogues is the historical Socrates. Although this character may draw on the historical Socrates, the precise relationship between the two remains controversial. See Annas and Rowe (2002) on this debate. Reading a Socratic-Platonic break into the *Symposium* would require the historical Socrates to be the Socrates of Plato's elenctic dialogues, a debate which lies outside the scope of this book.

the dynamics of philosophical argument, which is commonly figured throughout the dialogues by precisely these terms.[39] In such passages *euporia* is, in some sense, in play, too. Clearly, an interlocutor must be 'able to say' something and in that sense, might be said to experience *euporia* (Ion, for example, claims *euporia* many times in the opening part of the *Ion*, cf. *Ion* 532c3, 533c6). Meno, too, in the opening stretch of the dialogue, clearly has an ability to expound at length, and with ease, on the subject of virtue. But this experience of *euporia* is shown to be illusory, in part, because it is not based on an awareness of the difficulties of giving an account of the subject. Even when an interlocutor attempts to remedy a deficiency perceived by Socrates in his previous answer (as Meno himself does), these further attempts are often not based on an awareness that the interlocutor does not know the answer. They rather assume that the answer is still forthcoming. One might term this 'pre-aporetic *euporia*'. In many dialogues, we see a pattern of pre-aporetic *euporia* (*Meno* 71e1 ff., *Laches* 190e4, *Euthyphro* 4b9–5e2), which is shown to be misguided as the difficulties are teased out of a particular thesis, and then *aporia* follows (*Meno* 79e7–80b4, *Laches* 193d11–e6, *Euthyphro* 11b6–8). We do not tend to see *post*-aporetic *euporia* in such a discussion, since most of these dialogues typically end with *aporia*.[40] This is one of the reasons why Meno's complaint at 80a–b is such a compelling one, and why it is often held that dialogues such as the *Meno* and the

---

[39] For examples of *aporia* and *euporia* in an elenctic context, see *Charm.* 167b7, *Euthyd.* 290a8, *Ly.* 219c9, *Hip. Ma.* 298c7, *La.* 194c5. In the *Laws* these terms appear together and are linked with definition (861b1 ff.). There are many more examples of one or other of these terms in an explicitly elenctic context, but an exhaustive list would take up too much space, and my immediate concern is to illustrate the way in which *aporia* and *euporia* may work together in an explicitly elenctic context. Clearly these terms may simply refer to the ability or inability to speak about a given subject where the context is not an elenctic one (e.g. *Symp.* 198b2). I see no significant distinction between the claim that *aporia* and *euporia* operate in philosophical characters and the claim that they figure in the dynamics of philosophical argument. It is, strictly speaking, the characters who participate in these arguments who experience *aporia* and *euporia*.

[40] Whether and in what sense there is any genuine *euporia*, understood in terms of whether there is success in gaining even a part of the definition sought, is a controversial issue for many elenctic dialogues. The *Euthyphro* is a good example of such controversy. Allen (1970) 56–8 and Shorey (1933) 78–9 deny that any progress is made towards a definition of piety. This is in contrast to the views of McPherran (1985) 283–309 and Rabinowitz (1958) 108–20.

Phaedo—and I would add, the *Symposium*—are forging a more constructive model of the philosophical character.

Those dialogues that furnish parallels to the way in which *aporia* and post-aporetic *euporia* operate together may clarify the importance of this characterization of the philosopher. I begin with the *Meno*. In this dialogue, Socrates dispels Meno's aporetic despair by demonstrating with one of his slaves that *aporia* is the first positive sign of progress. Socrates questions the slave about a geometrical problem the answer to which he is, at first, confident that he knows. As Socrates says to Meno, he supposes he knows when he does not. Socrates' questions reveal to the slave that he, in fact, does not know the answer to this problem (84a). Socrates exclaims that this is the first sign of real progress (84ab). This realization creates the desire in the slave to remedy his lack, with the result that 'he will now go and search for [knowledge]'. The *Meno* passage makes it clear that it is a necessary condition of inquiry that one not believe that one already knows, a condition that also made explicit in the *Symposium* at 203d–204a, and for the very same reasons, namely that it is the realization of ignorance that leads to a search for wisdom (204a6–7). Similarly, in the *Meno*, it is this condition that leads the slave on to inquiry. Being aware of a lack of wisdom, he now 'longs for knowledge' and, further, he now has a better sense of the sort of answer that would satisfy the search for an answer. Here, too, there is the pattern of lack, informed desire, and search.

Part of Socrates' attempt to encourage Meno out of his post-aporetic despair is to show how the slave is led on from *aporia* to make progress. After reducing the slave to *aporia*, Socrates exclaims enthusiastically: 'Now look how he goes on from this state of *aporia* to discover as he searches with me' (84c9–d1). The slave experiences *aporia* and Socrates shows him how to remedy his ignorance by encouraging him to answer questions, in an orderly way (82e12–13), about the problem in hand. Socrates is the one with deliberative skill here (much like Diotima in the *Symposium*), but the slave's progress is nonetheless his own, for these ordered series of questions provide the occasion for the slave to reason out the answer logically for himself (82d). The progress Socrates initiates results in the slave having a correct belief (85bc). Socrates concludes that we should be optimistic about inquiry (86b6–c2): *aporia* is a necessary precondition of real progress. In this episode we see that the slave can remedy his ignorance with help from Socrates (an experience of *euporia*), after an experience of *aporia*. This results in genuine progress—a correct belief (what, in the language of the *Symposium*, might be one of the πoριζόμενα). Socrates says that at present these correct beliefs have been stirred up in him 'like a dream' (85c9–10); they are without knowledge, having which is like being awake.[41] The slave must be questioned many times, and in many ways, before this opinion becomes knowledge (85c10–d1). Later in the dialogue Socrates explains that knowledge differs from correct belief because this dreamlike state of belief is unstable, whereas knowledge renders a belief stable by 'reasoning about the explanation' (97e5–98a8). An explanation, we infer, provides one with reasons for why one's belief is correct, reasons, one is led to suppose, which allow one to stabilize one's belief in the flux of argument against any objections or challenges which may well have been met in the process of formulating the explanation. Such a belief will not 'escape from a man's mind', or 'flow away'. The slave's correct belief is, then, only a part of his progress towards knowledge, and places him in an intermediate position between knowledge and ignorance. Further progress must consist in a fresh *aporiaeuporia* dynamic, in a realization that this kind of explanatory *logos* is lacking, and in the attempt to provide such a *logos*. The slave needs to weave new argumentative devices, hunt down further reasons for his thesis, and display the courage that characterizes the philosopher in the *Symposium* (203d5), and that Socrates encourages Meno to display later in the dialogue (86c).

The *Phaedo* also displays a sophisticated argumentative dynamic between the *aporia* of Simmias and Cebes, and a subsequent state of *euporia*. Simmias and Cebes hold numerous beliefs about the nature of the soul, but they have doubts that need to be addressed. Simmias is persuaded by Socrates' argument that the soul is something beautiful and divine, but doubts that this is enough to prove that the soul is not destroyed with the body, since it could be like the attunement of a lyre that perishes with its instrument (86a–d). Cebes is

---

[41] Socrates ascribes the same status to his own 'wisdom' on arrival at Agathon's: 'My own wisdom is of no account—just like a dream' (175e4).

persuaded that the soul lasts longer than the body, but has doubts about whether the soul 'wears out' many bodies and, on leaving the last body, is eventually destroyed (87a–88b). A perceived deficiency in the argument creates *aporiai* for Simmias and Cebes. Socrates encourages them to explain these *aporiai* which, he says, warrant deliberation (86e2), and promise progress if they are successfully addressed. Again, we can see a similar pattern of a perceived argumentative deficiency, a desire for further inquiry which is informed by this realization, deliberation, and progress.

The portrayal of Socrates' philosophical character in the *Phaedo* furnishes a good parallel to the portrayal of the philosopher in the *Symposium*. Phaedo reports that many of those present were depressed at certain stages in the argument since they had been quite convinced by preceding arguments, and new problems confused everyone again. They 'drove them to doubt not only what had already been said, but what was about to be said' (88cd). Echecrates, who has been listening to this report of the argument, says that he himself is now 'quite in need, as if from the beginning, of some other argument to convince me that the soul does not die along with the man' (88de). But Socrates tackled the argument with no distress: 'he recalled us from our flight and defeat, and turned us around to join him in the examination of their argument' (89a). Few of Socrates' interlocutors have the courage to respond bravely in the face of argumentative defeats. Only when there are no more perceived argumentative deficiencies does the search cease (*Phd.* 107a). 'I have nothing more to say against that, Socrates, nor can I doubt your arguments', says Cebes. 'I have no remaining grounds for doubt', agrees Simmias. But Socrates encourages them to go over the arguments 'even though they are convincing, follow the argument as far as a man can, and if the conclusion is clear, you will look no further' (107bc). This is what it is to have *erōs* for wisdom, to scrutinize beliefs, perceive argumentative deficiencies, and to proceed on that basis to a more informed position until there are no remaining deficiencies to be remedied. This is the mark of the *Symposium*'s philosopher (203de).

The fact that parallels are to be found in the *Meno* and the *Phaedo* for the way in which *aporia* is wedded with some notion of progress suggests that the *Symposium* shares their positive picture of the philosopher. One might even say that the story of Eros' dual parentage is a response to gibes such as Meno's. But if so, then questions should be emerging. In the *Meno* and the *Phaedo*, Socrates responds to the experience of *aporia*—that is, he expresses *euporia*— by means of methodological innovations. In the *Meno*, for example, he responds to Meno's criticisms first by displaying the technique of knowing how to ask questions correctly and in order, and then by employing the method of hypothesis. Furthermore, in both the *Meno* and the *Phaedo*, the account of philosophical progress takes place within a context of an epistemologically optimistic psychology: there is something about the nature of the mind that supports such endeavour. So we should have the following questions for the *Symposium*: What does 'knowing how' to get wisdom consist in, and what methodological procedure is it informed by here? Further, what, if anything, ensures that genuine progress can be made? Answers to these questions will prove crucial to the positive account of philosophical progress in the *Symposium*. They will also prove crucial to the dialogue's central concern with showing that *erōs* is of great benefit. For if philosophical *erōs* can deliver the benefits praised by the previous speakers, then it had better be resourceful in its pursuit of beauty and wisdom and not just an aspiration towards these things.

3

Socrates' Speech: The Aim of *Erōs*

The aetiological story of Eros has described the experience of *erōs* as one where we are confronted with our deficiencies and yet we also awaken a more than human ability to transcend that nature and to strive towards a divine state of possession. In this state, we experience a needy, mortal, aspect to our natures and also a divine ability to extend ourselves towards the objects of attraction. Now Socrates still needs to give a more precise account of what it is that desiring agents are lacking and striving towards and why they strive towards this thing. We have already had a strong indication that *erōs* strives after good and beautiful things (203d4–5), and that this involves striving after wisdom, since it is one of the most beautiful things (204b1–3). But we still need to know why *erōs* pursues beauty (of whatever sort) and how this issues in the beneficial effects previously claimed for *erōs*. Or, as Socrates puts the question next: If it is the nature of *erōs* to pursue beauty, what use does it have for human beings (204e7)? The answer will be a complex one. In clarifying why we pursue beauty Socrates will be providing an account of what it is that we aim to achieve in that pursuit. But Socrates, in fact, specifies three aims of *erōs*: the good (206a11–12), reproduction in beauty (206b7–8, e5), and immortality (207a1–4). It will be the task of this chapter to discern how, if at all, those three aims are related.

Socrates' account of *erōs*' aims is a unified one. In the first section, we shall examine the claim that the aim of *erōs* is *eudaimonia*, the everlasting happiness characteristic of the divine. According to Socrates we desire a good whose possession we believe to constitute that state, and one which can be had in an enduring way. In the second part of the chapter we will address the question why Socrates' account moves on to discuss reproduction in beauty. Tracing Socrates' argument carefully will show that the desire to reproduce in beauty and the desire for the secure possession of the good are not independent desires; rather, the former is the way in which the latter makes itself manifest in human beings. Reproduction in the presence of beauty is the *ergon*, the characteristic activity, of the desire for the good. This, of course, calls for an explanation and in the third part of the chapter we move on to Socrates' account of human nature which explains why the desire to possess the good manifests itself in this way. Socrates explains that unlike the divine, human nature cannot possess things in any straightforward way; it needs to be productive. Productive activity is the mortal approximation to the divine state. The reason, then why the desire for *eudaimonia* manifests itself in creative activity in the presence of beauty is because this is the distinctively mortal way in which it can achieve a share of divine happiness.

In reaching this conclusion Socrates addresses the puzzling relationship between *erōs*, creativity, and the good that emerged from Agathon's speech. He also subtly reworks Aristophanes' claim that *erōs* pursues the *oikeion*. The creative activity in beauty characteristic of *erōs* is an attempt at self-fulfilment, as we shall see; but this is not pursued for the sake of the self as such, but for the sake of the self expressed, or realized, as good. Socrates' novel claim will be that there is an intimate relationship between realizing human nature in productive activity, pursuing our good, and achieving a share of divine *eudaimonia*.

1. ERŌS AND EUDAIMONIA

Socrates begins the account of *erōs'* aims with *erōs'* characteristic pursuit of beauty. If it is the case, as Agathon had claimed, for example, that *erōs* pursues the beautiful, then what do desiring agents hope to achieve in that pursuit? Socrates' initial answer is that they desire to possess it (204d7). But he is stumped as to why one should desire to possess that (204d10). When prompted to consider why anyone should pursue good things, however (e1), he finds this much easier to answer: they promise to deliver *eudaimonia*, and we all, ultimately, want *that* (205a1–3). There is no further need to ask why human beings pursue the good things they take to lead to, or constitute, 'happiness', for it is taken as obvious that all human beings want happiness. This, Socrates agrees, is the *telos* of all erotic pursuits (a3). Notice that it would not be a final answer to claim that human beings desire good things, or a good, which is not constitutive of, or conducive to, happiness. The finality of the answer rests on the assumption that the ultimate aim of all desire and action is happiness. If so, then what would satisfy our erotic pursuits is the kind of good, or goods, whose possession is thought to be conducive to, or constitutive of, *that*. This criterion will clearly restrict the kinds of goods, or good, desiring agents ought to pursue. If the ultimate aim of *erōs* is *eudaimonia*, then what would satisfy it must be a good whose possession no longer requires us to ask of the agent what she wants in pursuing it: a final good, we might say.[1]

There are two implications of this thesis that Socrates draws out next. First, if it is the case that *erōs* aims at the good things that are believed to constitute, or are central to, happiness—and it always does so (205a7)—and this desire is common to all human beings (205a6–7), then all human beings are, in fact, lovers. The term *erōs* has, in effect, been subject to a semantic confusion (205d1–8). For one aspect of *erōs* has been thought to be constitutive of erotic experience as a whole and it is only those who are devoted to one special kind of *erōs*—sexual *erōs*—who are called lovers exclusively. Herein lies the mistake, for examples of the desire for good things and happiness range from the love of money-making and the love of sports to the love of wisdom (205d4–5). According to this account, all these activities fall under the generic sense of *erōs* as the desire for good things and *eudaimonia*.

---

[1] I am taking *telos* here in a substantive sense, indicating not just the end of this particular line of questioning, but the *summum bonum* of *erōs*. Although Alcinous (*Idaskalikos* 28) asserted that Plato postulated a *telos* in the sense of *summum bonum*, it is not clear whether *telos* was used in this sense in the Platonic dialogues. If *telos* in the *Symposium* is connected with a unitary notion of good—that for the sake of which every action is pursued—and it is (cf. 210e5–6), then it seems that already in the *Symposium* a more technical sense of *telos* is emerging. I thank Tad Brennan for drawing my attention to this issue. For further discussion, see his '*Telos*' in the *Routledge Encyclopedia of Philosophy* (1999).

One might object that Socrates is changing the subject here—from sexual *erōs* to the goal of human desire and action more generally. But this would be to misconstrue the issue. Rather, Socrates is locating sexual desire within a larger context which explains what this desire is a desire *for*. Sexual *erōs*, apparently, is just one manifestation of a definitive longing for happiness. The claim that there is some relationship between *erōs* and *eudaimonia* should not be controversial, at least within the context of offering an encomium to *erōs*. Indeed showing that there is a relationship between *erōs* and happiness is crucial to the expressed agenda, namely, to show that *erōs* is good and does good things. This is borne out by the ample references to *eudaimonia* in the previous speeches (180b7, 188d8, 193d5, 194e6, 195a5, 205a1). Aristophanes, for example, cited *eudaimonia* as the end achieved by those who found union with their other half (193d6). What will be in dispute here is the sort of thing thought to satisfy *eudaimonia*, and the role and status of sexual *erōs* therein. According to Socrates it will not be merely a semantic confusion to think that sexual lovers are desiring agents *par excellence*, but a deeply misguided idea to think that sexual union with another person will satisfy *erōs*. Sexual *erōs* is an early stage of our awakening towards the good things we desire but is not capable of satisfying the desire for *eudaimonia* (*pace* Aristophanes). Whatever the role and status of sexual *erōs* will turn out to be on this account, though, it is nonetheless a manifestation of the desire for good things and happiness and so very much within the evening's agenda.[2]

A further implication of the claim that the aim of *erōs* is *eudaimonia* is the central place that it allocates to the good. For since good things deliver happiness, and we all want that, we all, in fact, desire the good, and nothing but the good (206a1).[3] If this is the case, as Socrates goes on to explain, then Aristophanes was mistaken to think that we desire the *oikeion* and should search for our other half. After all, people are willing to amputate their own limbs if they think they

---

[2] Cf. Rowe (1998*b*) 243: 'Since sexual desire is itself an aspect of human desire in the broader and broadest sense, the account of human desire also provides us with a treatment of sexual desire.'

[3] For other dialogues where Socrates argues for this claim, see *Grg.* 468a–b, 499e, 509d–510a, *Meno* 77b–78b, *Euthyd.* 278e3–6, 280b6, 281b4–e5.

are harmful; it cannot, then, be the *oikeion* as such that attracts them, but the good (205d10–e7). This supports the claims of the last chapter that Socrates is here concerned only with rational desires, that is, those based on judgements about the value of the object in question. Happiness is the ultimate aim of all our rational pursuits and the task is to ensure that we make the correct judgements about the sorts of goods, or good, that will deliver that.

At this stage in the account it is unclear whether there is just one good, or many good things that are central to our pursuit of *eudaimonia*, and just what the relationship is between this good, or goods, and *eudaimonia*. If Socrates thinks that there is a certain kind of good, or goods, the possession of which constitutes *eudaimonia*, then how is this to be understood? Is *eudaimonia* something that follows from the possession of the good (but is not identical with it)? Or is there a kind of good whose possession just is *eudaimonia*? Whatever the answers to these questions will turn out to be, the kinds of goods that Socrates mentions both here and later suggest that he takes there to be one kind of good that is central to each person's pursuit of happiness. He cites the desire for money-making, athletics, or wisdom (205d5).[4] Later in the account, the issue that divides the lower and higher mysteries of *erōs* is the competing claims of honour and wisdom, in particular (208c3, 211d2); Socrates will argue that the life of contemplation is the best human life (211d1–3). This division of different kinds of goods suggests that Socrates is searching for a single good that is the end of all our rational pursuits. It is not clear why he should make this assumption. Why not suppose that there is a series of different goods that taken together constitute a happy human life? We will return to this issue when we explore the life of contemplation as the happiest life and examine whether, and in what sense, it involves the valuation of goods other than contemplation. But already at this stage the suggestion is that Socrates is searching for the kind of good that will figure prominently in a person's life and which constitutes their conception of *eudaimonia*; for this is the *telos* of *erōs* (205a1).

---

[4] The threefold characterization of desires here has been seen to echo the threefold division of the soul in *Republic* 4. This should be treated with caution. For a full discussion of this issue, see Appendix.

Socrates goes on to make a further, and rather striking, claim. It is not just the case that we always desire the good, we also desire to possess the good always (206a11–12). There is a difference in the scope of 'always' in these two claims. Earlier 'always' had been applied both to the possessing of good things, and to the desiring of good things: we always *desire* the good (henceforth G: 'the generalization thesis) and we desire [*to possess*] the good always (henceforth P: 'the permanency thesis').[5] Given the way in which 'always' moves around in the claims that 'everyone desires to possess good things always' (P: 205a6–7 and 206a9–10), and 'everyone always desires to possess good things' (G: 205b1, 206a11–12 with 206b1), one might suspect that this ambiguity in scope has led to a fallacy. One suspects that Socrates is trying to derive the claim that we desire to possess the good always from the claim that we always desire to possess the good. But it does not seem to follow from the fact that everyone always desires to possess the good (G) that they desire to possess the good always (P). For G claims that at each moment I desire to possess the good and P claims that I desire to possess the good at all moments. I might always desire to have children, but only in a few years' time. In that case I will desire to have children in a few years, time, but I will not desire to possess that good at all times in my future: there is a planned child-free gap in that future (so, not P). The premiss may be true, but the conclusion is false. So the argument is not valid in virtue of its having this form.[6]

It may be the case that the argument is restricted to a consideration of certain kinds of goods, the possession of which involves temporal extension in the sense required by P. If so, then there would be something special about the nature of this good that one desires to possess, such that desiring to possess it at any given moment involves desiring to possess it at all moments. Since *erōs* has been defined as aiming at happiness (205d1–3), or rather, the good whose possession constitutes that state (cf. 202c10–11 with 206a1–2), perhaps there is

---

[5] Cf. 205a6–7: πάντας τἀγαθὰ βούλεσθαι αὑτοῖς εἶναι ἀεί, 'everyone wants to possess good things always'; 205b1: πάντες τῶν αὐτῶν ἐρῶσι καὶ ἀεί, 'everyone desires good things and always desires them.' At 206a9 ἀεί seems to qualify εἶναι (with τὸ ἀγαθόν as the subject of εἶναι) indicating that everyone desires that the good 'always' belongs to them.

[6] I thank Arif Ahmed and Nick Denyer for useful discussion of this argument.

something special about this particular good as an object of desire. Whilst one may be able to possess certain kinds of good for only a short time, perhaps it is just not the *eudaimonic* good that one is in possession of if one's possession of that good is not had at all future times. For a Greek, it would at any rate seem peculiar to claim that someone was *eudaimōn* for a brief time (whereas we would have no difficulty in describing someone as happy for a brief time). *Eudaimonia* was not conceived as a state of felicity, or a transitory feeling of pleasure or contentment, but whatever it is that makes one's life a worthwhile and flourishing one. That is why the account leads towards the specification of contemplation as the life worth living for human beings (211d1–3). Socrates is concerned here with whatever it is—some good—that makes a life a happy one in that sense. If so, then rather more plausibly perhaps, he may claim that if one desires to be *eudaimōn* at any time (G), then one desires to be *eudaimōn* at all subsequent times (P), for that is just what it is to desire this particular good. It is the kind of good that must be possessed at all times if one is to have it at all.[7]

Later, the claim that we desire to possess the good always leads to the claim that we desire immortality with the good. It is necessarily the case, Socrates claims, that we desire immortality with the good, if we desire to possess the good always (207a1–4). This move is also tricky. If I say that Cinderella lived happily ever after, I do not mean that she is still living happily and will continue to live happily; rather I mean that so long as she lived she lived happily. Similarly, if I desire the possession of *eudaimonia,* the nature of that desired good may require my desire to be temporally extended throughout my life, but not for eternity. If so, then it would not follow from the fact that I desire to possess the good at all future times that I desire immortality with the good. But Socrates must be making the stronger claim that the desire for *eudaimonia* is one that extends to *all* future times (i.e. even those beyond my death), otherwise it would not follow that we

---

[7] Compare Solon's claim that one should count no man happy until he is dead where, the point, I take it, is that happiness it the kind of thing that cannot be judged until one has lived an entire life. *Eudaimonia* is the kind of thing that has to be had at all times in one's life, for one to be said to have had it at all. Cf. Aristotle, *Nicomachean Ethics* book 1 and Aristophanes' *Frogs* 1180 ff., for example. I thank Nick Denyer for this reference.

desire immortality with the good. And if the claim is that we desire to possess the good at *all* future times, then this just sounds like another way of saying that we desire immortality with the good.

Notice that on this way of reading the introduction of immortality into the account, Socrates is not positing immortality as a separate goal of *erōs*.[8] There is no separate argument for this claim. There is instead the introduction of a tremendous assumption, namely that we desire to possess the good at *all* future times. Now, even if we take it that goods such as chocolate, cigarettes, and red wine are ruled out in this claim, and that Socrates is concerned with those goods whose possession we believe to constitute our happiness, we might still be puzzled by the strength of this claim. Why suppose that a desire for *eudaimonia* is a desire for the sort of good that can be had at all future times in this strong sense?[9] Why not (with Solon and Aristotle, perhaps) conceive of *eudaimonia* as the sort of good that is measured over an entire life, such that the desire for this sort of good is the desire to possess a certain good at all times in one's life? And just what is involved in desiring to possess *eudaimonia* at *all* future times (even those beyond my life)? If the desire is a desire to possess and enjoy some good then the desire may be, among other things, a desire to be around at all future times (i.e. to be immortal). But a desire for other goods, such as for one's children to prosper and to carry on the family name, or for certain projects or ideas to come to fruition, do not seem to involve immortality (in the sense of one's continued existence, at any rate). If they do not, then it is not clear how one's *eudaimonia* can be affected by their flourishing or demise after death.[10] To resolves such issues we shall need a clearer account of what *eudaimonia* consists in and how it is achieved. At this point we know only that our desire for whatever good we take to be central to *eudaimonia* is one that involves the desire for that good to be had in

[8] Contra Rowe (1998a) 184, who writes: 'While it is reasonable enough to say that someone who desires (literally) permanent possession of something must also desire immortality, it might seem less reasonable to suggest that it is immortality that we desire. Socrates next, in 207a5–209e4, reports how Diotima once tried to convince him that we do.'

[9] Aristophanes seems to make a similar assumption. The lovers in his speech want their union with one another to be everlasting and to survive death (192d8–e4).

[10] Cf. the discussion of posthumous fortune in Aristotle and the possibility of its effect on *eudaimonia* (*NE* 1. 10–11) with Scott (2000b) 211–29.

an enduring way—for all future times. The paradigm of the happy life, as we learnt earlier, is the life of the gods (202c10–d5) and that life is clearly one where good and beautiful things are possessed in a stable and secure manner. As the description of *erōs'* intermediate nature suggested, in our aspiration towards this state we are aspiring to the everlasting happiness of the divine.[11]

2. THE *ERGON* OF *ERŌS*: HUMAN NATURE, CREATIVE ACTIVITYAND THE GOOD

So far, then, Socrates has explained that *erōs* aims for *eudaimonia*, or rather, for a good whose possession is believed to be constitutive of, or central to, that state. This is a desire for a certain kind of good— one whose possession no longer requires us to ask of the agent what she wants in pursuing it—and it is a desire with temporal extension. We desire a good whose possession is central to *eudaimonia* as the *telos* of all desire and action—a final and secure good. It will be important to bear the above criteria in mind throughout the rest of his account. For if we know what a good must satisfy to meet our desire for happiness as the end of *erōs*, then we can use those criteria to evaluate different kinds of goods. We will also be in a better position to clarify the competing claims of the previous accounts. In the next chapter we will turn to Socrates' attempt to evaluate goods such as honour and contemplation in light of these criteria. But before we do so we would surely like to know what has happened to the beautiful as an object of *erōs*. For it will not have gone unnoticed that the previous discussion of *erōs'* aims substituted the good for the beautiful as the object of pursuit because Socrates could not explain why *erōs* pursues beauty (204e8–9). Now that he has

---

[11] This feature of *erōs* was already suggested by the description of *erōs* being between the mortal and the immortal (202e1–2). In the aetiological story this intermediate nature derives from his mixed parentage from the mortal Penia and the divine Poros. The lack of beautiful and good things is characteristic of the mortal, but the ability to remedy that state is derived from the divine Poros. We now learn that the way this is manifested in human beings is in the aspiration towards *eudaimonia*.

specified the aim of *erōs* as *eudaimonia,* or the secure possession of the good, he returns to a consideration of the role of beauty. The fact that we return to the role of beauty after specifying *erōs'* aim as *eudaimonia* suggests that this aspiration will form an important part of the explanation for *erōs'* characteristic pursuit of beauty.

Socrates' answer is complex. We are familiar with the idea that *erōs* pursues beauty, but Socrates specifies the manner of that pursuit as *reproduction in* beauty (206b1–2). This is unfamiliar territory and indicated to be so (206b9). What is also puzzling is the nature of the relationship between reproduction in beauty and possessing the good things that are supposed to deliver happiness. This recalls a similar problem in Agathon's speech. Agathon had claimed that good things arise from *erōs* for beauty and that, typically, the way they arise is that *erōs* manifests itself in creative activity of various kinds (197c1). What we need is an account of why and how it does so. Whether or not Socrates does any better in clarifying this idea depends on how one understands the shift to a discussion of reproduction and the corresponding focus on beauty in place of the good at this point. This has proved notoriously difficult.[12] Some have suspected that the account moves away here (206b1–2) from the generic account of *erōs* for good things and happiness towards an account of an *erōs* for beauty which aims at immortality. For it is said that reproduction is 'something everlasting and immortal' (207a1) and although it is said that we desire immortality with the good, the subsequent discussion of reproduction is one where the good appears to drop from view. It is said that generation allows the living being to partake of immortality (208b3), and that everything values its own offshoot for the sake of immortality (208b5). If so, the objection runs, reproduction would appear to be a value-neutral mechanism that aims at continued existence. If we want the continued possession of the good, then this will be some further thing to be striven for by reproducing something of value. Read in this way there is an uncomfortable gap between reproduction (as an apparently value-neutral activity) and the desire it is supposed to be the manifestation of (for the good and *eudaimonia*). It is just this gap which might lead one to suspect that

---

[12] See, for example, Price (1989) 26; Ferrari (1992) 254, Waterfield (1994) 86; Rowe (1998*b*) 247.

there is a shift in the account at this point. If there is a shift away from an account of *erōs* for *eudaimonia* to an account of an *erōs* for (reproduction in) beauty which aims at immortality, then this section of the account will not, after all, explain the connection between *erōs*' characteristic pursuit of beauty and the desire for good things and happiness.[13]

We have certainly not been prepared for any shift in the account. Reproduction in beauty is introduced as the characteristic activity

---

[13] R. Waterfield (1994) 86, argues that the shift to γέννησις returns to sexual ἔρως, rather than the generic account just outlined. I agree with Rowe that τοῦτο at 206b1 refers most naturally to (generic) ἔρως. As Rowe says, 'if there is a transition back to specific ἔρως, why should Socrates be stumped, as he is (b5–6), for an answer to the question about what sort of activity goes with ἔρως, obviously, *sex*'; Rowe (1998*a*) 182 n. on 206b1–3; K. Sier (1997) 221. For Rowe, part of the confusion at this point is that Diotima 'treats the universal ἔρως according to the paradigm provided by its specific counterpart. In other words, while the subject shifts to the universal, the description of the universal is determined by the specific'; see Rowe (1998*b*) 248. He continues: 'The whole approach is built upon a deliberate and artificial conceit, i.e. one which treats human desire in general as if it possessed the same structure as sexual desire, which she, and Socrates know (and we know that they know) that it does not ... we have passed from the limits of *literal* truth into the realm of metaphor; here in 206e–207a, in effect, Diotima simply breaks cover, as she manufactures what she needs in order to continue the metaphor'; Rowe (1998*b*) 251. Since 'literal truth' is apparently left behind with the introduction of γέννησις, the apparent shift to immortality as an end of ἔρως is not 'literal truth' either, but a metaphorical substitute for the good; Rowe (1998*b*) 257. Diotima is '[attempting] to persuade Socrates that our desire is for immortality, to which the means is procreation in beauty'. So, Rowe also sees a 'substitution of immortality for the good as an object of all human desire ... despite the *kai* in 207a3 ("... of immortality as well"); by the end of Diotima's discourse, certainly, the good just is what would give us the best approximation to immortality of which humans are capable'; Rowe (1998*b*) 249 n. 23. In order to deal with the tension between immortality as an (apparent) aim of ἔρως and the 'Socratic account of the good', Rowe (1998*b*) 249–51 then opens a gap between Socrates and Diotima, and claims that the substitution of immortality is 'ironic', designed in part to appeal to the symposiasts (1998*b*: 250–1). He argues that Socrates does not record his agreement to these aspects of Diotima's discourse, but rather expresses puzzlement and amazement. This is a popular strategy for scholars who are puzzled by the relationship between the good and immortality after this point: see O'Brien (1984) 185–205, esp. 186. O'Brien and Rowe note that εἶεν (206e6) is used disparagingly at *Republic* 350e, and ὦ σοφωτάτε [Διοτίμα] (208b8) has ironic parallels at *Republic* 339c and *Gorgias* 495d. But as O'Brien notes, Socrates says that he is persuaded by what Diotima told him (212b1–5). This most naturally refers to all of his speech, and not just select parts. He also says at 198d–199b that he will speak the truth about ἔρως. As both scholars note, εἶεν at 206e6 is not decisive, and driving a wedge between Socrates and Diotima is not without difficulty. On this issue see above, Ch. 2, sect. 5.

(the *ergon*) of the desire just outlined (206b1–4); in other words, it is the characteristic activity of the desire for good things and happiness. Socrates is, in fact, following correct encomiastic procedure in describing first what *erōs* is like, and then his activity (cf. 201e). This indicates how we should read the shift of focus from the aim of *erōs* to its effects, or work (206b1 ff.). It is a shift of focus entirely appropriate to the standards of an encomium and provides no evidence that the aim of *erōs* has shifted to another goal. Rather, the account moves on to illuminate the characteristic activity of the *erōs* under consideration so far: *erōs* for *eudaimonia.* The challenge is to work out how it does so.

We are, in fact, given a twofold answer to the question why we desire reproduction. Careful analysis of both aspects of this answer should show that reproduction is not a value-neutral mechanism that falls away from the desire for good things and happiness. First, it is said that we desire to reproduce because all human beings are pregnant in both body and soul (206c1–4; 206e1–2). Second, we learn that (re)productive activity allows us to partake of the divine in the way in which living beings are able (207c5–208b5). Examining both features of this account of reproduction should show that the desire to reproduce in beauty and the desire for the good are not independent desires. The first part of the answer, I will argue, amounts to the claim that there is something (potentially) good and divine about human nature which it is the task of our erotic *ergon* (reproduction) to realize in actions and productions of various kinds. The second part of the answer explains that we are the sorts of living beings that require such productive work; production is the mortal approximation to the divine state. Once both aspects of reproduction are taken into account, we can appreciate that, far from falling away from the desire for good things and happiness, reproduction in beauty is the way in which living beings manifest their aspiration towards everlasting happiness.

(*a*) Pregnancy and giving birth

To explain the relationship between the desire to reproduce in beauty and the desire for the good, let us take the first part of the above explanation for our desire to reproduce. Apparently erotically dis-posed human beings desire to give birth in beauty because:

All human beings are pregnant both in body and in soul, and when we come to be of the right age, we naturally desire to give birth. We cannot give birth in what is ugly, but we can in what is beautiful. The intercourse of a man and a woman is a kind of giving birth. This matter of giving birth is something divine: living creatures, despite their mortality, contain this immortal aspect, of pregnancy and procreation. It is impossible for this to be completed in what is unfitting and what is unfitting for everything divine is what is ugly, while the beautiful is fitting (206c6–9).

Part of the explanation for the desire to give birth is a pre-existing state of pregnancy, which desires expression at a certain age. The expression of this pregnancy can occur only in the presence of beauty and this is why *erōs* pursues beauty: to engage in its characteristic reproductive work. Notice the 'strange reversal' of pregnancy and procreation here. The encounter with beauty does not make one pregnant, but delivers a pre-existing state of pregnancy. Since the *ergon* of *erōs*—reproduction in beauty—assumes a state of pregnancy any account of this *ergon* and its relationship to the good must begin with an account of this state.[14]

The dual claims that *all* human beings are pregnant, and that when we reach a certain age we *naturally* desire to give birth (206c1–4), suggest that pregnancy and delivery are part of our natural make-up as human beings. For if this reproductive *ergon* were not grounded in our nature it is hard to see why we should naturally desire to give birth when we reach a certain age (presumably at a certain level of maturation). So, all human beings, it would seem, have an *ergon*, or characteristic activity, whose task is to deliver what we have long

---

[14] On this 'strange reversal' see Burnyeat (1977), from whom I take the phrase. Normally, of course, κυεῖν follows συνουσία, cf. Apollonius, *Lexicon Homericum* 106.3: Κύπρις ἐπίθετον Ἀφοδίτης, οὐ μόνον ἐκ τῆς νήσου Κύπρου, ἀλλά καὶ ἀπὸ τοῦ τὸ κύειν πορίσκειν, ὅ ἐστιν ἐκ τῆςσυνουσίας. Although the phrase τόκος ἐν καλῷ sug-gests begetting (literally) in beauty, as if desiring agents were ejaculating inside a beautiful object in a sexual encounter, τόκος is ambiguous between ejaculation and delivery. Since the role of beauty is to preside over childbirth (206d1), and one begets 'in proximity to the beautiful' (περὶ τὸ καλόν, 206e1), beauty is better described as the creative environment in which one begets a pregnancy, where the ἐν indicates being in the presence of, rather than literally inside, beauty. Price notes a similar use of 'in' to signify occasion rather than precise location at *Phaedrus* 228e4 (Price 1989: 41 n. 45).

carried by nature in the work of reproduction. This suggests an intimate relationship between our *ergon* and our nature.[15] That there is some relationship between our *ergon*, our nature, and our good, is suggested by the evaluative language used to characterize pregnancy and birth. The reason, the passage suggests, why pregnancies cannot be brought to term in the presence of ugliness is that they are a good and divine aspect of our nature. After all, if this were not so, why does our reproductive *ergon* require a harmonious and beautiful medium?

In order to substantiate the suggestive overtones of this passage and to clarify the relationship between our reproductive *ergon* and the good, we need to consider what it might mean to say that all human beings are pregnant; for our *ergon* delivers a pre-existing state of pregnancy, as we have seen (206c1–3). Whatever this natural state of pregnancy is, it is evidently something that comes in degrees. For although it is initially said that all human beings are pregnant in both body and soul (206c1), we learn later that some human beings are more pregnant in soul than they are in body (209a1–2). Those who are pregnant in body are said to carry physical offspring (208e3), whilst those pregnant in soul carry 'what it is fitting for a soul both to become pregnant with and to beget'—wisdom and the rest of virtue (209a1–4). We learn later that only some of these pregnancies result in genuine wisdom and virtue (212a1–5). So, all human beings are pregnant to varying degrees with children and wisdom and virtue, and only some of the latter type have a successful manifestation.

As it stands this is a puzzling picture. But if we construe these states of pregnancy as potentialities for these things, then we can begin to grasp how some people can have more of a certain type than others, and how the deliveries of different lovers can be better or worse expressions of the same sort of pregnancy.[16] If what it means to

---

[15] This is picked up, perhaps, in Socrates' concluding claim that *erōs* is the best 'co-worker' with human nature (212b3).

[16] One might compare the idea in Aristotle's biological writings that κυήματα reach different stages of completion—and only some are capable of higher degrees (cf. GA 736[a–b]). There is an analogue for both of these points. First, the pregnancy of the desiring agent of the higher mysteries reaches a higher degree of completion than that of the person engaged in the lower. Second, the idea that only some κυήματα are capable of higher degrees can be compared to the distinction between those who are pregnant in their bodies and those who are pregnant in their souls more than in their bodies. Those who are pregnant in their bodies, we infer, are much less capable of higher degrees of completion on the psychic level, i.e. the virtuous activity of those who are more pregnant in their souls. I owe this suggestion to Alan Code.

be pregnant is to have a potentiality of a certain sort, then one can account for the fact that this pregnancy can be put to good use if it is properly realized, and an inferior use if its development is thwarted. In a certain sense, of course, this is rather obvious. For just as a physical pregnancy is a potentiality for human life, so a psychic pregnancy should also be a potentiality of a certain sort. Since the soul is pregnant with *wisdom* and the rest of virtue (209a2–5), and needs philosophical development for its successful expression, this potentiality is clearly a rational one. This is confirmed by the fact that a proper expression of this potentiality is *knowledge* of beauty and true virtue (211d1–3, 212a1–3). Since the encounter with beauty releases what one has long been pregnant with (206c3–4, 209c2–3), it seems plausible to construe the reproductive work of *erōs*—the *tokos*—as a realization, or expression, of this potentiality. Part of the explanation for our erotic *ergon*, then, is that we are all pregnant in body and soul, and when we reach a certain age we naturally desire to beget (206c1–4). Put differently, human beings have various natural potentialities, which emerge at a certain level of maturation, and it is the task of our productive *ergon* to bring these into being.

So far, then, we have a working sense of pregnancy (as a natural state of potentiality) and giving birth (as its expression). What we need now is to give some content to this notion of potentiality by considering the nature of these pregnancies and their expressions. Once we do so it should be clear that there is indeed an intimate connection between our productive *ergon* and our good. Clarifying this is crucial to explaining the connection between birth in beauty and possessing the good. Now there are three groups of desiring agents under consideration in the account. There are those pregnant in body—with children (208e3), and those pregnant in soul more than in body—with 'wisdom and the rest of virtue' (209a4). Those more pregnant in soul are then subdivided into those who engage in productive activities such as law-making and poetry, who occupy the so-called lower mysteries of *erōs* (209a4–e4), and those who engage in philosophical activity and occupy the highest mysteries (209e5–212a7). It is only the latter group who manage a successful expression of their potentiality for wisdom and virtue: wisdom and *true* virtue (212a4–6). It seems natural to read the specification of '*phronēsis* and the rest of virtue' as a general description of the nature of a psychic pregnancy. This, we are told, is what it is fitting for a soul to be pregnant with (209a1–4). We do not know what such virtue or *phronēsis* consists in at this stage. The phrase '*phronēsis* and the rest of virtue' suggests a plurality of virtues which could be the cardinal Greek four. But the emphasis on *phronēsis* amongst these virtues may suggest a more 'Socratic' emphasis, a suggestion which is borne out in the ascent, where we learn that virtue must be grounded in knowledge. Initially, though, the description is underdetermined. The fact that we have to wait for a discussion of the productive activities of different desiring agents to clarify the nature of this wisdom and virtue further suggests that one's productive activity in some important sense determines the nature of the offspring. In order to learn more about this '*phronēsis* and the rest of virtue' we shall have to wait and see how such resources are employed.

So how, then, are these pregnancies expressed in each case and what, if anything, has this to do with the desired good? Expressions of the first (bodily) pregnancy type produce children who are thought to provide 'immortality and memory and *eudaimonia*' for their produ-cer (208e4). The first group of those who carry the latter pregnancy type—'wisdom and the rest of virtue'—deliver 'manifold virtue' (209e2–3), amongst which is included law-making (209d4–e1), the production of poetic displays (209a4), political activity (209a6–8), and educational conversations (209b8). And the third group of de-siring agents, who carry a psychic pregnancy but manifest this very differently in philosophical activity, produce *kaloi logoi* (210a8, 210d4) and, finally, true virtue (212a4–6). In all three cases we can see that the *ergon* of *erōs* works for the good of the agent. In the first case children are thought to provide immortality and memory and *eudaimonia*, clearly a good thing. In the second case, the actions and productions expressive of a soul pregnant with 'wisdom and virtue' are also good things; they are manifestations of virtue (variously conceived). And in the third case (those who manifest their potenti-ality for wisdom and virtue in philosophical activity) the philosoph-ical *logoi* are explicitly described as beautiful and they lead to the delivery of true virtue; again, clearly a good and beautiful thing.[17] Poems, laws, and philosophical *logoi* alike are all ways in which the potential for 'wisdom and the rest of virtue' is made manifest.

[17] Socrates describes virtue as a beauty of soul at *Republic* 444e. Cf. *Gorgias* 503a–504a.

That is to say, all of the aforementioned reproductive activities—heroic deeds, law-making, and philosophical activity—are ways in which a certain *good* is expressed for the particular desiring agent in question. For each type of desiring agent, then, giving birth in the presence of beauty is a way of attaining beautiful and good things.[18]

The precise sense in which pregnancy and giving birth provide good things will differ in accordance with the way in which each desiring agent conceives of the relevant good. Both of the first groups of desiring agents, that is, those pregnant in body and those more pregnant in soul who engage in practical activities such as poetry and law-making are explicitly said to be honour lovers (208c3).[19] They are also said to desire 'immortal virtue' (208d7), an 'immortal memory of their virtue' (d5–6), and *kleos* (208c5), all of which, I take it, are various ways of describing their definitive desire for honour (208c3). For reasons that remain obscure at present, Socrates places the honour lovers in the lower mysteries of *erōs* (208c1–209e4). This stands in contrast to those who make virtue the goal of their actions, and believe that wisdom is somehow central to its possession; these are those who follow the highest mysteries of *erōs* (210a1–212a7). Now since the former type think that the good central to a happy life is honour, they employ their reproductive *ergon* in certain ways to achieve this aim. Such types produce the sorts of products that they believe will provide this good for them: having children, making laws, engaging in educational conversations, and making poems are all examples of 'manifold virtue' produced to secure honour (or *kleos*, or 'an immortal memory of their virtue'). Since they are produced as a way of procuring honour, it would seem that there is a gap between their good products (e.g. heroic deeds,

---

[18] These products are truly or apparently good and beautiful. Some of these offspring are an image of genuine virtue (212a4–6). But this does not affect the point. Even if people engage in the wrong sort of productive activity and produce inferior products, these are still attempts to secure good and beautiful things for the producer and so are cases where one can see the reproductive *ergon* of *erōs* working for the good (however that is conceived) for the desiring agent in question.

[19] One should not be surprised at the inclusion of those who are pregnant in their body and beget physical offspring amongst the honour lovers (209a2–3). In the *Laws* the desire to be remembered by one's descendants is cited as a reason for marriage and the production of offspring (721b–d). See also *Rep.* 618b, for the fame which derives from one's ancestors.

poems, and laws) and the goal of honour (208c3). Having children, or engaging in virtuous actions and productions, would appear to be a means to honour. Virtue may not always play this instrumental role. For those included in the highest mysteries of *erōs* there will be no gap between their final product and their goal, and this will provide a reason for the superiority of their productive activity, as we shall see. But even in cases where the products of reproductive activity are instrumental to the desired good, the point is that they are nonetheless related to the good of the agent in each case (however that is conceived). So, when it is said that *erōs* is not of the beautiful, but of reproduction in the presence of the beautiful (206e1–5), the claim seems to be that *erōs* is of those beautiful and good things that are produced in the presence of beauty. For it is these things that promise the desired '*eudaimonia* for all time to come'.

There is no evidence so far that the aim of *erōs* has shifted to immortality—even for the honour lovers of the lesser mysteries. But a difficulty with my reading might seem to be suggested by the following line used to describe the desiring agents of the lesser mysteries: 'the better the people, the more they will do, for they love the immortal' (208d8–e1 ὅσῳ ἂν ἀμείνους ὦσι, τοσούτῳ μᾶλλον· τοῦ γὰρ ἀθανάτου ἐρῶσιν). But there is no need to translate τὸ ἀθάνατον as 'the immortal' meaning 'immortality' here: it may just as well mean 'the immortal thing' (whatever it is).[20] Given the earlier coupling of 'immortal' with 'virtue' (d7) and with memory (d5), such a construal would make the best sense here. 'The immortal' should be read as referring to the particular type of immortal good in question thus far—honour—since 208e1, in effect, summarizes the thesis that it is this particular type of good which permits this particular group 'to possess the good forever' (as they believe, 208e4). Further, the notions of 'being good—generating more deeds—immortality' are clearly intimately related in this sentence. The first part of the clause expresses the idea that good people will perform many more deeds where, given the previous catalogue of particular virtuous deeds, we can take it that these are all virtuous deeds. It is because Achilles is a better man than Diomedes, say, that he performs many more heroic deeds on the battlefield. This could be for two reasons. It could be

---

[20] Cf. Lamb in the Loeb edition.

both because Achilles is a better fighter than Diomedes that he performs more virtuous deeds, and because Achilles has a *better life* than Diomedes (since he has more virtue, or honour), that he desires to express that life in action more than Diomedes does. His life is more choice-worthy. This is the kind of view that Aristotle has in mind when he writes 'decent and blessed people desire [life] more than others do; for their life is most choice-worthy for them, and their living is most blessed' (*NE* 9, 1170ª27–9; trans. Irwin). Heroes, poets, and politicians are more productive because they have better lives which they desire to express in actions and productions of various kinds. In other words, this confirms the point that it is not continued life as such that is desired in each case, but *good* life.

If it is the case that *erōs* is not of the beautiful, but of those things that are produced in the presence of beauty (for these promise *eudaimonia*), then we have gone some way towards explicating the relationship between our nature (which is pregnant), our *ergon* (reproduction), and our desired good (variously conceived). All human beings carry potentialities for children and wisdom and virtue (albeit to varying degrees), and it is the task of our *ergon* to express these in actions (e.g. heroic deeds) or productions (e.g. poetic displays, or educational *logoi*). Having children, performing heroic deeds, creating poems, and making laws are all examples of reproductive activity. Such activities not only express the producer's nature (they 'deliver' a certain pregnancy type, 209a1, b2, 5–6, c3–4); various actions and productions make a certain good (e.g. psychic virtue) manifest for the desiring agent in question. Poems, heroic deeds, law-making, and educational conversation are all expressions of a potential for 'wisdom and the rest of virtue' and (re)productive activity brings that virtue into being. This, then, is the reason why reproductive activity is desired: it enables the producer to realize himself in a certain good way and in so doing to secure the sorts of things believed to provide '*eudaimonia* for all time to come' (209e4–5).[21] Giving birth in the presence of beauty is the way that desiring agents try to attain possession of the beautiful and good things that

---

[21] Cf. Aristotle, *Ethics* (1168ª7–8): 'Thus the producer loves his product, because he loves his own being. And this is natural, since what he is potentially his product manifests in actuality'. Cf. Price (1989) 28–9.

promise *eudaimonia*. And if that is the case then the good has not dropped from view in this discussion of reproductive activity.

(*b*) The role and status of the *kalon*

Now why we need to go about attaining possession of such good and beautiful things in quite this way remains to be seen. To answer that we need to consider the second part of the twofold answer to why reproduction is desired. Before we do so, however, let us see what the account of the *ergon* of *erōs* has made of the role of beauty in *erōs*. As we have seen, this eluded Socrates earlier in the account, and beauty is reintroduced after specifying the aim of *erōs* as *eudaimonia* (204e7) and the *ergon* of *erōs* as reproduction (206b1–2). Beauty reappears as the creative environment in which desiring agents try to procure the beautiful and good things that promise *eudaimonia*. Now that we have a better sense of reproductive activity, let us take a closer look at the role of beauty therein—with a keen eye on its relationship to the good—in order to complete our account of how the *ergon* of *erōs* works for our good.

The productive activities of different desiring agents suggest that the pursuit of beauty in each case is determined, in part, by natural endowments. Those pregnant in body turn towards the beauty of women (208e1–3), produce children, and thereby try to procure honour for themselves (208c3, 208e4). Whilst those pregnant in soul, who (I have supposed) have a more developed potentiality for wisdom and virtue, pursue the kinds of beauty that allow them to realize themselves in a way fitting to their nature (their psychic pregnancy). They turn towards the beauty of soul (or a combination of bodily and psychic beauty, 209b6 with 210b6–7) and produce *kaloi logoi* and/or virtue (209b8 with c6, e2–3 and 210a8, 210d4, 212a4–6). The role of beauty, we might say, is to arouse each desiring agent towards the realization of its nature in the best way possible for that person (i.e. depending on the pregnancy type they carry).

It is not just a person's natural endowments, but also their goal that determines the pursuit of beauty in each case. The issue that structures the division of Socrates' account into the lower and higher mysteries of *erōs* is the goal thought to be central to *eudaimonia*.

Those in the lower mysteries desire honour (208c3), whilst those in the higher mysteries make virtue their goal and evidently think that its attainment has something to do with wisdom (see further below). Now, if one specifies the good that one perceives to be central to a happy life as honour, then one's pursuit of beauty will be appropriate to that chosen good end. Such types, as Socrates explains, pursue the kinds of beauty manifested in fertile women, or promising students and flourishing cities, in which their chosen good can be realized by the production of children in the former case, or educational discourses and laws in the latter (209b8–9).[22] If, by contrast, one makes virtue the goal of one's actions, and believes that wisdom is somehow central to its possession, then one will pursue beauty in a way that allows one to be productive of that good end (e.g. by reflection upon its nature). This is the kind of pursuit described in the ascent to the form of beauty, the creative environment appropriate to the possession of wisdom and true virtue, as we shall see. In each of these cases, the pursuit of beauty is determined by two factors: the predominant tendencies in one's nature (whether one is more pregnant in body or soul) and one's specification of *eudaimonia*. Pursuing certain kinds of beauty just is the way in which different desiring agents pursue their chosen good and, depending on the good in question, different kinds of beauty will be better, or worse, at satisfying that pursuit. Beautiful souls, for example, will enable one to realize a desire for honour or virtue better than beautiful bodies; for in the presence of a beautiful soul one can produce the sort of thing that is conducive to the attainment of that end (e.g. educational conversations).

Since it is in the pursuit of beauty that we can realize ourselves in a certain good way, it is clearly closely related to the good; the pursuit of beauty in each case is fitting to an agent's particular conception of the good. Various actions and productions that result from the encounter with beauty (e.g. children in bodies, laws in cities, or *logoi* in souls) are ways in which a certain good (honour in these cases) can be realized, or manifested, for oneself. Beauty may be misleading in this role; it may not, in fact, deliver the desired good. Part of the philosophical work Socrates will advocate attempts to

---

[22] Cf. Dover (1980) 151–2 on the beauty of cities as the creative environment for Solon and Homer.

ensure that we desire the sorts of beautiful thing(s) that really do lead
to the good we desire. Nonetheless, it is in the encounter with beauty
that one can be productive of one's (real or apparent) good and the
beauty pursued will be appropriate to that desired end. If so, then
perhaps we can understand the description of beauty as 'fitting' with
everything divine (206d) in this way: beauty is 'fitting' to one's
specification of divine *eudaimonia* (cf. 202c10–d5).

There are also indications in the dialogue that the reason why one's
choice of beauty is fitting to one's conception of happiness is that it
embodies, or manifests, something one perceives to be of value. That
is to say, it is a visible manifestation of something one considers to be
good.[23] Consider the case of Socrates and his devotees, for example.
Apollodorus, Alcibiades, and Agathon are attracted to Socrates
because of his appearance of wisdom. This is what they perceive as
beautiful about Socrates (175d1, 219d5, 222a). When they are in the
presence of Socrates' beauty they are made aware of the wisdom they
lack and perceive to be of value, and they take steps to procure this
good for themselves (albeit in misguided ways). Socrates' beauty
resides in his ability to exhibit that value to them and in so doing
to prompt them towards the procurement of the good they desire. In
fact, he does more than prompt them towards this good. Because
he exhibits the desired value, his beauty provides an appropriate
environment for them to make that value manifest for themselves.
Intellectual intercourse with Socrates is productive of, or at least
conducive to, the attainment of wisdom. Compare other textual
examples. We might also suppose that, for an honour lover of a
certain sort, a beautiful woman exhibits something of value. This
will not be her looks, as such, but her honourable appearance,
perhaps, that holds out the promise of fine sons and a reputable
name for oneself; for this is what the honour lovers desire (208c3 and
e4). In a similar way, perhaps, a beautiful young soul exhibits honour
in its potential for an educator to cultivate excellence therein. If one
is a more intellectually inclined honour lover (more pregnant in soul,
that is), then this honourable quality exhibited by a young soul will

[23] It is in this sense that I agree with Dover (1980) n. on 201c that 'anything which
is *kalon*, i.e. which looks or sounds good (or is good to contemplate), is also *agathon*,
i.e. it serves a desirable purpose or performs a desirable function, and vice versa'. Cf.
Price (1989) 16. White (1989) 149–57, Ferrari (1992) 266, and Reeve (1992)102.

make you aware of the honour you lack at present and desire. Öu will then take steps to remedy that lack accordingly (by the production of fine discourses and laws, for example). And notice that these products will themselves be *kalon* to the extent that they perform this role and manifest the producer's commitment to a certain kind of good. In all such cases, the beauty is question is pursued because it is appropriate to the acquisition of the good desired in each case.[24]

Envisaging the following scenario may help to clarify this relationship between the beautiful and the good. Many people have the experience of encountering something beautiful and feeling what they call 'inspired'. Often what they seem to mean is that this encounter motivates them to get their own lives into shape in some way or another. If I visit the Grand Canyon, or see a beautiful painting I feel that somehow I want to do something beautiful and good myself. Why this is the case can be understood as follows. Both the Grand Canyon and a beautiful picture—though very different kinds of beauty—are ways in which (natural) things, or people, have realized themselves in certain good ways. I am a lover of the good, and although I may not want to (or cannot) manifest the kinds of good that they do, they make me aware of my own lack of self-realization and fulfilment nonetheless, and in so doing they motivate me to remedy that lack. It is then a further step for me to figure out how to realize myself in a productive way, which I desire, and of which I am capable. In this respect those beautiful media are not particularly helpful, or appropriate, to me procuring my good. But imagine encountering a more appropriate beauty, that is, one fitting to a conception of how human beings are best realized. If I believe that wisdom is somehow central to my flourishing life and then I encounter a person, or text, that manifests that quality, then this will be a dynamic and extremely productive encounter. For it will make

---

[24] Cf. the discussion of the *kalon* in Aristotle's *Ethics* by Richardson Lear (2004) esp. 125: 'According to Aristotle, actions are fine when their determination by the human good makes the agent's commitment to his good visible'. In the *Symposium*, the *kaloi logoi* of the ascent, for example, will, I take it, be beautiful insofar as they make his commitment to a philosophical good visible. The poems and laws of the honour lovers will be *kalon* to the extent that they manifest that desiring agent's commitment to honour. And so on. Or, as Lear puts it later (again with reference to Aristotle), 'fine actions are ones that are visibly appropriate to the agent's ideal sense of himself' (Lear (2004) 144).

me aware of something specific that I lack and desire (wisdom) and provide the very environment for me to procure that end.

Now, Socrates has clearly revised the role of beauty in *erōs*. For *erōs* is not of the beautiful (e.g. Socrates, the Grand Canyon, a beautiful boy), but of production in the presence of the beautiful and, we might now add, for the sake of the good. It is the good things that result from the encounter with beauty that promise *eudaimonia*. If that is the case, then although the *kalon* and *agathon* are closely related, there can be no straightforward identification of the two; the beautiful is not identical to the good, but a spur to its production. One chooses certain kinds of beauty (embodied in cities or souls, for example) for the sake of procuring certain kinds of goods.[25] In the case of the honour lovers of the lower mysteries, for example, the beauty of cities and souls is an occasion for the production of honour; it is not identical with honour. But this is unnerving as an account of beauty's role. For the best sort of good—the highest sort of virtue—that Socrates will advocate later will be one that makes the beautiful a *telos*; it is an object of contemplation and 'that for the sake of which' we do all that we do (210e5–6). And yet the *kalon* will also be playing its role as presiding over childbirth; it is also an occasion for the production of a psychic good (true virtue: 212a3–6). This suggests that caution is required before the *kalon* is regulated to a purely instrumental role as such. It may be the case that the *kalon* plays an instrumental role for certain sorts of desiring agents and a more complex role for others.[26] When Socrates' account reaches such a point we will have need to return to this discussion, but already at this point it should be clear that although the beautiful and the good are intimately related, there can be no straightforward identification at this point.

Be that as it may, the fact that the beautiful and the good are closely related in this account confirms that the account of the *ergon* of *erōs*—reproduction in beauty—is still functioning within the

[25] This is related to the problem raised by Vlastos concerning the status of the beautiful objects encountered by the philosopher in the ascent, and whether their status is purely instrumental. See below, Ch. 5, for further discussion.

[26] Cf. *Republic* 357c ff., where Socrates makes it plain that there are certain kinds of things that are valued for their own sakes and for their instrumental role. Cf. White (2004) 373.

larger account of the aim of *erōs*: for the good and *eudaimonia*. For in exploring the role of beauty we have seen that it has a central role to play in the production of virtue and happiness for all desiring agents.[27] Creative activity in a beautiful environment is the way in which we can be productive of our good. Since beauty has such a central role to play in the production of virtue and happiness, this might call for caution in another sense, too. For such associations lead to an altogether different conception of *to kalon* as the noble, or the fine, in Aristotle's *Ethics*, for example.[28] It is, perhaps, the fact that *to kalon* is associated here with reproduction, and appears as a 'spur' to creative activity, that lends itself most naturally to our conception of it as 'beauty'. But we should bear in mind that reproductive activities here include acts of heroism (208d3), law-making (209d4–e1), the production of poetic displays (209a4), political leadership (209a6–8), educational conversations (209b8), and the production of philosophical *logoi* and true virtue (212a4–6). And the beautiful environments which arouse these actions and productions include souls, cities, laws, and practices and, for a select few, the form of beauty. Further, the *kalon* is not just a spur, but also a genuine *telos*, as we shall see. And, the goal of these actions and productions aroused by the *kalon* is *eudaimonia*. If we continue to conceive of the *kalon* as the beautiful in the *Symposium*, we should not be blind to its range, or forget that what is at stake here is the role of the *kalon* in the attainment of virtue and *eudaimonia*.

3. THE *ERGON* OF *ERŌS*: PRODUCTION AS POSSESSION

Exploring the role of the *kalon* and its relationship to the good has confirmed that there is an intimate connection between reproduction in beauty and pursuing the good. Productive activity in a

---

[27] Even those pregnant in body are still concerned with *eudaimonia* (208e4).

[28] For a comparative discussion of the *kalon* in Plato and Aristotle, see Nehamas (2004). On the interpretation of the *kalon* as 'the fine' in the *Symposium*, see Irwin (1977) 170–2, 234–5.

fitting environment is the way in which we secure our good. But we should now have a further question. Why do desiring agents seek to *produce* something good and beautiful as a way of *possessing* something good and beautiful? If we fail to understand this, then we will fail to understand why *erōs* for the good manifests itself in the *ergon* of *reproduction*, rather than an attempt at a more straightforward mode of *possession*. This takes us to the second part of the twofold answer to why *erōs* manifests itself in reproduction. Socrates now explains that human nature cannot, in fact, possess things in any straightforward way (207c5–208b5). This inability on our part forms an important part of the twofold explanation for our desire to be productive. Let us examine this in some detail.

Apparently, a living being never has the same bodily and psychic parts but is always 'becoming new, whilst otherwise perishing' (207d6–8). Even though all bodily and psychic parts are subject to flux, a living being is called the same over time because it is able to replace what has been lost with another new, qualitatively similar, thing (ὅμως ὁ αὐτὸς καλεῖται, 207d7, ἀλλὰ τῷ τὸ ἀπιὸν καί παλαιούμενον ἕτερον νέον ἐγκαταλείπειν οἷον αὐτὸ ἦν, 208b1–2). The mechanism that allows us to retain our physical and psychic qualities in this way is generation (207d2–3). The explanation ends by distinguishing between the persistence that holds for changeable mortal beings, and that which holds for the non-changeable divine nature. Whereas the divine is not in need of constant renewal to persist, living beings do not remain the same without the work of generation (cf. the contrast at 208a8–b1, οὐ τῷ παντάπασιν τὸ αὐτὸ ἀεὶ εἶναι ὥσπερ τὸ θεῖον). It is by this device that mortal natures can participate in, or approximate to, immortality (θνητὸν ἀθανασίας μετέχει, 208b3).

The passage forms part of the account of our reproductive *ergon* by explaining that mortal creatures are the kind of beings that need productive work to attain anything at all. If we want to possess the good then this will have to be something striven for by productive activity of a certain kind. Before exploring this part of the account we need to broach an objection. For it might now appear that we have stumbled into our original problem concerning the relationship between productive activities and the good. Since the passage ends by claiming that generation is the way in which the mortal participates in immortality (208b3), and provides an account of apparently mundane processes, such as nutritional replenishment, it may seem as if generation is, after all, a value-neutral activity. There is no mention of the good here. This omission may be taken to suggest that if we desire to engage in this productive mechanism we do so because what we are really after is continued existence: generation 'such as oneself'. If so, then it will, after all, be unclear why *erōs* for the secure possession of the good should manifest itself in such an activity. Read in this way, the passage is in danger of reintroducing the gap between reproduction (as a value-neutral activity) and the desire it is supposed to be the manifestation of (for the good). The account of pregnancy and procreation just discussed suggested no such gap. Adding the two features of reproduction together does not diffuse the problem, for if it is the case that the description of reproduction in this passage is value neutral, then we have, at least one instance where reproduction is not working for the good. But if reproduction is the *ergon* of *erōs* for the good, and the passage in question is illustrating that mechanism in action, then it ought to manifest that concern. If it does not, then (so the objection runs) this may be taken as evidence for a shift in the account after all.

There are two strategies one might take here. Since teleological ideas are apparent in other Platonic dialogues (most notably, the *Phaedo* and the *Timaeus*), one might be tempted to read the account of the flux of mortal life as developing the kind of explanation of change and decay that the Socrates of the *Phaedo* desired to hear from the natural philosophers (97c–d). If so, then the good would be playing a role—even in apparently mundane natural processes—and we could thereby grasp how this part of the account explains generation as the *ergon* of *erōs*, that is, the *ergon* of the desire *for the good*. This is appealing since this very passage is drawn on by Aristotle, the teleologist *par excellence* (cf. *DAnima* 415ᵃ28 ff.). If the *Symposium*'s account of coming-to-be and ceasing-to-be were developing this sort of teleological account, then we might extrapolate that the cause of generation 'such as itself' would be the desire to exist as such-and-such a living being, because existing as such-and-such a living being is good for that living being. For example, a living being reproduces the part 'hair' because it is the kind of living being for which it is good to have hair. Hair, say, protects the scalp from the midday sun, and so enables that living being to function properly in its environment. In a similar way, one might say it is good for that particular living being to reproduce, say, pains and fears because such psychic states enable the living being to avoid harm and flourish safely in its environment. If the qualities regenerated are seen in this way, then the good might be understood as what is advantageous or useful for the living being in question.[29] Each act of generation would then be seen as contributing to a living being's good directly in that the results of generation would themselves be good. Read in this way, the desire to exist as '—' and the desire to possess the good sound like the same desire under different descriptions. In the case of animals and the processes of growth and decay the goal it contributes to (explicitly) is approximation to divine existence in the way in which such things are able to (208b3). The goal of *erōs*, in each case, will be specified differently, at least in part on the basis of the predominance of physical or psychic natural abilities. But everything, we might say, aspires to the condition of the gods, and each kind of thing (animals, those human beings who are pregnant in body, and those more pregnant in soul) tries to attain this goal in specific ways. Animals may strive simply to continue to exist—as their chosen good. Human beings, whose nature carries certain higher potentialities (rational ones) are able to partake of the divine life more fully. But in each case we could nonetheless see how generation works for a good and is therefore a fitting manifestation of *erōs* for the good.[30]

---

[29] Cf. Aristotle, *IA* 2, 704^{b}15–17, see also *PA* 2, 654^{a}19; 3, 662^{a}33, b3, 7; 4, 677^{a}16, 678^{a}4–16, 683^{b}37, 684^{a}3, 685^{a}28, 687^{b}29, 691^{b}1 with Balme (1987) 276 and Cooper (1987) 245.

[30] One might wonder how one would construe such purposive behaviour in the case of non-deliberating natural processes. Woodfield (1976) 163–4 compares internalist theories of teleological explanation (which assumes that there is 'a core concept of mental goal-directedness'), where having G as a goal involves wanting G, and a more general concept of goal directedness formed by extension from this notion, where there is a tacit appeal to 'an internal state analogous to wanting', i.e. a tendency. Cf. Kahn (1985) 183–207, esp. 203–5, who agues with reference to Aristotle that: 'the growth, nutrition and reproduction of living things, like the appetites which accompany some of these functions, turn out to be simply a special case of the universal tendency to realised form and continuous activity'. One would need to employ a similar notion to understand the non-rational processes included in purposive explanation for this reading of the *Symposium*.

What would settle the matter, of course, is some explicit statement to the effect that being is better than not being, or that all goal-directed activity aims at the *kalon.* And this we do not have here. But there is an alternative. In fact, *erōs* is nowhere ascribed explicitly to the nutritional replenishment of the body, for example, nor is the survival of a living being over time described as a form of *reproduction.* The earlier description of reproduction was quite distinctive: first, reproduction assumes a pregnancy is there to be delivered; second, it requires a harmonious and beautiful medium. If the cases of bodily and psychic replenishment are illustrative examples of reproduction in beauty—then where are we to locate the pregnancy? What acts as the harmonious and beautiful medium? Do hair and skin and blood experience *erōs,* carry pregnancies, and beget these pregnancies every time they regenerate themselves? The account of reproduction we were offered shows that it is not a mundane activity such as these; it is quite a specific kind of generation. Clearly the passage is introduced as part of the explanation for the desire to reproduce (207a8–9), but then generation quite generally (γένεσις) is described as a particular kind of mechanism that brings about immortality (207d2–208b2). It is not until the conclusion of this passage (208b4) that we return to reproduction proper (γέννησις) and are invited to consider the value we bequeath to our offspring. If this is the case, then, the passage is not considering reproduction directly. Rather the subject is generation quite generally, 'coming into being', and the way in which it contributes to the survival of a living being over time. This must still illuminate reproduction, since the latter is a specific type of generation. But just because all reproduction is a kind of generation, that does not mean that every act of generation is a kind of reproduction and thereby a manifestation of *erōs.* It is only if one assumes that *all* acts of generation are manifestations of *erōs* that the lack of any mention of the good and the focus on continued existence cause concern. Rather the passage is explaining the mechanism of generation in a general sense, which those of us who are erotically disposed employ in a very specific way: for the good and not just the *oikeion,* we might say.[31]

---

[31] Bury writes about the introduction of γένεσις at the start of the passage (207d1–2) as follows: 'τῇ γενέσει, if genuine, is an epexegetic supplement. Possibly we should excise τῇ γενέσει, with Vermehren; or else alter to τῇ γεννήσει. But the use of

Neither of the above readings requires a wedge between reproduction and the good. On the first reading, generation is a lower-grade form of reproduction, i.e. that *ergon* of *erōs* for the good. It is one of the ways that living beings manifest that desire in the way in which they are able to. On the second reading, the passage offers a general illustration of generation, of which reproduction is a specific kind. If so, then it is not illustrating reproduction *directly* and the omission of the good need cause no concern. There is, as yet, no threat to our understanding of how the *ergon* of *erōs* works for our good and, therefore, no evidence of a gap between the desire to reproduce and the desire for good things and happiness.

On either reading, one still needs to determine precisely what the account is offering to an explanation of our productive *ergon*. There are two ways in which we might read the contribution of the passage to this task. On the first, the passage provides a new theory of survival over time, which supports the claim that living beings can survive after death in their offspring, or products, in much the same way as they have done in their lives. Let us call this the strong reading. The explanatory force of the account is to explain how we can possess the good 'always' by reproduction: this mechanism functions by creating (physical or psychic) offspring (which somehow embodies our desired good), and which will go on and on and so allow us to survive (as possessors of that good) by proxy. This, apparently, is not dissimilar to the way in which we have survived in our lives by the regeneration of physical and psychic qualities.[32] Alternatively (and rather more minimally), the passage explains that production (i.e.

τῇ γενέσει above (206d) in the sense of "the process of generation", combined with the emphasis, by repetition of its moods and tenses, laid on γίγνεσθαι in the sequel (207d–208a), may make us hesitate to adopt any change'; Bury (1932) 115. Bury is, of course, right to point out that in the description of γέννησις at 206d1 γένεσις does appear, but in the context this must be the specific sense 'the process of generation' as opposed to the general sense 'coming into being', which is operative 207d2–208b2. There is no reason to read that specific sense into τῇ γενέσει at 207d1–2; what we are considering there is the everyday phenomenon of change and decay, i.e. 'coming into being' in a generic sense and its opposite.

[32] Of course, those who remain unconvinced by my arguments and think the good has dropped from view here would think the passage is just about plain old survival over time by reproduction for the sake of immortality. If so, they would drop the idea that offspring somehow embody our perceived good (unless that is taken to be the same as immortality).

generation) is the mortal form of possession, without specifying anything further about the nature of that production, or the precise form it takes (the weak reading). In other words, it does not specify that all reproduction functions by the creation of new 'person stages', or external products that enable us to possess the good by proxy. The explanatory force of the passage is simply to explain why human beings engage in creative endeavour: if we want to possess the good, this must be something *produced* if it is to be had at all. What precise form that production will take (e.g. whether it always involves the creation of external products, for example), and how long that possession or production goes on for, will be further questions dependent in part on how one conceives of the relevant good. The interpretative implications of this passage run deep, as we shall see. For how one interprets the import of this passage, and whether, and in what sense, one thinks it specifies the essential features of repro-duction, affects what stand one takes on the vexed question of philosophical virtue (for this is something produced), and that, in turn, affects how one conceives of the acquisition of *eudaimonia* by reproduction. For if this passage specifies, or implies, that all reproduction functions by producing something such as oneself which survives one (the strong reading), then we will have reason to expect an external product generated by the philosopher (perhaps 'in another', as is often held) that enables him to possess the good always by proxy. But if not, then our account of the final acquisition of virtue and happiness by reproduction will look very different. It will be worth our while to puzzle over the details of this passage.

Let us take the strong reading first: the 'redescription of survival in terms of replacement'.[33] The central idea is that the passage blurs the distinction between reproduction and the kind of generation involved in the maintenance of a living being in such a way that Socrates can claim that we can survive after death in our (physical or psychic) offspring. The idea is the following. For a living being to survive there must be: (1) another new thing which replaces the old ($\check{\epsilon}\tau\epsilon\rho\sigma\nu$ $\nu\acute{\epsilon}\sigma\nu$, 207d6), (2) which is qualitatively similar to the old thing ($\sigma\check{i}\sigma\nu$ $\alpha\mathring{\nu}\tau\grave{\sigma}$ $\mathring{\eta}\nu$, 208b2). If both these conditions are met, then a living being is said to survive over time. It survives by means of causal

---

[33] Price (1989) 31.

connections (one thing leaves behind another new thing) and qualitative continuities between itself at one time and another new thing at
a later time. Now, if the passage is claiming that all that matters in our
talk of survival over time is that a living being satisfies conditions (1)
and (2), and if reproduction enables us to satisfy conditions (1) and
(2), then we can say that a living being survives after death through
offspring. It does so in much the same way as it has done in its life, by
means of causal connections and qualitative continuities between itself
at one time and another new thing at a later time. If so, as Socrates
maintains at the end of this passage (208b4–5), we should not be
amazed that 'everything by nature values what springs from itself'.[34]

The strong reading provides an explanation of how reproduction
works to secure the continued existence of the producer. Indeed notice
how this reading works particularly well for those who claim that the
aim of *erōs* has shifted to another goal: immortality, in place of the
good. Even those who see no such shift, though, may (and do) appeal
to this sort of account because it provides an answer to how we
can achieve a substitute, or vicarious, immortality in our offspring,
and so extend our possession of the things we value into the
future.[35] If we consider the first two groups of desiring agents
considered above—both of whom desire honour—this sort of
account works quite well. The honour lovers employed their

[34] For a fuller discussion of such a position see Price (1989) 31–3 and Warner
(1979) 329–39, who both compare such a view to Parfit (1984) esp. ch. 12. The
Anonymous commentator on Plato's *Theaetetus* thought that Plato was here pro-
pounding a version of Epicharmus' growth paradox, see *In Tht.*, ed. Diels and Schubert
(1905), 71.12 ff., with Sedley (1982) 258. For puzzles raised by treating the passage in
this way, see Crombie (1962), i. 362. I doubt whether Socrates would want to raise such
puzzles in a substantive ethical treatise. *Euthydemus* 287b shows an awareness of the
problems that could result from such puzzles and their implications for philosophical
practice and ethical consistency more generally. Further, the passage makes better
sense in context without such puzzles. Even if one believes that the passage is providing
a new theory of survival, though, it could just be read as claiming that (1) and (2) are
what matters from the perspective of the physical and mental history that together
constitute a person's life, as Price puts it. One need not read into it the further claim
that the soul is nothing but these replaced states (as Price 1989: 24–5 notes). It is this
further claim that gives rise to some of the above puzzles.

[35] Hackforth (1950) 43, Kraut (1973) 346–9, Irwin (1977) 241, and Price (1989)
31 all talk of a second-best, or substitute, immortality, obtained in this way, though
Price (1989) 53 also entertains the possibility of an immortality 'not vicarious, but
proprietary.' Cf. also White (2004).

reproductive *ergon* to secure honour either by the production of children, or by the production of poems and laws. In the first case, children are an external product, thought to provide 'immortality, memory and happiness, for all time to come' (209e4–5) so, we might suppose, such offspring extend the possession of the producer's good (namely, honour) into the future by proxy. In the case of the honour lovers who created psychic offspring, too, there is a clear external product: *arētē* embodied in poems and laws which provide their producers with an immortal memory of their virtue, and honour in the form of cults and shrines. Their external products secure them a vicarious immortality insofar as their good progeny are possessed by students, or remembered by cities. The strong reading provides a neat explanation. Children are cases of leaving something behind (so, (1)), and they are such as the producer in the sense that they express his physical or psychic life, and are qualitatively similar to it (so (2)). They secure possession of the producer's good to the extent that the products continue to flourish and lay up a name for their producer. This good will not be something possessed, strictly speaking, but something produced. These desiring agents will survive as a producer of this good to the extent that their good actions and productions serve as memorials 'for all time to come', and their 'manifold virtue' endures in the memory of those who make it their practice to honour the producer in memory (209d3–e3). Achilles' virtue bears the mark of his life, and then Homer perpetuates a memory of that virtue in a similar way to that in which one recreates memories within a single life.[36] It is in this sense that the passage about generation provides an account of how one can survive in external products. It explains why we engage in productive activity by showing how it satisfies certain conditions for survival over time. And these need to be met in order to satisfy the desire to possess the good 'always'.

---

[36] As Halperin notes, we have already seen an instance of this preservative mechanism in action in the dialogue's prologue. Apollodorus perceives these sympotic *logoi* as good things to preserve (he only recalls those that are 'worthy of remembrance', 178a4) and his practice creates a memory which secures the survival of these *logoi* over a long period of time. They are such as their producers in the sense that they are expressions of the producers' thought and preserve a good for him insofar as they embody something of value. When reading the *Symposium* we remember Socrates, not as such, but as virtuous, and so his good being endures in that sense. See Halperin (1992), *passim*, who calls this the 'erotics of narrativity'.

The strong reading, then, assumes that creating an external product that somehow survives one is the salient property of reproduction quite generally. Leaving aside for the moment the philosophical problems involved in blurring the distinction between the kind of generation involved in the maintenance of a living being and reproduction, this reading has other problems. It leads us to expect much the same for all desiring agents, including those of the higher mysteries; for the philosopher, too, employs his reproductive *ergon* (212a4–6). But as we shall see in more detail in the next chapter, the strong reading does not work so well in the case of the higher mysteries. There is no mention of external products such as children, poems, or philosophical *logoi* at the highest stage, which provide memorials for all time to come. Even if we assume that the model from the lower mysteries should be applied to the higher[37] (a questionable assumption, as we shall see), the production of true virtue does not appear to require an external product (e.g. child, or a poem) in which it is expressed. It is, unlike honour, just not that sort of good, as we shall see. But even if the higher mysteries did not provide a reason for caution in the interpretation of this part of the account, the strong reading is not required to make sense of the passage in context so far. Let us turn back to the passage itself.

The central contrast drawn at the end of the passage is that between the divine, and living beings who do not have the same mode of being as the divine (οὐ τῷ παντάπασιν τὸ αὐτὸ ἀεὶ εἶναι ὥσπερ τὸ θεῖον, 208a8–b1). The divine is altogether perfect and changeless, but mortal nature requires productive work: it is constantly 'coming into being, whilst otherwise perishing' (207d6–7). Productive activity is the mortal approximation to the divine state (208b3). Read in a more cautious way, the passage is still concerned with the persistence conditions for living beings; that much is clear (207d5, 208a7–8). The point, though, is not to provide a new theory of survival over time which blurs the distinction between reproduction proper and generation, and grounds the conclusion that we survive after death in external products. The point is just that the mode of existence for the divine and the mortal is different, and that productive activity is an approximation to the divine state. On this

---

[37] With Price (1989) 29, 53 and White (2004) 374.

weaker reading, Socrates is not committed to any further claims about the specifics of how reproduction functions to approximate the divine, and whether it always involves the creation of external products. The point is just that for living beings productive activity is required to attain anything at all. If the salient point is to explain that production is the mortal form of possession, without specifying the manner in which we approximate to a divine state, then it will be an open question how exactly this works. Having an offspring may be (and clearly is) one of the ways in which living beings try to secure everlasting *eudaimonia* (e.g. for the honour lovers of the lower mysteries). But this will not be indicative of reproduction more generally. There may be other ways to participate in the divine. The point is simply that living beings require productive activity in order to possess anything at all. So, if we want the good, this must be produced if it is to be possessed. How long that possession will go on for, and in what shape or form, will depend upon the type of productive activity different desiring agents pursue. This, in turn, will depend upon their conception of the good, as we have seen. If one values honour, then one's productive activity will indeed be reliant upon external products left behind for its realization (i.e. as memorials after death). I will need to create an external product (a law, or poem) to secure that particular good. But there may be other goods (those of the soul) whose production does not function in this way.

Either way, we can see how this passage forms part of the twofold explanation for our desire for reproduction, and explains why 'everything by nature values what springs from itself' (208b4–5). The strong reading explains how we can survive after death by proxy and thereby forms part of the argument for how we can possess the good 'always' in that sense. But the weak reading is sufficient to explain why it is that we engage in reproduction: given that we are the kind of living beings that we are, we need to be productive. That is what Agathon missed when he made lovers altogether beautiful and good (204c4–6). If desiring agents were in that sort of abundant state they would have no need for creative endeavour. As it is, though, we are unlike the gods in this respect and need productive work to attain anything at all. If we desire to possess good things and happiness, or anything at all for that matter, this is something that must be realized in various actions and productions if it is to be had at all. That is why, on this reading, we value what springs from ourselves: productive activity realizes us and we love our own being, not as such, but insofar as it is good (205e1–5) and we realize ourselves in good ways in our productive activities.[38] We will argue this out further when we compare the productive activities of honour lovers and philosophers in the next chapter.

4. *ERŌS*, PRODUCTIVE ACTIVITY AND EUDAIMONIA

The aim of this chapter has been to chart a coherent path through Socrates' speech and to explain the relationship between the *ergon* of reproduction in beauty and the desire for *eudaimonia*, in particular. These two features of the account are not at odds with one another. The answer to why we desire to be creative in the presence of beauty is that this activity allows us to be productive of a perceived good and, given that we are the kind of living beings that we are, *production is the mortal form of possession*. (We will keep open for the moment the issue of how long that possession will go on for, or in what shape and form.) This explains why desiring agents manifest their desire for happiness in productive activity, and so it resolves the puzzling relationship between *erōs*, beauty, and creativity that emerged from Agathon's account. It also explains the relationship between the apparently disparate parts of Socrates' speech.

For reasons that remain unclear at present, Socrates divides the productive activities of different desiring agents into the lower and higher mysteries of *erōs*. In each case we have seen that the encounter with beauty allows the producer to realize himself in a certain good way ('deliver his pregnancy') by the creation of children, laws, educational conversations in the lower mysteries, or philosophical *logoi* and true virtue in the higher. All such productions are somehow thought to provide *eudaimonia*. The success of this activity depends

---

[38] Again, compare Aristotle, *Ethics* (1168ª7–8): 'Thus the producer loves his product, because he loves his own being. And this is natural, since what he is potentially his product manifests in actuality.'

upon a person's conception of the good and, in part, on the predominance of certain natural abilities (whether they are more pregnant in body or soul). We need to ensure that we have a correct conception of our good and the actions appropriate to its procurement, as we shall see. But already at this stage we know that *eudaimonia* will reside in a productive activity of the soul that expresses 'wisdom and virtue', for actions and productions expressive of that are explicitly said to be superior to physical offspring (209c6–7). And yet the placing of the productive activities of the poets and law-makers in the lesser mysteries of *erōs* suggests that the correct conception of the good is not honour. There is a better way to employ one's productive *ergon*, which we shall examine in the next chapter. Even when desiring agents go wrong in that pursuit, though, they are nonetheless pursuing their *eudaimonia*—their self-realization in the best way possible—and *erōs* is directed towards the achievement of *that* aim.

In exploring the twofold answer to why *erōs* manifests itself in productive activity, I have argued that there is an intimate relationship between our nature (our pregnancy), our *ergon* (reproduction), and our good (variously conceived). A further implication of Socrates' account, then, is not just a clarification of Agathon's claims about the relationship between *erōs*, beauty, and creativity, but also a clarification of Socrates' rebuttal of Aristophanes (205e1–2). If it is the case that all human beings are pregnant in body and soul and we naturally desire to give birth when we reach a certain age (206c1–4) in reproductive activity, these dual claims suggest that *erōs* is the natural way in which we express our nature. We have also seen that realizing our nature in productive activity and pursuing our good are intimately related. This gives us reason to suppose that Socrates was onto something important when he implied that we only desire what is akin to ourselves insofar as that is good (205d10–206a1). We can now appreciate that there was a sense in which Aristophanes was right: *erōs* does pursue the *oikeion*—but not as such; what we desire is not just ourselves, but ourselves realized in our productive activities as good. That is what *eudaimonia* consists in, and it is the task of our productive *ergon* to effect this self-transformation, and of beauty to inspire each thing towards the realization of its own nature in the best way possible. It is time to turn to Socrates' account of how this can best be achieved.

4

Socrates' Speech: The Activity of *Erōs*

So far, Socrates has argued that *eudaimonia* is the ultimate aim of all desire and action, and that this aim makes itself manifest in various actions and productions that issue from the pursuit of beauty. Since *eudaimonia* is the aim of all *erōs*, our choice of good must be one that will satisfy this desire: it must be a good whose possession no longer requires us to ask of the agent what she wants in pursuing it. It must be pursued because it will satisfy the desire for *eudaimonia*—which is chosen for its own sake—as the *telos* of all erotic pursuits (205a1–3). Further, we must find the pursuit of beauty appropriate to the possession, or rather the production, of this good; for production in beauty is the mortal way in which we can possess good things. Now we have already had a suggestion that *eudaimonia* resides in a productive activity of the soul that expresses wisdom and virtue. For psychic offspring—that is, the actions and productions expressive of a soul pregnant with 'wisdom and the rest of virtue'—are explicitly said to be superior to physical offspring (209c6–7 with 209a3–4). But the pursuit of honour in beautiful cities and souls, amongst which is included the ordering of cities and households (209a7) and the productions of poems and laws, yields only an image of true virtue (212a4). Such types are relegated to the lower mysteries of *erōs* and their pursuits are said to be 'for the sake of' something higher (210e5–6). The implication is that there is a superior good and a better way to employ one's productive *ergon*. In the so-called higher mysteries of *erōs* we learn that there is, in fact, just one kind of pursuit desired for its own sake (210e6), and that issues in genuine wisdom and virtue: the pursuit of the form of beauty. The life of contemplation, as opposed to the life of honour, is revealed as the best human life

(211d1–3). It will be the task of this chapter to examine why this satisfies the desire for *eudaimonia* to the greatest extent.

Since Socrates argues that it is in the pursuit of the form of beauty that one can be productive of the best life for a human being, in the first two sections of the chapter, I examine this ascent to the form. The aim will be to clarify the distinctive features of philosophical activity and its relationship to the productive activity in beauty that characterizes all desiring agents. In the third section I turn to the relationship between contemplation of the form, producing virtue, and *eudaimonia*. I argue that contemplating the form just is to be productive of true virtue and happiness, and this good can only be realized in the encounter with the form of beauty. Finally, we will be in a position to compare the philosopher with the honour lovers of the lower mysteries in order to evaluate how philosophical virtue, above all, is supposed to deliver happiness.

1. OUR *ERGON* AND KNOWLEDGE: PRODUCTION IN BEAUTY AND REFLECTION UPON BEAUTY

Let us start with an outline of the distinctive features of the desiring agent who occupies the higher mysteries (henceforth DHM) for this is the account of the proper activity of *erōs*, as we shall see. The DHM engages in a method that leads to knowledge of the form of beauty:

a beauty that always is, and neither comes into being nor perishes, neither increases nor diminishes, one that is not beautiful in this respect but ugly in that, nor beautiful at one moment, but not at another, nor beautiful in relation to this, but ugly in relation to that, nor beautiful here, but ugly there, because some people find it beautiful while others find it ugly (211a1–5).

Different classes of beauty are surveyed in the area of body and soul 'correctly and in the right order' (θεώμενος ἐφεξῆς τε καὶ ὀρθῶς τὰ καλά, 210e3) in a way that leads to the form of beauty. There is evidently a focused method to this pursuit of beauty.[1] The search for

---

[1] The importance of a structured movement from an ἀρχή to a τέλος is emphasized throughout the passage; cf. 210a1: τὰ τέλεα καὶ ἐποπτικά, ὧν ἕνεκα καὶ ταῦτα

beauty proceeds to the form through the use of particular examples, or kinds, of beauty. This procedure has certain structural features in common with Socrates' procedure in certain other dialogues that attempt to explain some general term. In many of these cases, where the method proceeds through a systematic review of the thing in question, Socrates talks as if he were examining all the different instances. When Socrates implies that he has given a complete review of every case, what the context suggests he means is that he has examined different cases of the thing in question by means of a review of different classes (cf. *Gorgias* 474d–e; *Charmides* 159–60; *Meno*, 87e–88e). This procedure typically follows a division into bodily and psychic goods, which seems to be the case here, too.[2] The initial division that structures this pursuit of beauty appears to be into physical beauty (210a5–b6) and psychic beauty (210b6 ff.). The classes of laws, practices, and knowledge appear as subclasses of objects that are related to psychic beauty insofar as they are things that concern the soul (by appearing to make the young better).[3] Turning one's attention to the beauty of soul provides an important occasion to turn to higher kinds of beauty, and to reflect upon their

---

ἔστιν, c3: ἵνα, c5: ἵνα, c7: ἵνα, e3–4: πρὸς τέλος ἰὼν, e5–6: οὗ ἕνεκεν πάντες πόνοι ἦσαν, 211b7: τοῦ τέλους, c1: ἕνεκα, c7: τελευτῆσαι, c8: γνῷ αὐτὸ τελευτῶν ὃ ἔστι καλόν.

[2] On this procedure, see Robinson (1953) 37: 'Besides the inference where we obtain the universal by inspecting every one of its particulars, there is the inference where we obtain it by inspecting every one of the subuniversals or species into which it divides according to a given principle of division... Thus the division of human affairs into bodily and psychical often enables Socrates to review them all compendiously.' In the *Gorgias*, for example, Socrates takes Polus through beautiful bodies first, then shapes, colours, and sounds, and then laws and practices in his examination of beauty (474d–e). See also *Charmides* (159–60) and *Meno* (87e5; 87e–88e). The body–soul division has also played a role in earlier parts of Socrates' speech (206c2–3). Socrates explained that all human beings are pregnant καὶ κατὰ τὸ σῶμα καὶ κατὰ τὴν ψυχήν, and he says of the state of flux that affects mortal creatures καὶ μὴ ὅτι κατὰ τὸ σῶμα, ἀλλὰ καὶ κατὰ τὴν ψυχήν (207e1–2).

[3] Cf. *Laches* (185e1–6), where it is said that one examines 'learnings' for the sake of the souls of the young. Highlighting the body–soul division explains the following textual points here. First, we are told that the DHM comes to realize that psychic beauty is worth more than physical beauty (τιμιώτερον... τοῦ ἐν τῷ σώματι, 210b7) and he searches 'for such λόγοι as make the young better', a search which compels him to look upon the beauty in practices and laws (cf. ἵνα ἀναγκασθῇ αὖ θεάσασθαι τὸ ἐν τοῖς ἐπιτηδεύμασι καὶ τοῖς νόμοις καλόν, c3–4). The way in which the interest in laws and practices follows from the DHM's search for λόγοι that will make the

nature (210a7, c3). On each encounter with beauty the DHM focuses his attention on the common quality of beauty (τὸ ἐπὶ πᾶσιν τοῖς σώμασι κάλλος, 210b3, τὸ ἐν ταῖς ψυχαῖς κάλλος, b6–7, τὸ ἐν τοῖς ἐπιτηδεύμασι καὶ τοῖς νόμοις καλὸν, b6–7), and draws generalizations about beauty on that level. On the first level, for example, he comes to realize that insofar as they are beautiful, bodies are closely related (κατανοῆσαι ὅτι τὸ κάλλος τὸ ἐπὶ ὁτῳοῦν σώματι τῷ ἐπὶ ἑτέρῳ σώματι ἀδελφόν ἐστι, 210a8–b1, and then that they are one and the same (ἕν τε καὶ ταὐτὸν, b3, ἰδεῖν ὅτι πᾶν αὐτὸ αὑτῷ συγγενές ἐστιν, c4–5). The systematic process of drawing generalizations on each level enables the DHM to develop a synoptic vision that forms the basis of a theoretical understanding of the nature of beauty (210c7–d1: βλέπων πρὸς πολὺ ἤδη τὸ καλὸν μηκέτι τὸ παρ' ἑνί, with 210d3–4: ἐπὶ τὸ πολὺ πέλαγος τετραμμένος τοῦ καλοῦ καὶ θεωρῶν). This recognition of unity on each level is essential preparatory training for the apprehension of an entity that is essentially one and the same: the form of beauty itself (αὐτὸ καθ' αὑτὸ μεθ' αὑτοῦ μονοειδές, 211b1). The result of this procedure is that the DHM is able to understand the nature of beauty (211c8–9) and to produce true virtue by grasping this truth (212a3–5).

This is evidently quite a distinctive type of productive activity in the beautiful. We have already seen that giving birth in beauty is a way of attaining the good and beautiful things thought to lead to, or constitute, *eudaimonia*. And we are now trying to determine why this is best satisfied in the kind of activity just outlined, as opposed to the productive activities of the honour lovers of the lower mysteries. For these latter activities, as we have seen, are relegated to an inferior status. But if production in beauty is a way of attaining the good,

young better, which in turn follows from his interest in psychic beauty, suggests that the interest in laws and practices lies in extension of the concern with psychic beauty. There is no step here which corresponds to that between body and soul at 210b8; rather, the interest in laws and practices is forced upon the DHM because of his interest in the soul (b8–c4). Moreover, after examining laws and practices, the DHM comes to think that physical beauty is σμικρόν τι (210c5). Why, if the laws and practices are not to be thought of as, in some way, subclasses of soul, would the DHM be compelled to make a comparison with physical beauty after this step? Further support for this suggestion comes from the summation of the DHM's progress. The steps mentioned are bodies, practices, and learnings (211c); no mention is made of soul. The lack of any explicit mention of soul here might seem problematic unless fine practices and laws are, in some sense, related to psychic beauty.

then how exactly does this relate to the activity of reflection upon beauty and acquiring knowledge of the form? What is the relationship between *reflecting upon* the nature of beauty and *reproducing in the presence of* beauty? Since such reflective activity leads to knowledge and the production of true virtue, we shall also need to clarify the relationship between *knowing the form* of beauty and *producing virtue* in the presence of beauty. If we fail to clarify these issues then we will fail to understand why—*as a lover of the good whose ergon is to reproduce in beauty*—the DHM is engaged in this kind of activity at all, let alone why it is the best of all productive activities.

Both the nature and the result of the DHM's search suggest that an intimate relationship must hold between the desired good in this case and knowledge and that this is part of the explanation for the distinctive pursuit of beauty in this case. The predominance of cognitive terms in the higher mysteries is noteworthy (κατανοῆσαι (210a8), πολλὴ ἄνοια (b2), ἐννοήσαντα (b4), ἡγήσασθαι (b7), θεάσασθαι (c3), θεωρῶν (d4), διανοήματα (d5), θεώμενος (e3), θεωμένῳ αὐτὸ τὸ καλόν (211d2)), as is the fact that the outcome of this reflective encounter with a range of beautiful objects is knowledge ὃ ἐστι καλόν, and true virtue. The DHM appears to value wisdom and (either he or his guide) believes this to be intimately related to the production of genuine virtue. Knowledge is, at least, a necessary condition of virtue; but the description of the DHM's progress gives no reason to doubt that knowledge is also a sufficient condition of virtue.[4] When the DHM comes to understand the form of beauty, his delivery of virtue is the direct result: he produces true virtue by grasping the truth (212a3–5). This is not just any bit of truth; it is knowledge of the form of *beauty*. If we suppose that laws, practices, and knowledge are beautiful insofar as they lead to the acquisition of virtue, then we can begin to grasp why, as a lover of the good, the DHM is concerned to know about the sorts of activities that are conducive to the attainment of this end. If virtue requires knowledge of beauty, then any attempt to produce virtue will require such knowledge, and progress towards it will surely involve reflection upon the nature of beauty. If so, then we have begun to clarify the

---

[4] From other Socratic dialogues we are familiar with the idea for which Socrates often argues, that virtue is knowledge (*La.* 194d1–2, *Prt.* 361b1–2).

relationship between a productive activity that aims at a good (wisdom and virtue) and the distinctive nature of the pursuit of the *kalon* in this case.

It must also be the case that the *kalon* sought is believed to be one thing, and something shared by the many beautiful things encountered in the ascent. Otherwise it is difficult to see why the DHM should be trying to recognize unity between different cases of beauty (210a 8–b1, c4–5). Although, at the initial stages, the DHM is attracted to the sorts of beautiful bodies that many other lovers might happen upon in their lives, the manner of his pursuit is not something that would occur naturally to most lovers. Again, note the cognitive terms that characterize the pursuit of beauty here: κατανοῆσαι (210a8), ἐννοήσαντα (b4), ἡγήσασθαι (b7), θεάσασθαι (c3), θεωρῶν (d4), διανοήματα (d5), θεώμενος (e3), θεωμένῳ αὐτὸ τὸ καλόν (211d2). The DHM is said, for example, to realize that the beauty of all bodies is 'akin' and that 'if he is to pursue beauty in accordance with the *eidos*, it would be mindless not to realize that the beauty of all bodies is one and the same' (210b2). Although *eidos* can refer simply to outward form, or physical appearance, it is difficult to see what would be mindless about not realizing that things are 'one and the same', unless one was committed to pursuing the feature that all cases of beauty have in common.[5] It does not seem to be the case that people generally speaking pursue the beauty of the young, come to sophisticated realizations about their unity, and then pursue this process in a variety of cases. If that were so, then many people would be engaged on this path and not just a select few. The DHM is being guided in a search for the nature of beauty from the start, though his destination may not always be clear to him. He proceeds 'correctly and in the right order' (θεώμενος ἐφεξῆς τε καὶ ὀρθῶς τὰ καλά, 210e3), through a range of classes of beauty because of certain assumptions about the relationship between virtue and knowledge

---

[5] In the *Meno* where Socrates explains the form a definition should take, the pursuit of the εἶδος is connected to the realization that its kinds are ἕν τε καὶ ταὐτόν: 'The same is true in the case of the excellences. Even if they are many and various, all of them have one and the same form (ἕν γέ τι εἶδος ταὐτόν) which makes them excellences, and it is right to look to this when one is asked to make clear what excellence is' (72c).

of beauty and about the nature of beauty itself (e.g. that there is one common quality that is the same in all cases).

The metaphysical assumption behind the pursuit of the form appears to be that beautiful laws and practices, for example, are not always beautiful, or beautiful in every respect (cf. 211a1–5). Beautiful laws and practices, as Pausanias had already intimated, are many and various and dependent upon different societies and the changeable views of their citizens (182b–c). Stable knowledge about the *kalon*— if there is to be any at all—cannot then be had from experience of these alone. If one is to acquire virtue, and this involves knowing about 'the sort of thing the good man must be concerned with, and the activities such a man should pursue' (cf. 209c1), then one cannot base such understanding on the perspectival and changeable nature of everyday experience. One needs to know the changeless and perfect form. Since this is the source of all beauty (211b1–5), such knowledge will enable its possessor to discern in any and every case where the *kalon* lies. If virtue requires knowledge of the *kalon*, then, producing the good for oneself will require knowledge of the form of beauty. Since other beautiful things are beautiful insofar as they participate in the nature of the form (211b1–5), reflection upon their nature can lead to its source. And, if that is the case, then the proper functioning of our productive *ergon* will be in the pursuit of the form that is, in reflection upon beauty and in producing the sorts of *logoi* that are conducive to the attainment of this end. Put differently, if it is only in the presence of the form that we can (re)produce a genuine good—wisdom and true virtue— then philosophical activity of just this sort will be *erōs'* proper expression.

Without an *erōs* that responds to the value of intellectual activity, and the above assumptions, it is difficult to grasp why one would be engaged in this ordered and reflective response to beauty at all. There is a distinctive methodological procedure that informs this encounter with beauty. It is difficult to suppose that this kind of procedure is something one just happens upon because of an attraction towards the beautiful—in any ordinary sense, at least. Even at the very lowest level of the ascent, we should not suppose that the DHM is simply (or solely) experiencing *erōs* for the boy in a sexual (or particularly interpersonal) sense just because of the fact that he experiences *erōs* and this is focused upon a beautiful body. We need to ask: What sort of *erōs* is this? A good way to answer that question is to focus on the manner of his engagement with this beautiful body, and the other objects of his *erōs*. Once we do so it is clear that the DHM is reflecting upon the nature of this beauty. This reflective activity is indicative of the kind of *erōs* that characterizes this desiring agent: the DHM values wisdom. If this were not so, then why and how would he perceive the beauty that all beautiful bodies have in common, since this requires intellectual engagement? This is the kind of *erōs* which is directed, albeit briefly, to the beautiful body, even at the first stage of this process, and this is presumably why he reflects upon its nature (as opposed to seeking other kinds of intercourse with this body).[6] He engages with the beautiful bodies and souls in this distinctively reflective way because of some conception he has—however vague—of the value of this kind of activity. And this reflective activity just is how *erōs* is manifested for this particular desiring agent. This is a description of the philosophical character in action from the outset.[7]

Since the DHM starts from early youth on this journey (210a5), it seems reasonable to assume that it is the guide more experienced in 'erotic matters' who holds such views.[8] The DHM himself may just be a promising young man full of potential (more pregnant in soul

[6] I am in agreement with Moravscik (1971) 291 about the emphasis on intellectual activity in the ascent, but I fail to appreciate why he divides up the ascent into R steps for reasoning activity and E steps for his erotic responses. For the point is surely that there is no distinction between reflecting and loving. The claim is that reflecting is the kind of loving involved here, it is a manifestation of a particular kind of *erōs*, for wisdom.

[7] The explanatory force of this reading will become clear when we turn to the interpretation of how the 'ascent' is made. But one might raise the following objection. On my reading do we not lose the 'erotic pedagogy' of this account (for which see Frede (1993)). That is to say, do we not lose an account of how one can be led from our ordinary lives and loves to more abstract ones. For on my reading of this passage, the DHM is intellectually inclined from the outset. I am not claiming that one can never move from one kind of *erōs* (e.g. sexual *erōs*) to another kind of *erōs* (e.g. intellectual *erōs*). I am simply claiming that this is not what we see in the ascent. Perhaps Plato thought that he could motivate the copulating lovers in Aristophanes' speech to ascend to the form. But when prompted to reflect by Hephaestus these lovers do not appear keen to move anywhere other than deeper into each others arms.

[8] I take it that the guide is an ideal lover, one who knows about 'erotic matters', much like Diotima, or (the experienced) Socrates.

with 'wisdom and the rest of virtue', 209a4), and the sort of person who values wisdom as one of the *kallista* (cf. 204b1–5). Even if the DHM is amongst those who value wisdom as one of the *kallista*—as his willingness to participate in such a process suggests—this will not be sufficient to explain why he engages in reflection upon the feature that a given class of beautiful objects have in common, rather than in the production of rhetorical displays, for example. Pausanias held that there was an intimate relationship between virtue and wisdom (184d7–e1), and so he could be described as one of those who value wisdom as one of the *kallista*, but he did not advocate anything like the ascent. There are certain substantive views that guide, if not motivate, the pursuit of beauty in the ascent.[9]

If that is the case then we can understand the relationship between the philosophical activity of the ascent and the productive activity in the beautiful that characterizes all desiring agents. Pursuing wisdom just is for this particular desiring agent to pursue his chosen good. And reflecting upon beauty is the way in which the DHM reproduces in beauty and thereby hopes to procure that good. For if virtue requires knowledge of the form of beauty, one can only be in the beautiful environment appropriate to the attainment of that end by reflection upon beauty. Knowing the form of beauty just is the way in which one comes to be in this particular creative environment (compare the sexual union required to be with, and reproduce in, physical beauty). The description of the form of beauty as an object of knowledge is not at odds with the description of beauty as a creative environment, or midwife, for productive activity more generally (cf. 206d–e). The description of the form as an object of knowledge (211c8) is a specification of how one comes to be in the appropriate creative environment. One comes to be in the presence of the form of beauty by understanding beauty. And it is in this environment alone that one can produce a genuine good for oneself: wisdom and true virtue (212a1–3).

---

[9] Cf. Rowe (1998*a*) 193: 'Since his development is a philosophical one, it seems reasonable to say that he is a philosopher, and that the one leading is also a philosopher, only more experienced than him.' See also Price (1989) 42, Nussbaum (1986) 179, and Gill (1996) 388 on the importance of the guide in motivating the ascent.

2. MAKING THE ASCENT

Socrates' account is becoming increasingly complex. The pursuit of beauty in the ascent involves substantive views about virtue and knowledge, and about the proper objects of such knowledge and how they are encountered. We are, after all, in the highest mysteries of *erōs*. Now Socrates has set himself quite a task here. If the point of his speech is not only to tell the truth about *erōs*, but (like those of his peers) in such a way that we are persuaded of its beneficial nature and effects, then we need to know how it is possible to attain so lofty a prize. If our aspiration towards the good and the beautiful leads to the form as the ultimate source of value, and the only creative environment in which we can be truly productive, then how exactly do we get there? It is time to turn to the details of how one makes the ascent.

Since the DHM's progress is structured by repeated acts of producing *logoi* (210a7, c1, d5, 212a3, 5), it is reasonable to think that these play an important role in his progress. There are two features of the DHM's activity we need to take into account. First, since he produces *logoi*, we need to consider the role that *logoi* play in his progress. Second, since he is expressing a pregnancy (note the use of the verb τίκτειν here), we need to appreciate the relationship between these *logoi* and the pregnancy he carries by nature and of which these *logoi* are the expressions. For, as we have seen (Chapter 3), *erōs*' reproductive activity assumes a state of pregnancy (206c1–3). Examining both features of the account will provide answers to how *erōs* can attain its goal.

Let us take the role of the *logoi* first. It seems reasonable to think that there is some relationship between the DHM's appreciation of the common quality of beauty in each class and the production of *logoi*. These *logoi* are, after all, part of the DHM's progress towards knowledge, and that progress involves the appreciation of similarity and unity amongst different classes of beautiful objects. Socrates explained earlier that knowledge involves the ability to give a *logos* (202a5–9). Since the ascent describes progress towards knowledge it must involve the attempt, or attempts, to provide a *logos*. Since knowledge is not had until one comes to know ὃ ἐστι καλόν,

211c8–9, it is suggested that the *logos* needed is a definitional one. This need not be taken to suggest that attempts at a definitional *logos* are the only *logoi* produced in the ascent; 'the sorts of *logoi* that make the young better' (cf. 210c), do not sound like strict definitional ones. The point is just that the ascent must at least involve the attempt to provide such a *logos*, since this is required for knowledge. Conversing with the young about the sorts of activities that make men better may not be reducible to definitional *logoi*, but may well involve attempts at such definitions, if they are to be *logoi* that aid progress towards (real) virtue (namely, knowledge).[10]

Although it is difficult to pin down precisely when the DHM attempts to produce just these sorts of *logoi*, at a certain stage it is clearly implied that the *logoi* produced are philosophical ones. After the DHM has proceeded through different classes of beauty in the area of body and soul, he is described as follows:

> ... turned towards the great sea of beauty and contemplating that, [he] may bring to birth many beautiful, even magnificent, words and thoughts in a love of wisdom that grudges nothing, until there, with his strength and stature increased, he may catch sight of a certain single kind of knowledge, which has for its object a beauty of a sort I shall describe to you ... (210d4–e1).

This passage indicates that, at least on this level of the ascent, that is, after the DHM has surveyed all the relevant classes of beauty and before grasping the form, he produces *logoi* in a love of wisdom, that is, philosophically. Although we have no clear and explicit description of what producing *logoi* philosophically involves, philosophical activity has already been described earlier in the account. As we saw in Chapter 2, Socrates argued that wisdom is one of the most beautiful things and *erōs* pursues beauty, so, *erōs* pursues wisdom (204b1–2). Those who pursue wisdom are those who have an intermediate status in relation to wisdom and ignorance: their nature is such as to experience deficiencies—*aporia*—and also such as to experience *euporia* in relation to wisdom. I provided an account of

---

[10] The *logoi* are themselves described as beautiful. Cf. Socrates' critique of his fellow symposiasts where it was suggested that a *kalos logos* is one that aims at truth (198e4). Since here the *kaloi logoi* are ones that aim at, and result in, truth, we may suppose that they will be *kaloi* to the extent that they enable the DHM to perform this particular task and reach an understanding of beauty.

how *aporia* and *euporia* might operate in the pursuit of wisdom, a dynamic, I argued, which was exemplified in the interaction between Socrates and Diotima in the presentation of this speech. Philosophical *erōs* involves the ability to scrutinize beliefs, perceive argumentative deficiencies, and respond to those with new and hopefully better answers. Now whilst *aporia* and *euporia* are not explicitly mentioned in the ascent, one would expect them to be active in the ascent since this is the highest manifestation of *erōs*, and *erōs* is essentially characterized in terms of the interaction of *aporia* and *euporia*. Further, the verbs *euporein* and *tiktein* were brought together earlier in the account (cf. the DLM εὐπορεῖ λόγων περὶ ἀρετῆς, 209b8); *euporia* is facility in delivery. So, when the DHM is said to 'give birth' (τίκτειν) to words and arguments in a love of wisdom and so on, we may take it that he experiences *euporia*. But since genuine *euporia—tiktein* is not attained until the final stage of the ascent (212a3–5), we may also suppose that the DHM experiences some difficulties. In order to clarify how the DHM ascends, we shall need to give a more determinate sense to how *aporia* and *euporia* might function in this particular context.

The fact that the DHM is said to produce *logoi* in a love of wisdom that grudges nothing (ἄφθονος φιλοσοφία, 210d5–6) suggests that other people are involved (at least at this stage). It suggests that the DHM is generous with his insights.[11] We can leave aside for now questions about whether this is the guide, or the beautiful soul encountered earlier. The important point for now is that producing *logoi* in a love of wisdom that grudges nothing suggests that the DHM is discussing his insights about beauty with another person, or persons. This other may well be providing the DHM with the opportunity to scrutinize beliefs, perceive argumentative deficiencies, and respond to those with new answers, in much the same way that Diotima provides an opportunity for Socrates to rethink his

---

11 ἄφθονος could just indicate 'unlimited' (as Dover (1980) suggests), but as Rowe (1998*a*) 197 argues, it seems reasonable to stick to the literal sense (compare the description of the good lover in the *Phaedrus* 249a2, where he is described as 'the man who has lived the philosophical life ungrudgingly, or who has united his love for his boy with philosophy' (ἄφθονος, 249a2). As Rowe (1986) notes, the latter part of the clause is a specification of what is involved in living the philosophical life 'ungrudgingly'. It is also clear from the context that the lover is having conversations with his beloved.

account of *erōs* at various points. Now if we take it that the aim of the ascent is to achieve wisdom and virtue, and it surely is, and this requires the ability to give a definitional *logos* ('for how could an unaccounted matter be knowledge?' 202a5–9), then we can begin to see how *aporia* and *euporia* might function in this context. If the DHM has already turned towards the wide sea of beauty when he produces philosophical *logoi*, we may suppose that these will be about the beauty explored so far. Since they are an important step towards an object that is one and the same (211b1), we may take it that they are attempts to articulate what it is that makes the vast array of different beautiful things before him a unity—a sea—though it is composed of various different kinds of beauty. For since the *kalon* sought is evidently one thing (for the DHM has been attempting to recognize unity between different cases), it seems natural to take it that the *logos* required for knowledge must reflect that unity as a mark of the DHM's synoptic understanding of beauty. If that is the case, then this will provide a criterion governing the provision of a correct *logos*. It will reveal how argumentative deficiencies might be perceived, and how one should go about remedying them, for example, by providing a more exhaustive and synoptic *logos*. The clear methodological procedure suggests that any sense of *aporia* is here coupled with a sense which the DHM (or the guide) has of where to go in order to remedy that deficiency and attain the object of definition. If the DHM produces a *logos* that falls short, then we can imagine how 'provisions' might 'flow away' in the flux of philosophical discussion and yet also motivate a more informed attempt to scheme further. (Compare Eros' 'provisions' in the aetiological story that were subject to flux (cf. 203e4 with Chapter 2).)

If knowledge is construed in terms of the ability to give a definitional *logos*, then one can see how both *aporia* and *euporia* might function in a way that propels the lover on towards the form. We may take it (with Irwin and Patterson), that at least part of the progress is elenctic, in the sense that the *logoi* produced here will involve 'first (where necessary) an explicit and sincere recognition of one's own ignorance; second, an attempt to remedy that ignorance by appropriate investigation of a given subject'.[12] For this, as we have seen, is

---

[12] Patterson (1991) 213. Cf. also Irwin (1997) 168 and 170, and Reeve (1992) 108.

just the kind of activity that characterized the nature of philosophical *erōs* (Chapter 2), and we have good reason to assume that philosophica *erōs* is operative in the ascent. Unless the DHM can produce an account of the form of beauty and survive all refutation 'as if in a battle, striving to judge things not in accordance with opinion, but in accordance with being, and can come through all this with his account still intact', we will say that he does not know the beautiful itself. And 'if he gets hold of some image of it, it is through opinion and not through knowledge that he has got hold of it' (cf. *Republic* 534b8–c6 with *Symp.* 212a5–6).

Notice that this reading avoids the claim that it is dissatisfaction with objects encountered on the lower levels that motivates ascent to another level. This causes difficulties because the DHM only realizes the inferiority of lesser beautiful objects after he has arrived at a more elevated state of awareness: that sense of the lower state, then, cannot be what enables him to reach the higher. At any rate, the only object explicitly said to be unsatisfying to the DHM is the [beauty of] body (210b5–6).[13] I have argued the following. The DHM is pursuing his good and either he or his guide believes this to reside in a certain kind of knowledge of the *kalon*. Since an unaccounted matter cannot be knowledge, the DHM needs to provide the right sort of *logos*, one which is reflective of a synoptic understanding of beauty. This provides a criterion governing the provision of a correct *logos* in accordance with a method that leads to such knowledge. At least at the level where we are told that the DHM produces *logoi* in a love of wisdom, we may take it that this activity brings to light deficiencies *in one's logoi*. This may well be related to the fact that the DHM has not yet found the proper object of definition, but dissatisfaction with the beauty of previous objects is not what is motivating here.

I have also argued that producing *logoi* in the philosophical way outlined above propels the DHM on towards the form, in particular. For this is the stage at which he is said explicitly to produce *logoi* philosophically. Although the evidence for the elenctic interpretation will be restricted, then, this is surely the central move to be explained.

---

[13] Irwin (1977) 168 and 170 seems exposed to such pitfalls: 'at each stage the pupil tests his aspirations against his present objects of admiration, and though he was not previously aware of it, finds the objects inadequate to the aspiration'. But see Patterson (1991) 196, who emphasizes (correctly, it seems to me) the role of *logos* in the ascent.

There does not appear to be any particular difficulty in explaining movement within the previous stages. The summation of the DHM's progress suggests that there are, strictly speaking, three stages on the ascent: body, soul, and form. As we have seen, laws, practices, and so on are examined in extension of an interest in the beauty of souls. If the DHM is interested in beauty of soul, he will be interested in the kinds of activities that are responsible for the creation of beautiful souls and are themselves, accordingly, beautiful instances of those kinds. If so, then an interest in the beauty of soul is enough to motivate those subsequent steps.[14] This interest, as such, is not a particularly sophisticated one. Pausanias had already drawn our attention to the beauty of soul long before Socrates' speech (184c3–4). Within the larger methodological context there will be sophisticated reasons for why one should move from body to soul (cf. 210b2). If one is to pursue the *eidos* of beauty, one needs to be systematic in one's review of different classes of the thing under consideration (cf. *Gorgias* 474d–e, *Charmides* 159–60, *Meno* 87e5, 87e–88e).[15] The search for the *eidos* provides the criterion against which progress is measured and the motivational focus for further inquiry. For this is an account of the progress of a lover of wisdom. The real difficulty, then, is not to explain how one moves from the beauty of body to that of soul and so on. It is rather to explain why the DHM proceeds in the reflective manner that he does at all (for which, see above), and how, within that structure, he moves from reflection upon beautiful particulars to knowledge of the form.[16]

The attempt to articulate the one thing that all cases of beauty have in common motivates the DHM to develop the synoptic grasp of beauty which is preparation for the apprehension of an entity that is essentially one and the same (211b1). But this is not sufficient to explain how one moves to the form. That, after all, is something that happens 'suddenly' as a result of proceeding correctly and producing

---

[14] If this is what Patterson (1991) 210 means by the aitiological interpretation, then I am in agreement with him on this point. See also Moravscik (op. cit.). I find it difficult to extend this interpretation to the move from body to soul, however (though at *Republic* 401 grace in body is said to be a *mimēmata* of a sound mind, as Patterson notes).

[15] See above, n. 2 with Robinson (1953) 37.

[16] Cf. Chen (1992) 42–3, who argues that there is, strictly speaking, one ascent: from the particulars to the form.

the right sorts of *logoi* 'in a love of wisdom' (210e4). And here we are up against a further difficulty. There are numerous examples from the dialogues which show how difficult it is to articulate the salient features of the thing under consideration. It is one thing to say what is similar about a given class of objects (for example, that the beauty of all beautiful bodies is akin, ἀδελφόν, 210a8–b1), but quite another to say what it is in virtue of which these objects are 'one and the same' (ἕν τε καὶ ταὐτὸν, b3). It is commonly held that the DHM comes to have knowledge of the form by 'generalization and abstraction' from the beautiful particulars he encounters. Although some such process must clearly be involved, as we shall see, as it stands this is a puzzling picture.[17] For the distinctive characteristics of the form are conveyed by means of a derogatory contrast with sensible particulars (in a manner reminiscent of the *Phaedo* 78d–e). Whereas the form is stable, immune from change, and uniform, the sensible particulars which partake of this form are unstable and changeable, and exhibit opposite characteristics (211a1–b5). Given the radical contrast between particulars and form, how could the DHM get sufficient cognitive input about this form from the particulars? Since particulars are not 'one and the same' but many and various (cf. 211a1–5), it is difficult to see how it is solely in virtue of encountering these particulars that the DHM can acquire the ability to discern this feature. It is here that I want to turn to the second feature of the DHM's progress: the fact that the *logoi* delivered on each level are expressions of a soul pregnant with wisdom and virtue (206c3, 209a3–4). This feature of the DHM's progress may provide an answer to how genuine *euporia* can be had.

As we saw in Chapter 3, in the presence of beauty one delivers what one has long been pregnant with (206c1–5, cf. 209c3). Beauty is the creative environment in which one is able to be productive of good and beautiful things (206d–e). This same pattern of ideas holds for the DHM's ascent: in the presence of the beautiful objects

---

[17] The main advocates of this reading are Moravscik (1971) 290–3 and Price (1989) 39–40. Price 42 argues that this reading requires 'a little supplementation' and suggests that 'the lover must be fresh from a pre-natal apprehension of the Forms (cf. *Meno* 98a4)'. Cf. also Guthrie (1975) 389 and Bluck (1964) 50, Irwin (1977) 171, who all agree that the method requires some such supplementation. None of them develops this suggestion, or addresses the obvious objection that *anamnēsis* is not mentioned in the ascent. On this issue, see further below.

encountered in the ascent he delivers, or produces, *kaloi logoi*, which
are expressions of a soul pregnant with 'wisdom and the rest of
virtue'. In the last chapter I employed the notion of a cognitive
power, or potentiality, as a way of understanding this state of pregnancy. This seemed to be a plausible explanation of the fact that some
people can have more of a certain type of pregnancy than others
(209a1–2), and of how the expressions of different types of desiring
agents can be better or worse expressions of the same type of psychic
pregnancy (212a1–3).[18] If what it means to be pregnant with 'wisdom and virtue' is to have a potentiality for wisdom and virtue, then
one can account for the fact that this pregnancy can be put to good
use if properly realized and an inferior use if its development is
thwarted. The fact that the soul is pregnant with '*wisdom* and the
rest of virtue' (209a2–3) and requires the philosophical method of
the ascent for its successful expression suggests that the potentiality
has to be understood as rational. This is confirmed by the fact that
the proper realization of this potentiality (a successful *tokos*) results
in *knowledge* of beauty and true virtue (211d1–3, 212a1–3). Given
these considerations, it seems reasonable to take it that this ability for
wisdom and the rest of virtue is a rational potentiality to know the
form of beauty; for this is what marks its proper realization (the
successful *tokos*). In order to determine what role such a rational
potentiality might play in progress to the form we need to consider
the nature and status of this psychic resource in a bit more detail.

The figuration of this psychic state by the use of κυεῖν—a term
which applies exclusively to the female state of carrying a child in the
womb—suggests that this is a specific and determinate ability in the
soul.[19] For to say that someone is pregnant is not just to say that they

---

[18] The degree of continuity between the start of the DHM's progress and its finale
should also be borne in mind here: the activity of repeated begetting in the context of
a correct method and in response to different beautiful objects of desire does not
inspire the DHM to reconceive, but to *bring forth* the pregnancy he already carries
(note the exclusive use of τικτεῖν and γεννᾶν here). This might seem problematic
unless one takes it that this pregnancy carried 'from youth' is a potentiality, or
cognitive power of some sort, being developed.

[19] Cf. 206c1, 7, d4, 7, 8, 208e2, 209a1–2, b1, 5, c3 for κυεῖν, κυήσις, ἐγκύμων, a
verb used exclusively in Greek of females carrying a child in the womb. On the use of
this verb see Dover (1980) 147, Morrison (1964) 53, Vlastos (1981) 21 and Burnyeat
(1992 (1977)) 55–6. This verb is also used in the *Theaetetus* at 149c, 151b8, 184b1, in
connection with Socrates' art of intellectual midwifery.

are fertile and creative, but to say that they already have something in their bodies (or souls) which guides the course and nature of their physical (or psychic) development towards a certain end. Just as a physical pregnancy is structured and informed so as to develop towards a certain sort of end, a complete human being, so a psychic pregnancy, we may suppose, is informed by the *telos* of its development—knowledge of the form of beauty. Acorns grow into oak trees, foetuses into adult human beings, and, *given the right conditions*, potentialities for wisdom and virtue develop into knowledge and true virtue. Since this potentiality is only fully actualized in knowing the form of beauty, it would seem to be a power directed towards a certain kind of end: knowledge of the form. This is not to say that the power is not employed in relation to other objects: for it is evidently employed to some extent on every level when the DHM produces, and also when the desiring agents of the lower mysteries (henceforth DLMs) engage in productive activity in relation to their chosen beautiful objects. The point is rather that it only *fully* emerges in relation to the form of beauty (a psychic pregnancy is only successfully delivered at this point, 212a1–3). Since it comes into full being in relation to just this object, it seems to be a specific potentiality directed towards a certain sort of end—knowledge of the form of beauty. We might say, then, that to be psychically pregnant with wisdom and virtue is to have an innate disposition to grasp the form of beauty. When the DHM reaches such a point he is said to 'Look there and behold it with that by which he ought' (ἐκεῖνο ᾧ δεῖ, 212a1), a phrase which elsewhere in the dialogues is said to be *nous*.[20] If this phrase does refer to *nous*, then we can say that the developed understanding which marks the full realization of this innate disposition is *nous*.[21]

The explanatory force of this notion is that it can help to explain how, given a limited cognitive input from particulars, one can end up grasping a form that is categorically distinct from those particulars. *There is something about the soul itself which directs its growth,*

---

[20] Bury (1932) 132 notes the similarity of this turn of phrase with *Phaedrus* 247c, *Phaedo* 65e, *Republic* 490b, 518c, 532a.

[21] This must be innate since we are all pregnant *before* the encounter with beauty, albeit to varying degrees, and this potential emerges at a certain age of development (206c1–4).

development, and characteristic activity towards this specific end. The beautiful objects in the ascent create the appropriate environment in which to express and develop a specific ability to grasp the form. Beauty is Eileithyia at the birth: it occasions the emergence of something already present in the soul (206d2). And the implication of this aspect of beauty's role in an epistemological context is two-fold. First, we might suppose that the presence of a specific and innate power in the soul enables one to use the experience of beautiful particulars in a productive way, just as a foetus enables the body to use external factors such as food and warmth for its development towards a certain end. Second, the experience of the beautiful particulars does not, so to speak, provide the grounds for knowledge. Beauty causes the DHM to bring forth his pregnancy, which, I have suggested, is to say that it causes him to develop his ability to perceive the form, an ability which is innate, and the fullest expression of which is *nous*. This is then able to grasp the truth in an immediate and direct way: one 'sees' the form (212a1–3).

The beautiful environment(s) encountered in the ascent will play a crucial role in providing the appropriate conditions for the development of this power. Just as gestation develops towards the goal of a complete human being through a series of stages, so progress towards this step must proceed through a series of stages that enable the soul to develop in a certain way. The necessity for proceeding ἐφεξῆς τε καὶ ὀρθῶς in one's psychic development is perhaps also due to the difficulty of apprehending an object distinct in nature from the particulars that form the basis of our ordinary ways of thinking about beauty (cf. 210a1). As in the Mysteries, where the necessity for an ordered series of steps was in large part due to the need to accustom the initiate to the experience of τὰ τέλεα καὶ ἐποπτικά, so here, one must develop the ability to apprehend the form. It is natural that one does so by first encountering kinds of beauty that would already be familiar, and only from there moving on to the less familiar (from σώματα at 210a6 to αὐτὸ τὸ καλὸν at 210e4–5).[22]

---

[22] On the importance of the need to accustom the initiate in the Mysteries, see Burkert (1985) 285–90 at 288. The need to move appropriately from different classes of objects to the form is also crucial to the ascent to the form of the good in the allegory of the cave in the *Republic*, where there is a comparable emphasis on the need

Beauty, we should recall, is both Moira and Eileithyia at the birth (206d2). In the latter role beauty presides over the delivery of the offspring—the development of the soul's resources. In the former role, beauty determines the fate of the offspring in the sense that the quality of one's production is determined by the quality of the beautiful environment in which one is productive.[23] Without the right conditions, the soul's development is thwarted: grasping an image one gives birth to an image, grasping the truth... (212a1–5). Only the form can cause the proper emergence of *nous* because this is what that potentiality is a potentiality for. One needs to find the appropriate context for the application of that faculty for it to emerge. The DHM trains his cognitive powers on the perception of similarity and unity because *nous* is a specific ability to grasp a monoeidetic object (αὐτὸ καθ᾽ αὑτο μεθ᾽ αὑτοῦ μονοειδές, 211b1).

Integrating this feature of the account can aid an understanding of how one makes the ascent and the possibility of its success. And that is a crucial part of showing that *erōs* can work for our benefit. For if *erōs* can lead to the virtuous benefits previously praised—and this is construed by Socrates as knowledge of the form of beauty—then explaining how *erōs* can work for our good must involve explaining how *erōs* can lead to knowledge. And Socrates needs a large dose of epistemological optimism to perform that task. The notion of

for the prisoners to adjust their 'sight' to the light of the sun. If someone suddenly dragged a prisoner up out of the cave, the sun would be too bright and he would be unable to see. Socrates advocates a slower progression because the prisoner: 'would need time to get adjusted before he could see things in the world above. At first he'd see shadows most easily, then images of man and other things in water, then too, the things themselves... Finally, he'd be able to see the sun clearly and study it (*Rep.* 516a–b). Such a person sees the form only with difficulty, after a long time adjusting to the new light of the intelligible realm (517a1–2). The ability to see the form is something which requires arduous training, without which, the eyes and the soul are blinded. The prisoner trains his cognitive powers, beginning with the use of sense-perception and moving on through the use of ἐπιστῆμαι and τέχναι (533d). Because they require thought and not sense-perception, and are directed towards what is, these ἐπιστῆμαι and τέχναι have the power to awaken the soul's intellectual abilities (532c–d) and to turn it towards the intelligible realm (533d). In the *Symposium*, too, the DHM begins from perceptible examples of beauty (210a) and moves on through the use of νόμοι, μαθήματα, and ἐπιστῆμαι (210c4, c6), appreciation of which (we infer) requires the use of thought rather than sense-perception.

[23] For Moira's traditional role, see Pindar, *Olympians* 6.41–2, *Nemeans* 7.1 with Rowe (1998*a*) 183.

psychic pregnancy, I submit, is an epistemologically optimistic assumption which plays a role in that story and answers some of the questions posed at the end of Chapter 2. What ensures that genuine *euporia* can be had from the confused flux of experience is a noetic disposition in the soul to grasp the form. If we continue to employ *erōs* in the right (philosophical) way, this disposition will emerge and deliver knowledge.

One might object that the notion of pregnancy cannot serve as an epistemologically optimistic assumption of this sort because it is not sufficiently developed.[24] We would like, for example, to know whether the notion of a soul pregnant with wisdom and virtue indicates that the soul has embryonic knowledge (as the analogy with physical pregnancy might suggest), or whether, as I have suggested, it indicates a specific potentiality to develop in a certain kind of way—towards knowledge and true virtue. The latter is a more minimal view. Either way one might also like to know what this potentiality (however minimally it is construed) is grounded in. If we compare this assumption with Plato's best known variety of epistemological optimism, the theory of recollection familiar from the *Meno* and the *Phaedo*, we can see that at least that theory has a clear explanation for our ability for knowledge: knowledge is recollection of what the soul once knew. In the *Symposium*, by contrast, it is just baldly stated that all human beings are pregnant in body and soul, with little indication of how they came to be in that state and thus how they have the specific abilities they do. The dual claims that all human beings are pregnant (206c1–3) and that when we reach a certain age we naturally desire to give birth (206c1–4) suggests that a potentiality for 'wisdom and the rest of virtue' is part of our natural make-up as human beings. For if the development of our psychic pregnancy were not to some extent grounded in our nature, it is hard to see why we should naturally desire to give birth when we reach a certain age. If it is part of our natural make-up, then perhaps this power is grounded in the presence of a certain sort of psychic structure; for Plato elsewhere associates *nous* with order (*Phaedo* 99c4–6).[25] In this text we know that when the DHM fully realizes this power he has knowledge, a state (we may suppose) by which he can order the

---

[24] I thank William Prior for putting this objection to me.

[25] On *nous* as a cause of order, see Menn (1995) 2.

confused flux of experience. The power of *erōs* was earlier said to reside in its ability to establish harmonious relations between human and divine (202e3–203e8), one instance of which may be the bringing together of the world of mortal particulars and the divine form in a godlike state of understanding. (For *erōs* see 202e6–7: ὥστε τὸ πᾶν αὐτὸ αὑτῷ συνδέδεσθαι; for the DHM see 210c4–5: ἰδεῖν ὅτι πᾶν αὐτὸ αὑτῷ συνγενές ἐστιν; for the form as divine, see 211e3.) If so, then it is, perhaps, this psychic structure that is being activated in the encounter with beauty and that enables us to use our experience of beauty in a productive way. But this does not answer the question of how we came to possess such structure, that is, whether we have it in virtue of a pre-natal acquaintance with the forms, or whether it is just a brute fact about our nature. Since immortality does not appear to be a given state of the soul in this text (208b2–3), perhaps the latter. There are questions about this image that do not receive clear answers here. But this should not prevent us from integrating this feature of the account. This much is clear: the DHM's productive activity employs the resources of a soul already pregnant with 'wisdom and the rest of virtue'. Whatever this disposition is grounded in, it provides support for our productive endeavours. If we employ *erōs* correctly it can deliver the benefits claimed for it. And it can perform this role because it is a 'co-worker' with a nature predisposed to reach this very end (212b3–4).[26]

3. PHILOSOPHICAL VIRTUE: *NOUS*, NATURE, AND HAPPINESS

Having examined the ascent to the form and explored the possibility of its success we are now in a better position to tackle the relationship between philosophical virtue and happiness. I have argued that

---

[26] Guthrie (1975) 389 and Bluck (1964) 50, Irwin (1977) 171 and Price (1989) 42 all flirt with the idea that recollection is assumed in the *Symposium*. None of them explicitly argues out the evidence, but all agree something of this kind is required to make sense of the ascent. See Chen (1992) for arguments against the idea that recollection in the *Phaedo*'s sense of that term is involved in the ascent. For a fuller discussion of these issues, see Sheffield (2001*a*).

pursuing the form of beauty is the way in which the DHM pursues his good: the production of wisdom and virtue. Since one can only come to be in the presence of the creative environment appropriate to the attainment of this end by understanding beauty, reflecting upon beauty is the way in which the DHM reproduces in beauty and thereby hopes to procure that good. We have also seen that reproducing in beauty is the way in which the DHM (like all desiring agents) expresses his pregnancy, and I have argued that the developed understanding which marks the proper expression of this pregnancy is *nous*. So, we have three notions to account for in our understanding of philosophical virtue and happiness: contemplation of the form (211d1–2), *nous* (212a1), and producing true virtue (212a5–6). It is time to examine the relationship between these three notions.

The DHM is said to produce true virtue by grasping the truth (212a3–5). Given that nothing further is required to deliver true virtue, it is suggested that true virtue is knowledge of the form of beauty. And this involves, or is, to realize one's *nous*. For when the DHM achieves knowledge of the form, he is said to 'Look there and behold it with that by which he ought' (212a1–2), a phrase also associated with *nous*. He is also said to deliver true virtue by grasping this truth (212a3–6). In the noetic encounter with the form the DHM begets wisdom and true virtue; the DHM realizes, or expresses, the virtue of *nous*. The compressed description of contemplation and virtue suggests that there are not two distinct activities that need to be accounted for at the end of the ascent: contemplating the form (noetic activity) and begetting true virtue. Contemplating the form just is to beget the virtue of *nous*.[27]

One might object that in contrast to the virtue of the DLM, this does not sound much like moral virtue, the ordering of cities and households which was one of the ways in which the DLM expressed virtue. We must, for sure, ask to whom the benefit goes in this case

---

[27] For a parallel description which supports such a reading, see *Republic* 490a8–b7, where the philosopher is said to 'grasp the nature of each thing with the appropriate part of the soul'; he is also said to have intercourse with reality and 'beget *nous* and truth', a relief from 'birth pangs'. For *nous* as a virtue, see Menn (1995) ch. 3 with *Phaedrus* 241a3 and *Laws* 12. 963a6–9 (where *nous* is said to be the chief of the four virtues). Menn argues that *nous* is reason in a certain sense, 'reserved for infallible direct intellectual intuition', it is 'the virtue of thinking, not the faculty of thought'.

and whether it is to the DHM who acquires this virtue, or those who associate with him. For in the case of the DLM (the desiring agent of the lower mysteries) beautiful cities and souls were not just vehicles for the production of honour, but received some (apparent) benefit. We shall address this further in the next chapter where we shall see that progress towards the form does involve care and concern for others. But lest one object to the interpretation of philosophical virtue at the highest level as too egoistic to be a plausible account of philosophical virtue, one should remember that this account of virtue is connected to an account of *eudaimonia*. Although the relationship between virtue and *eudaimonia* can be a complex one,[28] we should bear in mind that the DHM, like the DLM, wants the virtues because they are good for him to have. They are good for the agent to have because they promise *eudaimonia* (205a1–3). The good of the agent is the goal of *erōs* (206a10). This need not be taken to imply that the agent is the sole beneficiary; the point is just that it explains the focus on the agent himself and the state of his own soul. In other words, if we accept that the account is a eudaemonist one (as it surely is) then we should expect the virtues to be measured in large part in terms of their contribution *to the good of the agent*. And the virtue of *nous* fulfils that function just fine, as we shall see.[29]

The rather compressed description of contemplation and virtue at the end of the ascent gives us no reason to think that there is anything further required for *eudaimonia*. 'It is here, if anywhere,' we are told, 'that life is worth living for a human being, in contemplation of beauty itself' (211d1–3). Contemplation of the form is that for the sake of which we do all that we do (206e10), the true end of all erotic aspiration. If it is the case that life is worth living in contemplation of

---

[28] For which, see Prior (2001).

[29] The eudaemonist framework of this account cannot have gone unnoticed. The real issue, I suspect, that makes people unwilling to adopt this construal of philosophical virtue is what has come to be known as the Vlastos problem. This is the apparent problem that the account of philosophical *erōs* makes no room for interpersonal love. If philosophical virtue were moral virtue and required engagement with others for its expression, then interpersonal relationships would have a privileged role to play in this account. Or, if there were two distinct events at the end of the ascent, with the philosopher generating knowledge and virtue in his own soul first, and then virtue in others (see Price (1989) and Eowe (1998*a, b*), for example), then this might also diffuse the Vlastos problem. The influence of this problem on the interpretation of this text filters through to a host of interpretative difficulties. This will be explored further below, Ch. 5.

the form, and that this is the best life for a human being, then contemplation would seem to be constitutive of the highest good for human beings. In other words, *eudaimonia* resides in contemplation of beauty; this is the highest virtue, the best good for human beings. At this stage notice that Socrates calls the acquisition of this good a *tokos*, thereby reminding us that this good is a final activity ('that for the sake of which we do all that we do...', cf. 206e10) that also expresses our nature.

Let us go back to the earlier part of the account and draw its threads together. All human beings carry various natural potentialities (206c1–3) which require productive work for their expression (206c1–8). Performing that work well is to express that activity in accordance with wisdom and virtue (209a3–4, c6–7), an activity best expressed in the ascent (212a1–6). Since this final end is achieved by our productive *ergon* working properly, and this is the realization of our nature, we can now appreciate why Socrates concludes at the end of the ascent that *erōs* is the best 'co-worker' with human nature (212b3). Expressing true virtue (delivering our pregnancy) in the work of reproduction is also to realize our nature. If so, then we might also say that our nature, properly speaking, is the virtue of *nous*, since this emerges when our nature is fully realized.[30] And we can now appreciate the sense in which pregnancy and procreation are divine things (206c6–7). Employing our *ergon* successfully allows us to grasp the divine form and to achieve the happiness characteristic of the divine. The successful achievement of this end results in a friendship with the gods (212a6). Although there is no explicit statement to the effect that the gods engage in contemplation themselves, we do know that they are paradigms of happiness (202a7–8) and human happiness, at any rate, resides in contemplation. It seems reasonable to suppose that the friendship of the gods is based on a kinship and likeness with themselves, which is achieved by employing our *nous* in the activity of contemplation. This divine element we are struggling to realize in our productive activities is *nous* and it is the task of our productive *ergon* to realize this divine element by an ascent to the divine form (211e3).[31]

---

[30] That is if one assumes a teleological view of nature according to which the true nature of a thing is exposed in its fullest stage of development.

[31] In this respect the account is continuous with other dialogues that specify the goal of human life as 'becoming like god'. On this issue, see Annas (1999) ch. 3, Sedley (1999) 309–28, and Armstrong (2004) 171–83.

It is perhaps this feature of the account that explains Aristophanes' thwarted interjection at the conclusion of Socrates' speech (212c5). Aristophanes' objection may have been this. Is the philosopher not in danger, like his globular men, of hubris in this ascent to the divine (compare Aristophanes' description of an *anabasis* at 190b8 with 211c1)? Will the gods send a further punishment and tear us asunder a second time? Socrates may have responded by claiming that what is *agathon* for us—an ascent to the divine—is also what is *oikeion* to us. As the *tokos* language suggests, true virtue is an expression of our nature properly realized. This, like all productive activities, is an approximation to the divine (208b3). The gods recognize and value a kinship with themselves and give us their friendship. True piety, then, must not reside in thinking mortal thoughts, but we should ascend to the task of thinking immortal ones. It is in this activity alone that we will find what is truly *agathon* and *oikeion*: our own godlike nature.[32]

4. THE GOODS COMPARED: HONOUR AND CONTEMPLATION

Now that we have a better sense of philosophical *erōs* and virtue, let us evaluate why contemplation of the form of beauty is supposed to be the life worth living for human beings (211d1–3). Why is this the best activity for *erōs*? Why does this satisfy the desire for *eudaimonia* to the greatest extent? Earlier in the account Socrates claimed that we are looking for a good whose possession is constitutive of *eudaimonia*, a final good, whose possession no longer requires us to ask of the agent what she wants in pursuing it (205a1–3). Further, this good is one whose possession we want in a secure way (206a9–10). We want the enduring possession of the good characteristic of the divine (202c). Since human nature is unlike the divine, however (207d1–208b5), we need to be productive of the things we value

---

[32] The idea that what is best in us (the *agathon*) is what we really are (the *oikeion*), is more explicit elsewhere. This leads to the claim that we should identify with the *agathon*, for in doing so we are finding what is really our own. See, for example, *Republic* 586e, and Aristotle's *Ethics* 9.8, 1168^{b}30 with 1178^{a}3. I thank Dominic Scott for these references and assistance in developing this idea. For a further response to Aristophanes, see below, Ch. 6.

and to realize ourselves in ways that make this good manifest to us. Production is the mortal form of possession. It is in the pursuit of beauty of various kinds that we can be productive and this pursuit will be appropriate to our specification of the good. In the philosophical case, it is the philosophical life, as opposed to a life of honour, that is deemed valuable, and it is in the pursuit of the form of beauty that the philosopher can make manifest that chosen good for himself (wisdom and true virtue). So, we have three features of the account that we can use to evaluate the philosophical good. (1) It must be a final good (if it is to be constitutive of *eudaimonia*). (2) It must be possessed in the most secure way possible for human beings. (3) Our choice of beauty must be appropriate to that chosen good end.

Let us begin by comparing the philosophical activity of the DHM (in the highest mysteries) with that of the DLM (in the lower mysteries). The description of the DHM cleverly mirrors the DLM. Both desiring agents seek out something beautiful in which to be productive (DLM: τικτεῖν τε καὶ γεννᾶν ἤδη ἐπιθυμῇ, ζητεῖ δὴ οἶμαι καὶ οὗτος περιιὼν τὸ καλὸν ἐν ᾧ ἂν γεννήσειεν, 209b2–3; DHM: 210a7, c1, d5, 212a5). Both engage in the activity of producing *logoi* (DLM: εὐπορεῖ λόγων περὶ ἀρετῆς καὶ περὶ οἷον χρὴ εἶναι τὸν ἄνδρα τὸν ἀγαθὸν καὶ ἃ ἐπιτηδεύειν, καὶ ἐπιχειρεῖ παιδεύειν, 209b8–c2, DHM: καὶ τίκτειν λόγους τοιούτους καὶ ζητεῖν, οἵτινες ποιήσουσι βελτίους τοὺς νέους, ἵνα ἀναγκασθῇ αὖ θεάσασθαι τὸ ἐν τοῖς ἐπιτηδεύμασι καὶ τοῖς νόμοις καλόν, 210c1–4). And the aim of both is to be productive of their good in an encounter with beauty (DLM: ἁπτόμενος γὰρ οἶμαι τοῦ καλοῦ καὶ ὁμιλῶν αὐτῷ ἃ πάλαι ἐκύει τίκτει καὶ γεννᾷ, 209c2–3, DHM: ἢ οὐκ ἐνθυμῇ, ἔφη, ὅτι ἐνταῦθα αὐτῷ μοναχοῦ γενήσεται, ὁρῶντι ᾧ ὁρατὸν τὸ καλόν, τίκτειν οὐκ εἴδωλα ἀρετῆς, ἅτε οὐκ εἰδώλου ἐφαπτομένῳ, ἀλλὰ ἀληθῆ, ἅτε τοῦ ἀληθοῦς ἐφαπτομένῳ, 212a3–5). These artfully constructed parallels serve to highlight the fact that both desiring agents are aiming for the same thing, and also to indicate the differences between the two. The search for beauty in which the DLM engages is far from the methodical ζητεῖν of the ascent: when he hits just the right age (καὶ ἠκούσης τῆς ἡλικίας, 209b1–2) the DLM is attracted to beautiful bodies (209b4–5), and if he chances upon a beautiful soul (περιιών; … εντύχῃ, b3–6) immediately issues *logoi* about virtue (εὐθὺς εὐπορεῖ, b8). The use of the term περιιών to describe the DLM's 'search' for beauty may be significant, for although the word is not always used in a derogatory sense, it is so used in the dialogues, particularly when paired with ἐντύχῃ.³³ The somewhat random activity of the DLM stands in contrast to the DHM, who starts from early youth (ἄρχεσθαι ... νέον, 210a5) and follows a method (τὸν ὀρθῶς ἰόντα, 210a4; ὀρθῶς ἡγῆται, a6; παιδαγωγηθῇ, θεώμενος ἐφεξῆς τε καὶ ὀρθῶς τὰ καλά, e3; τὸ ὀρθῶς παιδεραστεῖν, 211b5; τὸ ὀρθῶς ἐπὶ τὰ ἐρωτικὰ ἰέναι, b7; with πρῶτον ... ἔπειτα at various points in the speech). Although both are interested in the production of improving discourses (cf. 209b8–c1, 210c1–3), the DLM seems to care less about the quality of his production and more about its immediate delivery (cf. εὐθὺς εὐπορεῖ, b8).³⁴ In contrast, the DHM feels compelled to seek out such discourses (ζητεῖν, 210c2). Laws, practices, and 'knowledges' at 210c3–6 are examined as a consequence of the DHM's concern for the beautiful souls of b8–c1 and for the quality of the discourses he is inspired to produce (210c1–4). The method followed by the DHM here leads to knowledge of the form, and his delivery of virtue is grounded in that understanding (211c8). Both the DLM and the DHM may concern themselves with beautiful bodies and souls, but they approach these things very differently. The parallels and contrasts indicate that it is because the DLM does not engage in a method that leads to knowledge of beauty that he produces only an image of virtue. The honour lovers of the lower mysteries are revealed as shadow lovers, engaged in practices that imitate those of the DHM, but do not mark the proper realization of a soul pregnant with wisdom and virtue.³⁵

---

³³ Socrates uses it of his search for wise men in the *Apology* 23b5, 31c5, for example, a characterization which could, however, be artfully self-derogatory. For a pejorative sense of the term, see *Prt.* 320a2, where it is said that children have to wander around in search of a teacher of virtue. In the *Symposium* itself the term is applied unflatteringly to the wanderings of Alcibiades, humiliated after a failed seduction attempt (219e5), whilst a similar *peri*-verb is used for the aimless behaviour of Apollodorus before he met Socrates (περιτρέχων ὅπῃ τύχοιμι, 173a1).

³⁴ The adverb εὐθύς is also often used in the dialogues in a pejorative sense, to signal an opposition to a reasoned and well-thought-out response (see, for example, *Ion* 532c, 536b8, *Prt.* 357d1, *Tht.* 144e2, 186b11).

³⁵ Those who are puzzled by the apparently positive description of the poets as generators of virtue, and how it coheres with Socrates' disparaging treatment of the poets in *Republic* 10, should bear in mind the contrasts between DLM and DHM (cf. *Symp.* 209a5–7 with *Rep.* 599c–d). Asmis (1992) 338–65 argues that the *Republic* is a corrective to the positive treatment of the poets in the *Symposium*. But their inclusion in the lower mysteries does not give them more status than the *Republic*: their virtue

There is much in the description of the DLM that suggests that their productions manifest a kind of demotic wisdom and virtue.[36] The claim that the most beautiful part of this wisdom and virtue is concerned with the correct ordering of cities and households is reminiscent both of Meno's first definition of virtue (as emended by Socrates) in the dialogue that bears his name (*Meno* 73a7–b2), and of Protagoras' claim to teach the virtue that is concerned with the affairs of the household and the city (*Protagoras* 319a, 322e).[37] The description of the virtue of the DLM points to the virtues of the politicians and lawgivers which certain sophists professed to teach, and to the kind of wisdom to which Agathon refers in his speech as motivating all kinds of expert production (cf. 197a–b). Socrates frequently expresses scepticism in the dialogues about this sort of virtue in comparison to a superior kind based on understanding.[38] The parallels between the productive activities of the lower and higher mysteries here indicate just this sort of scepticism.[39]

is an image of true virtue (212a3–6). It is generated without *nous*, a description which fits with the characterization of Homer as one who does not *know* what practices make people better (an example of which is his failure to educate Creophylus).

[36] As has been noted for instance by Bury (1932) 121 and Rowe (1998*a*) 190.

[37] The phrase 'poets and craftsmen—so many as are said to be inventive' (ὅσοι λέγονται εὑρετικοὶ εἶναι, 209a5) may suggest that these types are those whom the *demos*, but not necessarily Socrates, held in high esteem as socially useful (those same types of wise men, incidentally, whom Socrates chose to examine in the *Apology*).

[38] e.g. *Men.* 99c3–5, e6–100a1, *Phd.* 68d, 82a, *Rep.* 401e, 500d, 506a, 518d–e, 554c; with Archer-Hind (1894) 149–55, and Scott (1995) 43–52. We should be cautious about pushing this analogy too far because the DLM are a quite extraordinary group of people: poets, law-makers, and *inventive* craftsmen. Their virtuous productions may pale in comparison with philosophical ones, but they nonetheless have some claim to be εὑρετικοί—as those who shape and form the habits and practices of the *dēmos*. As a parallel for the status of their virtue one might compare such types as Thucydides and Themistocles, who are mentioned at the end of the *Meno* (99b–c). They do not just possess virtue formed through the slavish adherence to tradition and hearsay (like those who are said to practise demotic virtue at *Phaedo* 82b1–2, for example); if they did, it would be difficult to see how they could fail to pass this on to their sons. These are rather the political leaders of the day, those who shape the habits and practices of the many.

[39] Those scholars who believe that the lower mysteries represent the views of the historical Socrates, and the higher mysteries of the ascent represent a Platonic break with these ideas, will find the previous assessment of the DLM too dismissive. See, for example, Cornford (1971) 125, 129; Markus (1971) 134; Vlastos (1981) 21 n. 58. Support for a Socratic–Platonic distinction is often found in the disparaging

Having explored the comparisons and contrasts between the desiring agents of the lower and higher mysteries it remains to return to the specific criteria for *eudaimonia*. Now the fact that the productive activities of the honour lovers are included in the lower mysteries suggests that they are not productive of final goods. For in the higher mysteries the form of beauty is said to be 'that for the sake of which' all other actions are done (210e5–6, cf. 210e4, 211c2), and a life in contemplation of the form is the best human life (211c1–3). If, in some sense, everything else pursued is pursued for the sake of the form (cf. 210e6), we must also take it that the objects pursued in the lower mysteries are for the sake of the form. Since we also know that the productions occasioned by lesser beautiful objects inherit the lesser value possessed by those objects (212a1–6), the implication is that the productions of the lesser mysteries, are not final goods. The philosopher's virtue is occasioned by the most beautiful object—that for the sake of which all previous toils were performed—and his virtue is good above all (212a1–3). It is true virtue and, we may suppose, that for the sake of which the lesser productions were occasioned (the *kaloi logoi* of the ascent). Since other productions are occasioned by objects pursued for the sake of the form, they will, in their turn, be productions for the sake of a further end. And if we take it that an end which is worth pursuing for its own sake is more final than one pursued for the sake of something else, then the implication is that the productions of the lesser mysteries fail to satisfy the condition of being a final good. They do not attain a genuine *telos* in their productive activities and, consequently, they are not

remark which Socrates reports having heard from Diotima (209e5–210a2). For an alternative explanation for this, see above, Ch. 2, sect. 5. Since examples of the DLM included poets, inventive craftsmen, and lawgivers, I would argue that the dismissal intended here is of Socrates' fellow-symposiasts, whose speeches celebrated Eros through such practices. The love of honour specified as the goal of the DLM makes it difficult to identify him with the historical Socrates—if we assume that the *Apology* can be used as evidence for the latter (208c3), a questionable assumption, perhaps. The distinction between those who value honour and those who value 'understanding and the perfection of the soul' is a crucial one for the Socrates of the *Apology*. (29d). The Socrates of the *Apology* is better identified, in many respects, with the DHM, whereas the DLM is reminiscent of those people with a reputation for wisdom whom Socrates examines in that dialogue (22 ff.).

productive of the sort of good that will satisfy the desire for *eudaimonia* as the end of *erōs*.

But we need some clarity here. If everything else pursued is pursued for the sake of the form (210e6), then it seems to be the case that the objects pursued in the lower mysteries are, in some sense, for the sake of the form. We may be able to see how the *kaloi logoi* produced at the lower levels of the ascent are for the sake of contemplation of the form in the sense that these *logoi* are an important part of progress towards knowledge, as we have seen. But how, if at all, might the actions and productions of the DLM be construed as for the sake of contemplation of the form? The DLM pursue the kinds of beauty (embodied in students or cities) in which honour can be realized for themselves (208c3). So the DLM do not do what they do for the sake of the form as an object of their desire. One might construe the point in the following way. Such types want to be honoured *for their virtue*. People envy the *good* poets (209d1–2), and the brave exploits of Achilles and Admetus (208d1–3). So virtue is the real end of their desire. As we have seen, such virtue is only attained in the encounter with the form, so the form is the real *end* of *erōs* in the sense that whether or not they are successful in their erotic pursuits is dependent upon the encounter with the form: grasping an image one gives birth to an image, but grasping the truth one gives birth to true virtue (212a3–6). We might also take it that, insofar as the actions and productions of the lesser mysteries are expressions of a soul pregnant with 'wisdom and the rest of virtue' (209a1–5), their pursuits at least attempt to embody a measure of wisdom. Although the virtue of such lovers is developed without the philosophical practice that leads to knowledge, this is, nonetheless, a quite extraordinary group of people: poets, lawmakers, educators, and inventive craftsmen (209a4–5, d1–e3). The virtuous offspring of these lovers may pale in comparison with philosophical offspring, but they nonetheless have some claim to be εὑρετικοί—as those who shape and form the habits and practices of the *dēmos*. Their creative activity is imperfectly realized in their (practical) pursuits in much the same way as their objects of pursuit imperfectly realize the form of beauty, but insofar as the true end of a soul pregnant with wisdom and virtue is an encounter with the form, they can be said to do what they do for

the sake of the form. For the DLM's desire for immortal virtue
(208d5–7), misconstrued by them as honour, is only satisfied in
an encounter with the form. That is to say, whether they really
are *good* poets, lawmakers, and educators—truly virtuous—will be
determined by whether they have wisdom. Their productive activities
are, ultimately, measured against the attainment of this end, as the
parallels and contrasts with the DHM illustrated.

That wisdom is the real end of *erōs*, and not honour, was perhaps
foreshadowed in the exchange between Socrates and Agathon earlier
in the dialogue (193c1–5). Agathon, a man who clearly values honour,
admits to Socrates that he feels shame in front of an intelligent group
of people. Socrates invites Agathon to reflect upon why he experiences
shame in the presence of this group of people, in particular. A
plausible answer might be that he has some sense that the real end
of his creative activity—the real measure of its value—is to be found
in the wisdom he perceives to be embodied in this sympotic gathering
and not the applause from the crowd. Agathon's revelation that he
desires honour *from the wise* (and not just the judges in the theatre)
may indicate an awareness of that fact. Perhaps this thwarted elenchus
is prompting Agathon to realize that the real end of his desire and its
object must come together if he is to achieve real success. For, as we
can see in the philosophical case, success is in large part due to the fact
that the object of desire (wisdom and true virtue) and its real end
(contemplation of the form) come together in the ascent.

I have argued so far that the issue that structures the division of the
productive activities of different desiring agents into the lower and
higher mysteries of *erōs* is what we might term a division of ends. The
DHM pursues that which is chosen for its own sake, and the DLM
pursues those things chosen for the sake of something higher. Philosophical virtue is occasioned by the most beautiful object, 'that for
the sake of which all previous toils were' and, consequently, his virtue
is good above all (212a1–3). If we are to take seriously Socrates' claim
that 'It is here, if anywhere, that life is worth living for a human
being, in contemplation of beauty itself' (211d1–3), then it would
seem that contemplation of the form of beauty is desirable for its
own sake. If this is the life worth living, then nothing further will be
sought beyond the activity of contemplation. Virtue in this instance
(the virtue of *nous*) is constitutive of happiness. Nothing further

seems to be required for *eudaimonia.* In the case of the desiring agents of the lower mysteries, by contrast, notice that their productive activities are desired for the sake of some further end. Their productive activities and virtuous actions are chosen for the sake of the honour that results (208c3) and the memorials and shrines in poetry or cult that provide them with honour (cf. 209d1–e3). Since the DLM do not desire the productions themselves, but the honour that results, it would seem that their good offspring are not ends in an unqualified way; for they have an end outside themselves (honour). If so, we may take it that these productions are less complete and final in this sense, too: they are not desired for themselves (insofar as they manifest virtue) but for the sake of the honour that results. If they are not ends in an unqualified way, in the sense that they are not desired for their own sake, then they cannot be the sort of good we are seeking. For the good we are seeking is one desired for itself, and not for the sake of something else. We are looking for a good that is constitutive of happiness as the *telos* of *erōs* (205a1–3).[40] Contemplation, by contrast, appears to be just this sort of good.

Contemplation is not only a more final good, it is also a more secure good in at least two senses. First, the virtue of the DHM is grounded in knowledge of an object that is changeless and altogether perfect. It has not been occasioned by objects subject to change and decay, beautiful at one time and not another, and to one person and not another. Since the quality of one's production is determined by the quality of the beautiful environment in which one produces (212a4–5), we are led to believe that this is responsible for the inferior value of the DLM's virtue. Solon may win the favour of the many today, but tomorrow it could be Pericles. Agathon may win the crowd today, but tomorrow it could be Euripides. None of these characters *know* the 'sort of thing a man should value or the activities a man should engage in' and so on.

---

[40] Cf. Aristotle, *Nicomachean Ethics* (1176^{b}2–9) and (1139^{b}1–4): 'Everyone who produces does so for the sake of something else, and his product is not an end in an unqualified way. But in the case of action it is different. For good action is an end.' And further (1140^{b}6–7): 'Producing has an end other than itself, but action cannot. For good action is itself an end.' In Aristotelian terms, the distinction between the DHM and the DLM would have to be understood as that between an action and a production. See further below.

They have based their experience of beauty on objects subject to shifts in perspective and growth and decay and, consequently, the productions that have been occasioned by such objects will not endure: grasping the truth one gives birth to the truth, grasping an image one gives birth to an image (212a1–5). The virtue of the DHM, by contrast, will endure as true—as really good—because it is based on an enduring object. Since his virtue is based on a 'beauty that always is, and neither comes into being nor perishes, neither increases nor diminishes,... is not beautiful in this respect but ugly in that, nor beautiful at one moment, but not at another, nor beautiful in relation to this, but ugly in relation to that, nor beautiful here, but ugly there, because some people find it beautiful while others find it ugly' (211a1–5), it will always, at any given time and to any (capable) onlooker, be true of the DHM that he is virtuous and that he 'knows the sorts of things a good man should concern himself with' and so on. The same could not be said of the DLM. If the DLM do not have a secure grounding for their virtue, then what ensures their virtue will be remembered at all times, and memorials preserved across the ages? By making virtue his priority, rather than honour, the DLM would, it seems, have had a better chance of securing this good.

The DHM has no such concerns. Contemplation is a more secure good for the DHM not just because it is grounded in knowledge of a stable object, but also because it is a good *of his own soul.* There is no further event upon which possession of the good relies in this case. Whether the DLM are successful, whether they achieve the goal of their *ergon*, depends upon others honouring them, for this is their expressed aim (208c3). Their happiness lies outside of the activity of child-bearing, law-making, heroic deeds, educative pederasty, as we have seen; it resides in the honour that results from these activities. In the philosophical case, by contrast, the goal does not lie outside of the DHM, it resides in the activity of contemplation itself: 'It is here, if anywhere, that life is worth living for a human being, in contemplation of beauty itself' (211d1–3).[41]

---

[41] One might object that the philosopher still needs external factors: he needs to be able to make the ascent which seems to involve other persons at numerous stages, and a guide. But the point is that his good—contemplation—once reached, is less dependent on external factors when compared to the DLM's, whose

But we might now appear to be up against a problem. If it is the case that there is no suggestion of the philosopher perpetuating his production in the memory of others, one might wonder how his good can be really enduring and satisfy the second criterion for *eudaimonia*, after all. How does he secure *immortal* virtue, the good for himself '*always*'? A popular strategy is to say that the philosopher passes on his mental life to a beloved or, more loosely, that he somehow lives on in his external works.[42] Price, for example, sees this as an extension of the description of the DLM, who was said to beget educative *logoi* and to 'join with the other person in nurturing what has been born', with the result that such people enjoy a firmer '*philia* between them, insofar as their sharing is in children of a more beautiful and more immortal kind' (209c4–6). But the DHM, by contrast, is described as follows: 'when he has delivered true virtue and nurtured it, it belongs to him to be loved by the gods, and to him, if to any human being, to be immortal' (212a3–5). Where the DLM was said 'to join with the other person in nurturing what has been born (συνεκτρέφει κοινῇ)', in the philosophical case the prefix συν- 'together' drops out and he is said (in the middle voice) to nurture true virtue by or for himself (θρεψαμένῳ). There is no indication that the DHM is producing virtue 'in another'. Further, the relationship of *philia* enjoyed by the DLM with his beloved is here transferred to the gods. The focus is exclusively on the lover's union with the form, his own delivery of virtue and a relationship of *philia* with the gods. If knowledge of the form of beauty and true virtue was essentially practical in nature, then we might have some evidence for the idea that the philosopher somehow propagates this virtue. If the philosopher were to 'order cities and households', or deliver 'educative *logoi*' on the highest level of the ascent, then we would have some reason for thinking that his *eudaimonia* at least involves other persons (cf. 209a7, b8). But there is no evidence for this at the highest level of the ascent. The philosopher contemplates, and this is said to be the life most worth living (211d1–3).

good (honour) depends on recognition by others. See below, Ch. 5, sect. 3, for further dissussion of this issue.

[42] See Hackforth (1950) 44, Irwin (1977) 342–3, Price (1989) 54, Rowe (1998*b*) 257, and, for the view that the philosopher lives on in external works in much the same way as Homer, see White (2004) 373.

One might say that the philosopher's superior knowledge and virtue is not propagated among men, but leads to a more stable kind of memorial: by the gods.[43] After all, the philosopher is said to win the friendship of the gods (212a6), a sign that the philosopher has achieved the goodness that forms the basis of such a relationship.[44] He is engaged in a godlike activity of contemplation and, we may infer, is, in this respect at least, like the gods. Perhaps, then, the gods recognize and value this kinship by keeping the philosopher in mind. This gives a significance to the name of the apparent creator of this speech—Diotima. She, or one who gives such a speech, is 'honoured by Zeus'. By delivering a speech in the guise of one 'honoured by Zeus', Socrates perhaps indicates that the philosopher will, like Diotima, be honoured by the gods.[45] The Mystery terminology that enshrines this part of this speech might also suggest the possibility of literal immortality. The friendship of the gods may result in immortality as a divine gift, just as the Homeric heroes could achieve both honour and apotheosis.[46] But this may be to provide too much. After all, it was said that productive activity is the way in which mortal natures *partake of* the divine (208b3), and there is nothing to suggest that we should not follow the account thus far: even the philosopher becomes immortal through a productive act, so he, too, partakes of immortality in some way.[47]

[43] Cf. Aristotle, *Ethics* 10.8, 1179ª22–30 with Rowe (1998*a*) 201, who writes on this line, 'his immortality will stem from his offspring whose true value will be recognised by the gods (and not by mere mortals, like those of the poets and politicians)'. Somewhat surprisingly, Rowe (1998*b*) 257 also argues for a donor–recipient relationship. See Xenophon, *Mem.* 4. 47–8 for the relationship between becoming θεοφιλής and the gods keeping you in mind.

[44] The friendship of the gods is a consequence of virtue in other dialogues, too. See *Eu.* 11a, *Rep.* 612e5–613b, *Phil.* 39e–40b, *Laws* 716d.

[45] In the *Iliad* it is said that honour comes from Zeus, τιμὴ δ᾽ ἐκ Διός ἐστι, cf. 2.297 and also 1.353, 510; 9.514, 608; 15.189; 16.84. Heraclitus also talks of honour coming from both men and gods: B24 with Hussey (1991) 523.

[46] On this issue, see O'Brien (1984). Nagy (1974) 190 argues that there is no tension in poetic traditions between the hero being transported into a state of immortality and being venerated in epic or cult.

[47] Those who argue that the philosopher achieves literal immortality in a way compatible with dialogues such as the *Phaedo* have to work hard to put some distance between the philosopher's final act of generation and the description of generation as the way in which the mortal partakes of the divine (208b3). This problem of compatibility has been raised most notably by Hackforth (1950) 43–5. See also Luce (1952) 139–41; Morrison (1964) 44; Price (1989) 21, 25. One of the most

We do need to make sense of the rhetorical build-up in the speech: if the philosopher is to win this prize above all human beings (cf. 212a7), then surely he must participate in divine immortality to the greatest extent. But we must do so whilst working closely with the text. The above options are far from explicit. What does seem to be strongly suggested is that *eudaimonia* resides in the contemplation of the form (211d1–3). If this were not so, why does Socrates claim that *this* is where life is most worth living? Contemplation of the form is the *telos* of *erōs* (211c6–d3). This surely indicates that the fulfilment of *erōs* resides there, that this is all that is required for *eudaimonia*. If so, then not only is there no indication of any further generative act required to produce external works, but the friendship of the gods would appear to be a result of that fulfilment, and not something required for its attainment. 'It is *here*, if anywhere, that life is worth living for a human being, in contemplation of beauty itself' (211d1–3). Immortality, then, which is part of his erotic aim, cannot be found in that friendship, but in the activity which is described as the *telos* of erotic striving. And if that is the case then we need to consider just what it is about contemplation that delivers the secure possession of the good.

popular strategies for compatibilists has been to exclude the soul from τἆλλα πάντα and include it with ἀθάνατον δὲ ἄλλῃ in the final lines of the discussion of generation, which read as follows, 'By this device a mortal thing partakes of immortality, both the body and everything else; but the immortal in another way.' This reading also excludes the soul from the claim that mortal nature can only be immortal by generation (207d3). However, we are told that this flux operates not only κατὰ τὸ σῶμα, ἀλλὰ καὶ κατὰ τὴν ψυχήν (207e1–2), and then given an extensive list of the psychic states that are subject to flux, which parallels the description of the body (e2–208a3). It thus seems quite natural as a summation of the entire thesis to claim that 'the body and everything else' (b3–4) includes the soul. Moreover, ταύτῃ τῇ μηχανῇ at b2 most naturally refers to τούτῳ γὰρ τῷ τρόπῳ at c7, which in turn refers to what happens in the soul when knowledge is replaced (a5–6). So the text does not justify a disanalogy between body and soul. Moreover, given that most of the subsequent account is focused on psychic creativity, it would seem odd for there to be an account of generative activity, which had no bearing on most of this discussion. As Hackforth noted, even the lover of the ascent becomes immortal τῇ γενέσει (212a5–7). I see no problem, in principle with supposing that the soul might be immortal in some stricter sense, as the enduring subject of the flux, perhaps (see Price (1989), for example). But if all one's mental and physical states are subject to this kind of flux, then it is not easy to see how the postulation of an immortal and presumably impersonal soul would be relevant to a discussion of *eudaimonia*. The focus here is surely on what matters in one's life.

We already have the tools for an answer. I argued that delivering true virtue is to beget *nous* and knowledge in the activity of contemplation. The DHM produces true virtue by grasping the truth (212a3–5). Since nothing further is required to deliver true virtue, it is suggested that true virtue is knowledge of the form of beauty. And it is further suggested, as we have seen, that this expresses, or is, the virtue of *nous*, for this is what emerges in the encounter with the form. If so, then to say that the DHM produces wisdom and true virtue is to say that he realizes the virtue of *nous*. And that is to say that there are not two distinct events here: contemplating the form and producing virtue. This explains why the delivery happens in the philosopher's own soul, and why there is not the slightest indication that his virtue resides in the external discourses perpetuated in memory by others.[48] We have no need to import another soul, or souls, in which the DHM produces, nor need we suppose that there are further productive acts required to secure his *eudaimonia*. And we should not be surprised that this marks a departure from the honour lovers of the lower mysteries. As the contrast between the two desiring agents illustrated, the DLM is no model for the DHM. The benefit of this interpretation is a firmer grasp on the security of the DHM's possession of the good. The goal of his productive activity resides in the activity of contemplation itself, as opposed to the DLM's where happiness lay outside of the activities of law-making and pederasty—in the cities or souls whose flourishing procures honour for the producer. The same also holds for those who produce physical offspring. Such types will secure no happiness unless their offspring turn out well. In the philosophical case, by contrast, since there is no further event upon which possession of this good relies, we can infer that it is more secure than others in this sense: it is a good of one's own soul not reliant upon others for its acquisition.[49]

---

[48] As, for example, White (2004) 366 argues: 'The virtue in question is not an internal state of the soul, but external discourse, and the immortality attained by the philosopher qua mortal consists in his living on in the philosophical works that he leaves behind him.' Compare Hackforth (1950), Price (1989), and Irwin (1977). But contrast Pender (1992) 85.

[49] Cf. Aristotle, *Ethics* 1100^{b}12–22 with Kraut (1976) 238: 'There is no danger that tomorrow the virtues will become irrational, unenjoyable, beyond our control, etc. By contrast, the superficial features of the virtues could, in certain circumstances, be lost. A good man can be falsely accused, punished or disgraced.' And, we might add,

This reading would certainly be clarified by an explicit distinction of the sort that Aristotle makes between *poiēsis* and *praxis* and a clarification of where the goal resides in either case.[50] In a case of *praxis* the *telos* is in the activity itself (compare the DHM). In a case of *poiēsis*, by contrast, the *energeia* of the student, for example, is one's *telos* as a producer in the case of the production of educational *logoi* (compare the DLM). To Aristotle who clarified the distinction between external products and internal activity and where the goal resides in either case, what really matters in the end is the internal activity—doing our own *energeia*, so to speak. So I want to suggest for the *Symposium*. The DLM produces a law-abiding city, or a good student, whose *energeia* is his own, where the *telos* of the production is in another city or soul whose flourishing secures him honour. But the DHM reproduces in himself, so to speak, where the goal of the production lies in his own soul. This makes good sense of the emphasis on the state of the agent at the highest level of the ascent.

We need, though, to return to the earlier account of generation (207c5–208b5), lest one object that it does not cohere with that description of productive activity.[51] For it might be thought that generation was earlier described as leaving behind something 'such as oneself' and yet the account I have given of philosophical productivity makes no mention of leaving something behind. But as I argued in Chapter 3, Section 3, it is not at all clear that reproduction—a special case of generative activity—necessarily involved the creation of an external product which will go on and on after one's death, *or* whether the point of the passage was simply that living beings require productive activity of various kinds in order to attain anything at all. If the latter then this leaves it open how reproduction proper functions exactly and whether it requires an external product. Since there is no external product that results from the activity of contemplation, I think we can take this as evidence in support of the latter. The ascent still shows a living being constantly 'coming into being' in new—and crucially, better—ways, as each production helps him to

Homer's poems go out of fashion, Solon's laws replaced, and Socrates accused of corrupting the youth.

[50] See *Nicomachean Ethics* 1140ª1–6, ᵇ6–7 with Scott (2000*b*).

[51] I thank Alexander Nehamas for putting this objection to me.

attain his end. Finally, the DHM recreates himself as 'godlike' in the activity of contemplation. The philosopher realizes his being in the best way possible for a human being. And the fact that human beings have to realize themselves in various ways is, I submit, the central feature of the account of (re)productive activity.

If we take this route we are following closely the pattern of ideas that has emerged thus far in the text. For recall that generation is the way in which the mortal partakes of immortality (208b3). Since the DHM fulfils his *erōs* by this means too (he employs his reproductive *ergon* to produce true virtue), this production is the way in which he, too, partakes of immortality. By realizing his noetic ability in the encounter with the divine form he achieves a genuine and secure good and in this respect becomes like the gods and so attains their friendship. On this reading, we are still prioritizing the nature of the philosophical good. The philosopher still *secures* his good, and in the best way possible for human beings, for it is a good based on an eternal truth and it will always be true of the producer that he has produced genuine virtue. And his virtue is a good of his own soul, not dependent on any further events for its acquisition such as the whims of those who dispense honour. The point is not that he will live on; immortality in this case resides in a perfection of soul. If *eudaimonia* resides in this then little can threaten his possession of this good. It will always be true of the DHM that he has produced genuine virtue.[52] This is more than most will ever attain and, it is suggested, the best possible for a human being.[53] One may conclude that this is an Aristotelian development, rather than a Platonic interpretation, and one that relies on clarifying the distinction between *poiēsis* and *praxis*, and where the goal of the activities resides in either case. But it is a view which accounts for the emphasis on the activity of contemplation as itself the end of the best human life.

---

[52] This does not require others to be around constantly predicating this of him.

[53] I am here in agreement with Bury (1932) xlv n. 2, who argues that immortality 'may be used not simply of quantity, but also of quality of existence'. This is probably the case in 212a: 'immortality is rather "eternal life" than "everlastingness", as connoting "heavenliness" or the kind of life that is proper to divinities. So, as the "spark divine" in man is the *nous*, immortality is practically equivalent to pure *noēsis*. On the other hand, in earlier parts of the discourse the word denotes only duration.'

If *eudaimonia* resides in a certain activity of the soul that best expresses 'wisdom and the rest of virtue'—contemplative activity—then unless there are alternative grounds for thinking that the soul is immortal it is not easy to see how this can continue after death. That does not imply that the philosopher will not affect others, or survive in their memory. The *Symposium* itself contributes to the survival of, at least, one virtuous philosopher. Or of a man who came pretty close, at any rate, and appears to have at least a measure of *eudaimonia* (cf. 173d6). Both the prologue and Alcibiades' speech are concerned with Socrates' influence on others. Indeed Alcibiades will later crown Socrates with the words: 'Socrates conquers all men with his *logoi*, not yesterday alone as yours did [Agathon], but always' (213e4). The dialogue itself can be seen as a testament to the survival of virtue, one that reflects the role of memory in preserving virtue in sympotic contexts more generally. But Alcibiades' speech also shows us ways in which the philosopher is misunderstood (221e6–222a1). If Socrates' *eudaimonia* were somehow dependent on the practice of Apollodorus and Alcibiades, this might be shaky ground. Elsewhere Plato emphasizes the degree to which philosophers are misunderstood and not appreciated by their fellow men (e.g. *Rep.* 517a–b, *Tht.* 174c–175b), so it would be surprising if he allowed the philosopher's highest achievement here to depend on such appreciation. The point is not that the philosopher, like Socrates, will not have beneficial effects after his death. The point is rather that this will not affect his *eudaimonia*. The practices of Apollodorus show that Socrates' life was a happy one, for that is responsible for the seductive pull of his characteristic conversations, as we have seen. The rehearsal of his characteristic conversations (in dialogues like the *Symposium*) continue to make that manifest to us. But this is not to say that Socrates' *eudaimonia* is dependent upon such practices. That is to be measured and determined whilst he lives and is not something to be settled later by the activities of others. The *telos* of a good life is to be found in a life, one lived in contemplation of—or, at the very least in pursuit of—the form of beauty.

Socrates has provided an account of the proper activity of our productive *ergon* in the pursuit of the form. If it is only in the presence of the form of beauty that one can be productive of the sort of good that will satisfy our desire for *eudaimonia*, then philosophical activity will be *erōs* proper expression. For one comes to be in the presence of the form of beauty by understanding beauty. The philosopher produces true virtue by grasping the truth about beauty, and I have argued that contemplation of the form just is the production of true virtue. I have also argued that the virtue of contemplation meets the criteria for *eudaimonia*. The philosopher's contemplative activity is a final good, not desired for anything beyond itself, and it is a secure good in the sense that it is true, and a state of the agent's own soul, not dependent upon external events for its possession. It is also the fulfilment of our nature and 'godlike'. At this stage we should have the following questions for this account. First, if *erōs* is best expressed in the activity of contemplation, is there room in the account for other-directed concern? A distinctive feature of some of the other speakers' accounts is that they take place within the specific context of the nature and goals of interpersonal erotic relationships. Has Socrates, after all, thrown the baby out with the bathwater? Second, as Aristophanes' thwarted interjection was perhaps going to question, to what extent is *erōs*' ascent to a godlike state of understanding an account of a characteristically human life? Is the philosopher in danger of hubris in making and ascent to the divine (cf. 190b8)? In the next two chapters I address both these issues.

5

Socrates' Speech: Concern for Others?

In the last chapter we examined the nature of the philosophical life as the happiest life. The philosopher pursues a truly beautiful creative environment, is able to produce genuine virtue, and so to attain the happiest life for himself—the life of contemplation. This account raises a question. If the highest virtue is contemplative virtue, then is there room in this account for other persons and, if so, in what form? This question has become a central one for the *Symposium*. In an influential article Gregory Vlastos argued that the ascent to the form of beauty instrumentalizes other persons as unworthy of love for their own sake, and nowhere indicates that the philosopher's creative activity will enrich the lives of others.[1] The article fuelled a vigorous debate about whether and, if so, in what sense, philosophical *erōs* involves loving other people. Is the love of other people superseded by *erōs* for the form of beauty, or is love of others compatible with *erōs* for the form?[2] There is now a widely held response to this view, namely that the philosopher needs to pass on his mental life to a beloved in order to secure his own immortality as part of his *eudaimonia*.[3] For if one takes the view that the philosopher needs to pass on his mental life to a beloved in order to secure his immortality, then it is argued that 'personal love is ... not supplanted, but

---

[1] Vlastos (1981) 3–34.

[2] For the former position, see Vlastos (1981) 19–34; Nussbaum (1979) 131–72. For the latter, see Hackforth (1950) 43–5; Irwin (1977) 267–72, 342–3; Price (1989) 45–9; Gill (1996) 385–9; Moravscik (1971) 293; Kosman (1976) 53–69, esp. 64; Rowe (1998*b*) 257.

[3] Although this view was first proposed by Hackforth, it has been revived more recently by Price (amongst others), in part, as a solution to the problem posed by Vlastos. See Hackforth (1950) 43–5; Price (1989) 45–9.

glorified'.[4] Since I have argued that there is no such transference of philosophical virtue, at the highest level of the ascent at any rate, this question re-emerges for my account with some force. In this chapter, then, I address Vlastos's problem. I argue that although misguided in setting an Aristotelian standard of *philia* as a measure of Platonic *erōs*, Vlastos is right to argue that the account of the philosopher's progress instrumentalizes other persons in relation to the form, but this need not be read as objectionable when see within the larger context of the account. Further, this is not the only manner of his engagement with others. Socrates' account is still firmly anchored in an account of interpersonal relationships and their role in a flourishing human life.

1. VLASTOS'S CHARGE

At the heart of this debate are numerous assumptions about the nature of interpersonal love. But what exactly is meant by 'love' both in the context of this debate and in the context of the *Symposium* is not always made clear. Since Vlastos has set the terms of the current debate, I begin with his argument. He starts with a discussion of Aristotle's account of *philia*, which he distils as follows: to love another person we must wish for that person's good *for that person's sake*, not for ours.[5] This, he argues will serve as 'a standard against which to measure Plato's concept of love'.[6] Although Vlastos shows a keen sense of the differences between *philia* and *erōs* earlier in his argument, they fail to play any significant role subsequently. In a discussion of *erōs* one does not traditionally expect the love of other

---

[4] Price (1989) 54; cf. Hackforth (1950) 44, Irwin (1977) 342–3, Rowe (1998*b*) 257.

[5] Such a view is found in the *Rhetoric* 1380^{b}35–1381^{a}1 and the *Nicomachean Ethics* 1166^{a}2–5; Vlastos (1981) n. 1 and 2. In an interesting footnote Vlastos notes that the phrase 'for his own sake' need not always indicate altruism, but can simply indicate loving another *for who he is* which neither implies nor excludes altruism. Vlastos seems to adopt a strongly altruistic reading of the phrase (1981) 33 n. 100. I am not concerned here with Vlastos's reading of Aristotle, but rather with bringing to light the assumptions that Vlastos brings to bear on his discussion of Platonic 'love'.

[6] Vlastos (1981) 6.

persons for their own sake to play a central role, nor again the reciprocity of affection that ideally characterizes a relationship of *philia*.[7] Eros, signifying an intense feeling of desire, most centrally refers to the feelings and experiences *of a lover* aroused by the stimulus of beauty. In the *Phaedrus*, when Plato is concerned to describe an interpersonal relationship based on *erōs* he creates a new term to include the experiences of a beloved: *anterōs* (255d8). Moreover, the tradition of pederastic *erōs* to which Plato is referring in this dialogue did not traditionally include the love of other persons for their own sake, but rather an exchange of benefit for both parties—*paederastia* for *philosophia*, as Pausanias puts it (181c–185d). Aristotle himself was well aware of such distinctions.[8]

But Vlastos takes Plato to hold a theory of love as unitary, with *philia* and *erōs* as two distinct species thereof, where *philia* is related to utility and *erōs* to beauty, but *erōs* is more intense.[9] It is this unitary conception that is reflected in Vlastos's translation of both terms by 'love', and that underlies his argumentative strategy as he moves between the *Lysis*'s notion of *philia*, with which he begins his examination of 'love' in Plato, and the *Symposium*'s notion of *erōs*—using his Aristotelian standard in both dialogues. The assumption that the discussions of *philia* in the *Lysis*, of *philia* and *erōs* in the *Republic*, and of *erōs* in the *Symposium* together constitute a Platonic theory of 'love' as a unitary phenomenon, is itself questionable. It is clear that Plato talks about—that is, his characters talk about—both *philia* and *erōos* in these dialogues, and it is also clear that those discussions exhibit certain similarities, such as appeal to the notion

---

[7] On this issue see Halperin (1986) 60–80 and Kahn (1996) 261. As Kahn (1996) 261 argues, 'In such a theory the object of desire is only initially or instrumentally a person. Reciprocal relations between persons would have to be treated in an account of *philia*, which Plato did not develop. If this distinction is kept in mind, many criticisms of Plato's theory are seen to be misconceived.' Cf. also Ferrari (1992) 248–9. For Vlastos's discussion of the distinction between these terms, see (1981) n. 4. There is some degree of slippage between the two terms. As Dover (1978) 43, 49, notes, although *erōs* and its cognates can apply to any intense desire and was frequently used to denote sexual activity, *philia* can also refer to sexual activity where the context is a loving and affectionate one.

[8] *NE* 8, 1157ᵃ6 ff.

[9] Thus he writes that Plato's theory is concerned with 'love for placeholders of the predicates "useful" and "beautiful"—of the former when it is only *philia*, of the latter when it is *eros*', cf. Vlastos (1981) 26.

of a 'first love', as we shall see; but this does not amount to a proof that these accounts provide, or were supposed to provide, a unitary and exhaustive 'theory of love'. Nor, then, does the absence from such discussions of the notion of love of others for their own sake demonstrate that such a notion was altogether missing from Plato's thought about love. Whether or not Plato did hold a unitary and exhaustive theory of 'love' is outside the scope of this study. My concern here is with the assumptions Vlastos employs in his argument and the way in which those assumptions have shaped an entire debate about interpersonal love in the *Symposium*.

Starting with the *Lysis*, Vlastos argues that Plato is there concerned only with 'utility' love. Since Socrates argues that if a person loves another he does so because of some benefit he needs from that other, on the grounds that 'if one were in need of nothing, one would feel no affection... and he who felt no affection would not love' (215b–c), Vlastos concludes that a person will be loved if and only if he produces some good *for the person who loves* (1981: 7). The *Lysis* thus appears to focus only on those features of Aristotelian *philia* that fall into the category of 'utility love', an incomplete or imperfect kind of *philia*. As Vlastos notes, Socrates also argues in the *Lysis* that there is a 'first beloved for whose sake all other objects are loved' (219d), later described as 'the good' (220b7). Many scholars have seen parallels here with the *Symposium*'s account of *erōs*. Socrates argues there that *erōs* is caused by a need in the lover (199c–201c, with Vlastos (1981) n. 20), a need and a desire which is always for the good (206a10). Moreover, in the notion of the 'first love—for the sake of which all other objects are loved' many, too, have found a parallel in the *Symposium*'s notion of a *scala amoris* to the form of beauty, 'that for the sake of which all previous toils were' (210e6). Vlastos is one such scholar and he subsequently moves, via the *Republic*,[10] to the *Symposium* in search of this 'first love'.[11] Since

---

[10] Vlastos (1981) 13–15 argues that the promotion of *philia* in the ideal city is compatible with his understanding of 'utility love' in the *Lysis*. On the notion of the 'first love', he argues with reference to the *Republic* 474c ff. that 'the first beloved is the Idea' (1981) 19–20. He then turns to the *Symposium* for an elaboration of this idea.

[11] I am not concerned here to analyse the relationship between the *Lysis* and the *Symposium*, rather my concern is with the kinds of assumptions that Vlastos brings to bear on the *Symposium*, and with the origin of those assumptions. For a discussion of the relationship between the *Lysis* and the *Symposium*, see Kahn (1996) 290–1.

both the *Lysis* and the *Symposium* are taken to be parts of a unified theory of 'love', and the *Lysis* failed to measure up to the Aristotelian standard of 'virtue friendship', Vlastos's question then is: How does the *Symposium* fare?

The 'first love' in the *Symposium*, it is argued, is the form of beauty itself. Thus Vlastos urges that other people are to be loved only insofar as they instantiate that true beauty which the lover seeks. Support for such a view is suggested by the description of the other love objects as 'steps' to be used in the lover's progress. We are told that:

This is what it is to approach love matters, or be led by someone else in them, in the correct way: beginning from these beautiful things here, one must always move upwards for the sake of that beauty I speak of, using the other things as steps from one to two and from two to all beautiful bodies, from beautiful bodies to beautiful activities, from activities to beautiful sciences, and finally from sciences to *that* science, which is science of nothing other than beauty itself, in order that one may finally know what beauty is, itself (211c1–d1).

The desiring agent in the *Symposium*, Vlastos argues, loves only 'a complex of qualities answering to the lover's sense of beauty, which he locates for a time truly or falsely in that person'.[12] The account of philosophical *erōs* in the *Symposium*, Vlastos continues, is not about love for persons: 'What it is really about is love for placeholders of the predicates "useful" and "beautiful"... the idea, and it alone, is to be loved *for its own sake*'.[13] This idea Vlastos finds objectionable and, given his unitary conception of Platonic 'love', he concludes that the account exhibits cold-hearted egoism that fails to do justice to the kind of love persons feel for one another.

If this was a fair objection, it would be quite an indictment of the account. This critique needs to be examined in some detail. The salient contrast Vlastos employs when examining Socrates' account of *erōs* in the *Symposium* is that between loving a person 'for their own sake' and loving a person 'as a placeholder of predicates'. The phrase 'placeholders of predicates' appears as the opposite of the preferred 'individual worth' in an earlier paper of his entitled 'Justice and Equality', which illuminates some of the reasons behind

---

[12] Vlastos (1981) 28.   [13] Vlastos (1981) 26.

Vlastos's interest in, and reaction to, Platonic 'love'.[14] In that paper Vlastos is concerned to defend 'equalitarian justice', as he puts is, as opposed to 'meritarian justice'. Persons, he argued, have 'intrinsic value as individual human beings'; he also expressed it by saying (with Kant) that men are 'ends in themselves'. This is evidently involved in Vlastos's reading of the Aristotelian phrase 'for his own sake'. Vlastos argues that treating persons as 'placeholders of predicates' necessarily involves abstracting a quality of merit from their individuality and disregarding the 'individual worth' of persons: 'If A is valued for some meritorious quality, m, his individuality does not enter into the valuation. As an individual he is then dispensable; his place could be taken without loss of value by any other individual with as good an m rating... No matter how enviable a package of well-rounded excellence A may represent, it would still follow that, if he is valued only for his merit, he is not being valued as an individual.'[15]

Vlastos is clearly right that persons in the *Symposium*'s ascent are desirable insofar as they exhibit the quality of beauty. On Socrates' account a desiring agent loves a particular beautiful person or thing because he finds the properties of that person or thing to be attractive. As we have seen, desiring agents recognize value and are moved towards the objects of attraction because of this recognition. We might not find this much objectionable. There is something that seems natural about saying that we are attracted towards certain objects because of valuable properties we perceive those objects to possess. Loving other persons as individuals without regard for their properties is the kind of the love that some traditions reserve only for God.[16] Vlastos rejects the idea that the beloved's valuable properties are the basis of love because, as the above quotation makes plain, he takes it that if one loves a person for his beauty then it is, strictly speaking, beauty that is the object of love and the person is merely an occasion for, or an instance of, this kind. One might begin to respond by claiming that there are some valuable properties that

---

[14] See Vlastos (1962) with Burnyeat (1992), who draws attention to this point.

[15] Vlastos (1962) 44.

[16] See, for example, the discussion of God's love in A. Nygren (1982) 76–7: 'It is only when all thought of the worthiness of the object is abandoned that we can understand what *agape* is.'

define who a person is, so that in loving them for such properties we are loving them as persons.[17] This might allow us to say that *persons* are valued on this account, but not necessarily that they are valued as unique individuals, or as whole (non-idealized) persons. There may be further conditions required for an interpersonal relationship besides the perception of valuable properties. But these will not concern us here, as they do not concern Socrates either, and for good reason; or, so I shall argue in the following.

Socrates relishes precisely the implication Vlastos finds objectionable. That is, that if *erōs* is based on the perception of beauty, we should not expect desiring agents to pursue one beautiful person or thing alone, but to desire any other person or thing that also exhibits the same, or more of, that property of beauty. If *erōs* is motivated by the apprehension of value in its object, then what reason would there be to focus on a single instance to the exclusion of all other valuable instances? If we are to be consistent, it would, as Socrates says, be mindless not to expand our horizons and consider all valuable things in the way the ascent requires (210b1). If *erōs* is universalizable in this way, then one should not be committed to particular things, but turn one's gaze to 'the wide sea' of beauty (210d4) and, ultimately, to the most beautiful object of all: the form. Now in order to assess whether this procedure is, in fact, an objectionable one, we need to clarify what desire we are trying to satisfy here, and why we are encouraged to look beyond a single person or thing. If we go back to the larger pattern of ideas at play in Socrates' account, then we can appreciate why Socrates advocates this kind of pursuit. He has argued that what we really want as desiring beings is to possess, or rather to produce, whatever good we take to be central to our happiness. The pursuit of, or production in the presence of, beauty is the way in which we are able to possess this good. That is the reason why we pursue beauty with such intense eagerness. Socrates' point is that if we want the possession, or production, of a good that will satisfy the desire for *eudaimonia*, then we need to ensure that we pursue the right kinds of beautiful objects, and in the right kind of way, to ensure that we

[17] Kosman (1976) 53–69, develops an argument along these lines. He argues that 'If I love A because of P, or love the P in A, I should not be said to love something other than A if P is what A is. Thus, to love A for its beauty, is to love A for itself'; see Kosman (1976) 64.

attain *that*. If *eudaimonia* is the aim of *erōs* and our pursuit of beauty is determined by that aim, it is not just a semantic confusion to think that *erōs* refers centrally to love for individuals, but a deeply misguided idea to think that a person or persons can satisfy our aspiration for good things and happiness. Only the most committed romantic would entertain such an idea.[18]

As Socrates made plain earlier in his account, *erōs* refers not just to erotic love for individuals, but to our pursuit of good things and happiness quite generally. Desire for a beautiful individual can awaken us to a longing for something more, like Aristophanes' perplexed lovers; but we misconstrue what *erōs* is if we fail to realize that there is something more central to human happiness than union with another individual. Examples of *erōs* for good things and happiness range from the love of money-making and the love of sports to the love of wisdom (205d5). Socrates is concerned with whatever it is that we deem to be of value in our lives and are moved towards, the things that define our pursuit of happiness and the good life and that determine the kind of people that we are. And that is ultimately why Socrates welcomes the more expansive encounter with beauty. If one is to become a good person and lead a satisfying life, one needs to ensure that one desires the right kinds of things—those things that are productive of genuine excellence and happiness—and that is what the wider encounter with beauty is concerned to ensure that we attain. One needs to move away from exclusive focus upon the beauty of an individual body or soul so that one may come to understand the nature of beauty, and cultivate a genuine psychic good (true virtue). Within the larger framework of the account, union with another body will lead to the production of physical offspring for the sake of fame, and unreflective union with another soul will lead to the production of an underdeveloped virtue. If one believes (as the majority of desiring agents do in this text) that psychic goods, or those activities expressive of the soul, are central to a happy life, then Socrates' point is that we need an expansive encounter with beauty in order to ensure that we attain that. That is, we need a wide and reflective encounter with those things we deem valuable in the area of body and soul so that we may come to

---

[18] I mean romantic in the common sense of that term.

understand the sorts of things a good person should pursue and produce a genuine good, that is become virtuous ourselves. Vlastes is right that the account of *erōs* in the ascent is not about love for persons. 'What it is really about is love for placeholders of the predicates "useful" and "beautiful".'[19] This is both explicable and, given certain assumptions about the relationship between virtue and knowledge, an appropriate way to proceed towards that end.

One might object to the epistemology/metaphysics of the account, and (with Vlastos) to the fact that an expansive encounter of this kind leads to the form as the ultimate source of value. But, when seen within the larger context of Socrates' account, the wider concern with those things we deem valuable does not as such warrant Vlastos's harsh conclusion. Socrates is concerned with the cultivation of virtue and happiness, and the role of the sort of relationships that were taken—by all the speakers at this symposium—to have a central role in that end.[20] Given the larger framework of this account it might be less misleading to translate *erōs* as 'aspiration', rather than Vlastos's 'love' or even 'desire'.[21] Socrates' point is that in our aspiration towards happiness we need to look beyond individuals. That, ultimately, is the reason why the account does not focus on 'love' for persons. Persons may still be valued for their contribution to the good life, and perhaps also loved for their own sakes. There is no incompatibility between giving *erōs* according to merit (beauty) and other forms of affection (e.g. *philia*) according to other criteria. All the *Symposium*'s ascent suggests is the former and, as I hope to have shown, for good reason. When it comes to considering what things are productive of our happiness, we need to think beyond individuals as the sole repository of all that is valuable in human life and to cut Socrates some slack when he does so.

Why doesn't Vlastos? Vlastos shifts the question from: What happens to the individual as an object of love? to: Does progress towards the form as the ultimate object of love accommodate love of

---

[19] Vlastos (1981) 26.

[20] Many of the previous speakers cited virtue as the proper outcome of *erōs* (179d1–2, 184d7, 185b5, 188d4–9, 196d4–e6) and *eudaimonia* was said to be the result of *erōs* correctly employed in almost all the speeches (180b7, 188d8, 193d5, 194e6, 195a5, 205a1).

[21] Cf. Moravscik (1971) 290.

other persons? Is the ascent to the form, at least, compatible with loving other persons *for their own sake*? Or does such progress exclude such a thing, as Vlastos himself concludes: 'it is not said or so much as hinted at that "birth in beauty" should be motivated by love of persons—that the ultimate purpose of the creative act should be to enrich the lives of other persons who are themselves worthy of love *for their own sake*'.[22] The nature of the question may have shifted to compatibility, but the standard of loving another person for that person's own sake has not. Although one would not typically expect an answer to such a question in an account of *erōs*, it is Vlastos's unitary conception of Platonic 'love' that brings the Aristotelian standard back into the fold. Given that the *Lysis* has apparently proved to Vlastos to have exhibited the features only of Aristotelian 'utility' love, his next question is: Does the *Symposium* do any better? This places a burden on the account that it is not designed to carry.

2. THE ROLE AND STATUS OF OTHER PERSONS IN THE ASCENT

The question whether the account of *erōs* in the *Symposium* is compatible with loving other persons for their own sake has taken hold of many scholars, even though the assumptions behind the question do not often come to the fore.[23] There seem to be two reasons for this. Even if we can agree that the account of philosophical *erōs* is not primarily about the love of other persons for their own sake, and agree that there is nothing objectionable about that lack of focus, we nonetheless hope that Socrates' account does not exclude such relationships. We may still wish to ask whether we can value other persons as part of a happy and fulfilling life and, if so, in what

---

[22] Vlastos (1981) 31.

[23] Thus Price, for example, who uses Vlastos's work throughout his own work on the *Symposium*, tries to reconcile the account of *erōs* there with the notion of loving others *for their own sake* (1989: 98), which suggests that Vlastos's Aristotelian standard is in mind.

sense. Socrates may still be concerned with the real end of the sorts of interpersonal relationships that typically took place at symposia, and with their role within a flourishing life. If we shift to this latter question, though, we need to do so in a way that is informed by the explanatory goals of this account of *erōs*, and not by preoccupations brought in because of assumptions we would do well to question. A further reason emerges from the hotly debated issue of the status of the philosopher's immortality. If one takes the view that the philosopher needs to create virtue in other souls in order to secure everlasting virtue and happiness, then it would seem that interpersonal relationships are essential to this account of *erōs* after all, and in a way that might meet Vlastos's criteria. But since I have argued that philosophical virtue is contemplative virtue, and requires no such transference of virtue to another, I need an alternative way to address such questions. In the following, I clarify the role of other persons in the ascent and develop an alternative response to Vlastos.

Price, who has argued most recently for an interpretation that attempts to 'reconcile personal love with developing interests', argues as follows:

The strongest ground in favour of interpreting the ascent as an exercise of personal love is its relation to what precedes: if it is to bear out Diotima's original definition of love in the specific sense as aiming at immortality through generation in beauty, it must have the task of completing the mental procreation, and in particular the educative pederasty described in the so-called Lesser Mysteries of 209. Though it is only the discourse of 210c1 that is specified as being educative (c2–3), the emphasis on discourse at every level (a7–8, c1, d4–6) confirms that communication is always the goal (cf. 209b7–c2). If the ascent passage has standardly been read as describing a discarding of persons for the sake of Forms, that is, if I am right, the result of two connected mistakes (whose effect is only slightly mitigated by an inclusive reading): confusing the loved one's rôle as an object of contemplation (in which he is soon largely superseded) with his rôle as recipient of thought, and taking the passage out of context.[24]

---

[24] Price (1989) 48–9. Cf. also Hackforth (1950) 44, Irwin (1977) 343–2, and Rowe (1998*b*) 257.

Price's argument—a dominant one in the literature on this sub-ject—rests on a particular construal of the nature and importance of educative pederasty in the lower mysteries. Why this should be taken as the standard and model for the desiring agent of the ascent is unclear to me. The contrasts between the lower and higher mysteries examined in the last chapter suggested that caution is required here. But even if we do assume that the behaviour of the desiring agent of the lower mysteries (henceforth DLM) is a model for that of the higher (henceforth DHM), it is unclear how this helps. As we have seen, when the DLM were introduced, love of honour was cited as the goal of their behaviour (208c3). Such types generate heroic deeds (208d1–6), poems (209a4), laws (209d5–e1), and educative conversations (209b8–c2) in the hope that they will be honoured and remembered for virtue and in that sense secure their good 'eternally'. Now on such a model, the beloved is not educated for his own sake, or loved for his own sake, but is rather a vehicle for the lover's self-glorification, a way to procure honour *for the lover.*[25] Notice further that educative pederasty is only *one* of the ways in which honour is procured, and not a paradigm case even for the DLM. But most significantly, the desire for honour is a self-regarding desire, but one Price describes as if it were other-regarding. The fact that the education of another happens to be one of the ways in which honour is achieved is not enough to ensure that a beloved is loved as an end in himself and not just as a means to the DLM's own end(s). Nor, therefore, is it enough to ensure that the beloved is loved 'for his own sake, not for [the lover's]' (Vlastos). One is surely inclined to conclude that such a person will be loved if and only if he produces some good—honour—*for the person who loves.* The lower mysteries, like the *Lysis*, then, would appear to describe only those features of Aristotelian *philia*—if, for the moment, we allow the assimilation of *erōs* to *philia*—which fall under the category of 'utility love'.

Price has an answer to this objection: 'If bequeathing a way of life is to satisfy, even to some extent, an innate desire for survival, I must

---

[25] Note that in the *Phaedrus* we are told that as philosophers lovers have a continuing basis for friendship whereas the *philotimioi* depend merely on pledges given and received (256c7–d1 with Rowe 1986: 190).

value its realisation in another as I value it in myself. If I view him as a means and not an end, then his happy life cannot count in itself as a success for me. The further we extend the desire for the good to belong to oneself always (206a11–12), the less we can oppose it to a desire that others should possess the good, and for their own sake.'[26] The (apparent) fact that desiring agents will continue to enjoy the good by proxy seems to ensure that the beloved is valued for his own sake, in the sense that if the beloved is seen as a future self (qua beneficiary of virtue and happiness), then he must be valued as one values one's current self. Price hopes that this model of virtue and happiness by proxy will ensure that the beloved is loved for his own sake, and will thereby meet Vlastos's Aristotelian standard.

For the sake of argument let us accept the possibility that a model of educative pederasty may involve loving another for his own sake, and try to determine whether there is any such model in the ascent. The evidence for educative pederasty in the higher mysteries rests on a particular construal of the DHM's *logoi* as educative, a construal which itself rests on the emphasis on the production of *logoi* at each level, and on the specification of those *logoi* as educative at 210c1. This supports the claim that educative pederasty in the ascent is an extension of the model of vicarious immortality described in the lower mysteries: 'Such verbal offspring offer a kind of immortality, so long as they are read or remembered, by their object or by others.'[27] Since the question naturally arises for such a reading why the DHM needs to ascend given that he is already 'propagating virtue' on the lower levels, Price goes on to argue that the DHM ascends because 'the propagation of virtue needs to be backed by knowledge'.[28] In answer to the further question: 'Why should vicarious survival be better served by propagating virtue with knowledge than without?' Price answers that: 'The *Symposium* itself contains no answer, and this, I think, is a major omission.'[29] For an account of a method which leads to knowledge of the form of beauty, this omission must be a grave one indeed, and its emergence constitutes one of the most serious objections to this interpretation.

---

[26] Price (1989) 98.   [27] Price (1989) 41.
[28] Price (1989) 41.   [29] Price (1989) 42.

I begin with the first claim, that the DHM is producing educative *logoi.* As we have seen, the DHM follows a method that proceeds to the form of beauty through the use of particular examples or kinds. On each level of the ascent the DHM focuses his attention on the common quality of beauty in each class, and draws generalizations about the quality of beauty on that level (210b3, b6–7; 208a8–b1, b3, c4–5). Since the delivery of *logoi* follows the DHM's realization of the common quality in each class, it seems reasonable to understand such *logoi* as, at least, involving an attempt to articulate that common quality, a process which is not complete until he encounters the form. If so, then the primary educative function of such *logoi* will be to aid the DHM's *own* progress towards knowledge. Part of the explanation for this emphasis on the DHM's own development is a polemic with the DLM. The description of the DLM contrasts with the description of the DHM in important respects. The DLM, when he hits just the right age (209b1–2), is attracted to beautiful bodies (209b4–5), and if he happens to chance upon a beautiful soul (b5–7) *immediately* produces *logoi* about virtue (b8). The readiness with which he engages in an educative relationship suggests that this desiring agent assumes that he already knows what virtue is and how to acquire it. The DHM, by contrast, starts from early youth (210a5) and follows a correct method which leads to knowledge of beauty itself (211c8). When the DHM shows a concern for educative discourses, he feels compelled to *seek* them out (210c2). At the end of the ascent it is made clear that it is only one who engages in this methodical search and educates himself about the nature of beauty who is able to deliver true virtue successfully. The DLM, by contrast, delivers only an image of true virtue (212a5). Since the DLM does not himself know about fine practices and activities, we infer that he has no business setting himself up as an educator of anyone else, a role that assumes he does know about such things. The DHM does not assume that he already knows what virtue is and how to acquire it; thus he does not set himself up as an educator, but rather positions himself as a pupil who seeks the knowledge he realizes he lacks. This is precisely the way in which Socrates positions himself before the delivery of his speech. In place of the confident stance of the rest of the speakers, Socrates presents

himself as the ignorant student, aware of his lack and eager to learn
from the wise Diotima (206b, 207c).[30]

Although the fact that the DHM produces *logoi* on every level
cannot in itself be taken as evidence for an other-directed educative
intent in the passage, nothing has been said so far to exclude the
possibility that such *logoi* might also educate another. The DHM
might be involved, as Price argues, in a search together with the guide
and the beloved simultaneously.[31] The strongest evidence in favour of
educative pederasty is the DHM's focus on the beauty of soul at
210b6 ff.

> The next stage is that he must consider beauty in soul more valuable than
> beauty in the body, so that if someone who is decent in soul has even a slight
> physical bloom, even then it is enough for him, and he loves and cares for
> the other person, and gives birth to the sorts of *logoi*—and seeks for them—
> that will make young men into better men, in order that he may be
> compelled in turn to contemplate beauty as it exists in kinds of activity
> (210b6–c3).

This passage appears to be evidence that the DHM is engaged in an
interpersonal relationship, both from the initial encounter at 210b8
and right through until the point when he begins his examination of
beauty in the area of laws and practices at c3–4, and the 'knowledges'
at c6 as a consequence of his interest in soul on this level and, in
particular, in the activities that make a decent soul better (cf. 210c1–
2). Thus Price concludes that the beautiful soul the DHM encounters
at 210b8 replaces the beautiful boy with whom he was enamoured at
the earlier levels and that this soul remains with the DHM throughout his progress as the recipient of his increased understanding of
beauty.

Crucial to understanding the nature and role of this relationship is
how one interprets the motivation at 210c1–2. Why is the DHM

---

[30] In the *Apology* 19d8–e2, 23a3–5 and the *Laches* 200e1–201a1 Socrates disavows
the role of teacher and in the latter text argues that one should first find a teacher for
oneself—and then for the young men. Socrates often declares a desire to become the
pupil of anyone that has knowledge; cf. Nehamas (1999) 47, 71.

[31] Price (1989) 56–7 argues that 'it seemed intended, though not always explicit,
that the ascent should involve three people (guide, lover and beloved) within all its
stages and so constitute a model at once of intellectual development and interpersonal relations'. Cf. Rowe (1998*b*) 257.

compelled to examine laws and practices and 'knowledges'? The future form ($\pi o \iota \acute{\eta} \sigma o v \sigma \iota$) at 210c2, in the line which reads 'he *seeks* for the kind of *logoi* that *will make* young men better', and the use of the plural 'young men', do not suggest that the DHM's search actually makes this one, particular 'decent' soul (the $\tau \iota s$ of 210b8) better here and now. The DHM has a response to the beautiful soul which motivates him to seek out improving *logoi*. The *logoi* the DHM is seeking have an educative *intention*, which is not necessarily something he carries through on this particular level of the ascent. The future form is itself explained by the searching ($\zeta \eta \tau \epsilon \hat{\iota} v$) which follows, and which suggests that the DHM searches for *logoi*—ones he has not yet found—which will (when found) make young men (plural) 'better'.[32] It is a result of this concern to seek out such discourses that the DHM is compelled to turn to laws and practices at 210c3–4, and 'knowledges' at c6, which are examined as a consequence of his concern for the beautiful souls of b8–c1, and for the quality of the educative discourses he is inspired to produce. He turns to the beauty of souls—and if he comes across a decent soul he will love and care for that person—so that he (the DHM) will be compelled to contemplate beauty in the area of laws and practices.[33] 'Soul love' provides an occasion for the DHM to turn to other bearers of beauty: laws and practices are beautiful insofar as they contribute to the moral education of the young soul. If the DHM is interested in beauty of soul, he will be interested in the kinds of activities that are responsible for the creation of beautiful souls and

[32] Along with Rowe (1998a) 195, and Sier (1997) n. on 210c2–3, I see no reason to bracket *kai zētein* at 210c3 with Dover (1980) 156. Dover says that 'the seeker has already found his partner... he does not "seek" arguments [*logoi* in the Greek: it seems more natural to keep to the more neutral "words"], and *toioutous* ["the sorts of"] obviously looks forward to *hoitines* ["that will"]'. But as Rowe argues, it is the search for the right sorts of *logoi* that compels the lover to contemplate beauty in kinds of activity. It is also what makes sense of the future ('that will make the young better'.)

[33] Kahn (1996) 270 refers to 'discourses that permit both the speaker and the auditor to comprehend the moral beauty of practices and laws'. In n. 15 he adds: 'There seems to be a confusion at 210c3. How can the production of educative *logoi* force the speaker to behold moral beauty?' See also Dover (1980) 155. Along with Rowe (1998a) 195 I take it that $\emph{\iota} v a$ $\emph{\dot{a}} v a \gamma \kappa a \sigma \theta \hat{\eta}$ $a \emph{\mathring{v}}$ $\theta \epsilon \acute{a} \sigma a \sigma \theta a \iota$ refers to the lover (c3–e1), and not to the beautiful soul of 210c1. The search for educative *logoi* leads the lover to practices and laws because insofar as they are *kala* these are the sorts of things one should know about if one is to learn how to improve young souls.

are themselves, accordingly, beautiful instances of those kinds. The emphasis here is on how the DHM uses his experiences and responses to beautiful objects as part of his progress. This is what it means, I take it, to use the loved objects 'like steps'.

To satisfy the conditions of interpersonal love laid down by Vlastos, the concern for the soul at 210c2 must be more than the *occasion* for the DHM's progress. So, is the DHM's educative intention fulfilled? It might be the case that later concerns prevent him from fulfilling the intention at a later stage in his progress. The DHM might discover that he does not any longer have the feelings and interests constitutive of the sort of person who expressed the intention at 210c2. The description of the DHM's subsequent development suggests that his feelings and interests have indeed changed. After examining the beauty in 'knowledges', the DHM is described as 'gazing now towards a beauty which is vast, and no longer slavishly attached to the beauty belonging to a single thing—a young boy, some individual human being, or one kind of activity—may cease to be worthless and petty, as his servitude made him, but turned towards the great sea of beauty and contemplating that, may bring to birth many beautiful, even magnificent, *logoi* and thoughts in a love of wisdom that grudges nothing' (210d1–5). The fact that the DHM is no longer attached to the particular seems to be an implicit reversal of his attachment to the decent soul encountered earlier who was the occasion for future educative concerns (the ἐπιεκὴς ὢν τὴν ψυχήν τις at 210b8). If so, then when the DHM reaches 'the great sea of beauty' any relationship begun at 210b8 is altered. If his educative intentions are still present at this stage, they must also include a wider concern for others too, lest he exhibit any 'slavish' attachment to a particular.[34]

So is there any evidence that the DHM's educative intention— albeit no longer an exclusive one—is fulfilled? After examining laws, practices, and 'knowledges', the DHM is said to produce *logoi* in a love of wisdom that grudges nothing (ἄφθονος φιλοσοφία,

---

[34] So Rowe (1998a) 197. This move also distances the DHM from the DLM's exclusive attachment (cf. 209b5–c7). It can be compared to the description of the bad lover in the *Phaedrus* who jealously guards his beloved, and to Socrates' description of Alcibiades in this dialogue (213c–d).

210d5–6).³⁵ These *logoi* appear as the outcome of the search started in 210c1. But the question is, *whom* do they benefit? Since the love of souls is an important part of the DHM's progress because it provides an occasion for him to turn to other areas of beauty, at least one beneficiary of these *logoi* is the DHM himself. But the description of the DHM producing *logoi* in a love of wisdom that grudges nothing (d5–6) does suggest that other people are involved; it suggests that one is generous with one's insights, a sentiment that contrasts with the previous, exclusive attachment to the beautiful soul, the *tis* at 210b8.³⁶ The *logoi* delivered ungrudgingly at 210d5 are—as the outcome of the search started at 210c2—educational (*that* is not being denied), but they are not exclusively concerned with one person. The DHM here generates *logoi* with all sorts of people—he is making young *people* better, and thereby we may suppose carrying out his earlier educative intention to make the young (plural) better (210c2–3) including himself. So, although the motivation for the ascent is DHM's own fulfilment (which, I have argued, is appropriate to an account of *erōs*), we have reason to agree with Price that this involves concern for others at this stage, at least.³⁷

I have teased out two main features of the account so far. First, the role of the bodies, souls, and laws and so on as objects of the DHM's *erōs* in his progress towards wisdom. Second, the concern for the soul encountered at 210b8 and its expression in a generosity of insight. In relation to the first I argued against the view that the DHM is realizing himself in the beautiful bodies and soul by the production

---

³⁵ ἄφθονος could just indicate 'unlimited' (as Dover (1980) suggests), but as Rowe (1998a) 197 says, it seems reasonable to stick to the literal sense (compare the description of the good lover in the *Phaedrus* 249a2).

³⁶ Compare Socrates' description of Alcibiades' jealousy (cf. φθόνος, 213d2, with 222b, on Socrates' philosophical promiscuity). This contrasts with the philosophical activity which grudges nothing (τίκτῃ ἐν φιλοσοφίᾳ ἀφθόνῳ, 210d5–6), and can be seen as dramatizing the move in the ascent at 210d5–6, when the DHM becomes 'promiscuous' in his educative concerns.

³⁷ An obvious question concerns the content of these *logoi*. Since the DHM does not assume that he already knows what virtue is and positions himself as a pupil who seeks the knowledge he lacks, then such *logoi* must be the *logoi* of one who is seeking knowledge. Since these *logoi* appear at a transitional point, after the DHM has surveyed all the different classes of beauty, and before coming to know ὃ ἔστι καλόν (211c8–9), perhaps these *logoi* are attempts at a definition of beauty.

of educational *logoi*, and provided reasons to agree with Vlastos that the beautiful bodies and souls have, at least, instrumental value. Even the soul encountered at 210b8 provides an occasion for the DHM to turn to other bearers of beauty and for him to make progress towards the form and *his* goal: better *logos* and, finally, wisdom and virtue. As Vlastos notes, the form is what all the previous toils were 'for the sake of' (210e6). There is, though, nothing in the account that states that the form is the only thing pursued for its own sake. There may be classes of objects that are pursued both for their own sakes and for the sake of something higher. Vlastos seems to take it that the beautiful objects are valuable only as a means to the form because he objects to the fact that the value of such attractions does not appear to be grounded in these beautiful objects, but in the form. Since the form is the ultimate source of their value, he takes it that they must be desired *solely* as a means to this end. But this does not follow. If we take it that the form is the only object that is desired for its own sake *alone* we leave room for the possibility that other objects may be valued for their own sakes, *and* for the sake of a further end.[38] One might value souls as good instances of beauty and as a step to the form because (like the DHM) in valuing that soul one comes to desire a deeper understanding of how persons come to exhibit the attractive qualities possessed by that soul. We have reason to entertain this possibility if we consider the way in which particular bodies and souls are beautiful. It is, of course, true (on this account) that the form is the ultimate source of value in the sense that it is the only object that embodies beauty perfectly and immutably. But the relationship of participation that holds between the form and its particular instances implies that particular beautiful things embody

They may be educative in the sense that the DHM is conversing with another as part of his search for the definition. Since he has not yet found this definitional *logos*, they cannot be attempts to transmit virtue he does not yet have, but are expressive of his progress towards knowledge. Since knowledge involves having a definitional *logos*, progress towards it must involve the awareness that one lacks such a *logos* and the attempt or attempts to provide it. They will educate others insofar as they help others, just as they help the DHM himself, to realize what is involved in giving a definition and in searching for knowledge.

[38] Socrates allows for classes of objects that are of instrumental and intrinsic value in the *Republic* 357c ff.

the character of the form: they have a share in its beauty (211b3). They do not exhibit beauty perfectly, or in every respect and so on; but as beautiful instances of this kind, they nonetheless exhibit the character of the form.[39] If beautiful bodies and souls embody the supremely valuable character of the form, then they will be worth valuing for their own sakes too and not just for their instrumental role.[40] Indeed, if we view the beautiful bodies and souls solely as a means to the form—as defective and imperfect—then we are not really seeing the beauty of the form embodied in them and cannot, after all, further employ them 'for the sake of' the form. It is by being enraptured by the beauty around us—the beauty of individual bodies and souls—that we *also* come to appreciate beauty as such.[41]

Pointing out that there is nothing to exclude the possibility that the objects may also be treated as ends in themselves might meet part of Vlastos's problem, but it does nothing to address the further objection that they are not treated as whole persons, rather than as 'placeholders of predicates'. But that objection is explained in terms

---

[39] Cf. Williams (1998) 41–2, who argues that the lesser beautiful objects in the ascent are still beautiful, and that it is a crucial part of Socrates' account that they are so. If they were not beautiful, then we could not use them as part of an ascent to the beauty of the form.

[40] Cf. Irwin (1977) 169: 'The lower stages are a means to the higher (210e5–6, 211c1–3), but Plato does not suggest that they are only means. The lower beautifuls partake in the form, and embody it imperfectly; but Plato does not claim that they are imperfect because they are purely instrumental, but only because they are incomplete expressions of beauty.' See also Adams (1999) 154 on ways to construe a teleological relationship which do not require one to view the proximate end solely as a means. He argues that one can construe the relationship between a proximate end and a final end causally, where one end is causally conducive to another as a means, or alternatively, one may take it that the proximate end is 'an exemplification or instance of the ulterior end'. Insofar as the proximate end exemplifies the valuable thing, it is worth valuing also for its own sake. For an application of this sort of idea to the problem of the relationship of ends in Aristotle, see Richardson Lear (2004) 3 and 207. In the case of the *Symposium*, the point would be that insofar as the beautiful objects in the ascent are 'incomplete expressions of beauty' they are to be used 'like steps' towards knowledge of the form of beauty and will play an instrumental role. But insofar as they participate in the form of beauty they 'exemplify the ulterior end'—an end which is intrinsically valuable—and so are worth valuing also for their own sakes.

[41] Cf. Adams (1999) 194, who argues that love for a finite good is an integral part of love for god: 'If we do not care for the light on the leaves, for its own sake, the divine glory will not be visible to us in this experience'.

of the larger explanatory goals of this account and has, I hope, been met by the arguments above (Section 1). Further valuation of the beautiful objects in the ascent is suggested by the second feature noted above. The concern for the soul and the production of *logoi* in an ungrudging love of wisdom suggested that one's *erōs* for wisdom involved, at least at this stage, another sentiment towards the objects of one's reflective *erōs*: concern, or care. Indeed the two appear to be related. For we are told that when the DHM considers beauty of soul to be more valuable than that of the body he cares for another soul (210c1). Now this is not a feature of the account that Plato dwells on here. The focus is on the fact that this motivates the DHM to search for improving *logoi*, and so to turn to other bearers of beauty, as we have seen. But the presence of this sentiment should be sufficient to show that there is nothing in the account to suggest that directing one's *erōs* towards an understanding of beauty is incompatible with concern for others. Indeed, the fact that it is care for the beautiful soul that motivates the DHM to explore beauty more widely provides evidence to the contrary. The DHM may well experience all sorts of feelings towards the 'placeholders of predicates' other than an arousal of his reflective *erōs*, but they are not the focus of the ascent for the reasons explored above. The aim of the guided ascent will surely not be to prevent the DHM from having a life, but to encourage him to reflect upon that life, and to use his experiences of beauty in a particular way, that is productive of knowledge. That is all the ascent shows.[42]

3. CONCERN FOR OTHERS IN THE PHILOSOPHICAL LIFE

So far I have discussed both the motivation and the grounds for *erōs*. But Vlastos raised another issue which arises, in particular, from my reading of the end of the ascent. Vlastos wanted some indication that

---

[42] Compare a therapeutic context today. A therapist will encourage reflection upon one's lovers, family, and friends. But treating such persons as objects of intellectual curiosity does not prevent one from engaging with them in a variety of other ways.

'the ultimate purpose of the creative act [will] enrich the lives of others who are themselves worthy of love *for their own sake*'. In other words, there needs to be some indication that the DHM's progress does not terminate in the encounter with the form. This is where the idea that the DHM needs to propagate his virtue in another soul to achieve *eudaimonia* would satisfy. For if it could be shown that the philosopher continues to engage in such relationships at the final stage 'just when his mental life most merits transmission', as Price puts it, then, personal love would indeed be 'not supplanted' by the ultimate object of *erōs*, but 'glorifed'.[43] But I argued that there is a discontinuity with the DLM, and one that thwarts our ability to take this option.[44] There is little indication that the philosopher is producing virtue 'in another'. The focus, as Vlastos noted, is on the DHM's union with the form, the production of virtue in his own soul, and his relationship of *philia* with the gods. Whatever involve-

---

[43] Price (1989) 49–50, 53. It is difficult to see what would be involved in 'transmitting one's mental life to another' (Price 1989), and using that other as a recipient of thought (Rowe 1998*b*). Since we are all already pregnant with virtue, and need to elicit those resources in the ascent, how would it help another to transmit one's own virtue? Price, for example, talks of 'aspects of his life [which] are duplicated and developed within another's life', and of the beloved as a 'recipient of thought'. But if all human beings are pregnant with virtue (209a3), then they already have the resources for virtue within themselves, and it is difficult to see how such a notion is compatible with them receiving aspects of a life from another. The suggestion that the philosopher is passing on his mental life to a beloved boy in order to secure his vicarious immortality would need careful analysis to render it compatible with such a model. One might respond that the aspects of the philosopher's mental life that 'are duplicated and developed within another's life' are those aspects that refer to knowledge of how to proceed correctly in erotic matters, that is, knowledge of how to make the ascent. This is the knowledge that Socrates himself claims when he says that he knows nothing but 'erotic matters' (177d, 198d1). As the ascent shows, 'erotic matters' is nothing other than knowing how to proceed correctly (211b8) to the form of beauty. If one does respond in this way, then it is not, strictly speaking, virtue that is transmitted, but knowledge of how to become virtuous oneself. The role which Socrates ascribes to himself as someone who knows about 'erotic matters' is the role of the guide who leads the DHM to the delivery of his own virtue. He also says that he attempts to persuade others of this account of erotic progress (212b1–c1), an attempt which clearly shows a concern with the education of others, as Gill (1996) 389 notes. Since just such a relationship is described in the ascent, there is no need to invoke an absent beloved to respond to Vlastos. See further below.

[44] Compare 209c4–6 for the DLM with 212a3–5 for the DHM. Where the DLM was said 'to join with the other person in nurturing what has been born (συνεκτρέφει κοινῇ)', the DHM is said to nurture true virtue by or for himself (θρεψαμένῳ).

ment the philosopher may have had with others is absent from this final stage. There is no indication that personal love at this stage is 'glorified'.

There is an alternative way to allay some of Vlastos's concerns. If we turn to a passage which was introduced earlier in the account to describe the workings of *erōs* as a *daimōn* there may be another response to Vlastos. The passage explained that the power of a *daimōn* is

> that of interpreting and conveying things from men to gods *and from gods to men*—men's petitions and sacrifices, the god's commands and returns for sacrifices; being in the middle between both, it fills in the space between them, so that the whole is bound close together. It is through this that the whole expertise of the seer works its effects, and that of priests, and of those concerned with sacrifices, rites, spells, and the whole realm of the seer and of magic. *God does not mix with man*; through this it is that there takes place all intercourse and conversation of *gods with men*, whether awake or asleep; and the person who is wise about such things is a demonic man (202e3–203a5; my emphasis).

The 'rites' are here revealed as the rites of the ascent ($\tau\epsilon\lambda\epsilon\tau\acute{a}s$, 202e3–8, with the description of the ascent as $\tau\grave{a}$ $\tau\acute{\epsilon}\lambda\epsilon a$ $\kappa a\grave{\iota}$ $\grave{\epsilon}\pi o\pi\tau\iota\kappa\acute{a}$, 210a1). Eros' daimonic nature 'binds the whole together with itself' by bringing together the mortal world of particulars and the divine form in a godlike state of understanding, and by successfully communicating with the divine in a relationship of *philia*.[45] This relationship of *philia* is the culmination of the successful functioning of the *daimōn* Eros who, like all demonic characters, brings together men and gods. But notice that the function of a *daimōn*—and therefore also that of a demonic man—does not operate simply one way—from men to gods, but *back again*. What could this communication consist in? We have one example of a demonic person, Diotima 'honoured by Zeus'. Her work, at least here, has been to persuade Socrates, as Socrates wants to persuade others (212b5), of correct erotic practice. Socrates' intention is both educative and interpersonal, just like Diotima's role as a guide. Such types might also enjoy a more stable *philia* than the DLM because of the greater virtue they generate

---

[45] For Eros see 202e6–7: $\H{\omega}\sigma\tau\epsilon$ $\tau\grave{o}$ $\pi\hat{a}\nu$ $a\mathring{v}\tau\grave{o}$ $a\mathring{v}\tau\hat{\omega}$ $\sigma\upsilon\nu\delta\acute{\epsilon}\delta\epsilon\sigma\theta a\iota$; for the DHM see 210c4–5: $\mathring{\iota}\delta\epsilon\hat{\iota}\nu$ $\H{o}\tau\iota$ $\pi\hat{a}\nu$ $a\mathring{v}\tau\grave{o}$ $a\mathring{v}\tau\hat{\omega}$ $\sigma\upsilon\nu\gamma\epsilon\nu\acute{\epsilon}s$ $\grave{\epsilon}\sigma\tau\iota\nu$; for the form as divine, see 211e3.

(cf. 209c6). If one is concerned that this account of *erōs* does not envisage the possibility that the creative act might enrich the lives of other persons, then one had better take account of the care and devotion of the guide who leads the DHM to the fulfilment of his *erōs*. And this, I suggest, manifests *erōs* working back from gods to men.

This response to Vlastos draws on one of his own suggestions put forward as an attempt to mitigate the egoism he saw as inherent in Socratic eudaemonism.[46] Vlastos considers a proposed definition of piety in the *Euthyphro*. Euthyphro claims at 13d7 that piety is service to the gods, but is unable to answer what sort of service this would be. Socrates remarks that if this question had been answered correctly, the definition would have been complete. As Vlastos notes, this is only a hint, but he interprets that hint along the lines of the *Apology*, where Socrates describes his philosophical practice as a 'service to the god' (30a). He argues that piety, for Socrates, is 'doing on the god's behalf, in assistance to him, work the god wants done and would be doing himself if only he could'.[47] A general definition would then be something like: Piety is doing god's work to benefit human beings (work such as Socrates' philosophical service to his fellow men). Vlastos urges that this characterization of philosophical practice releases Socrates from the egocentricity he sees as inherent in Socratic eudaemonism, where happiness is understood as one's own personal happiness: 'To the spiritual toxins in eudaemonist motivation high religion here provides an antidote.'[48] The description of *erōs* as a communicator from men to gods and gods to men suggests another such an antidote. The gods themselves cannot provide services to men without the help of intermediaries (cf. 'God does not mix with man', 203a1–2). But they are able to communicate with mortals through the help of people like Diotima, those demonic beings whose function is to communicate both from men to gods, and back again from the gods *to men* (a2–3). For the one who has made the ascent, then, if he is to fulfil his demonic nature, he must perform this demonic work and descend back again from gods to men. He must, in short, help others to achieve what he has done (i.e. become a guide himself). To the egocentricity inherent

---

[46] Vlastos (1991a) 157–79.   [47] Vlastos (1991a) 175.
[48] Vlastos (1991a) 177.

in this account, the mediatory nature of *erōs* may provide the necessary antidote.[49]

But one might have the following objections to this reading as a
response to Vlastos. First, to what extent can one be said to guide
another ('communicate back from gods to men') for that other's own
sake? The work of guidance may require other-directedness, but there
is no logical connection between other-directedness and loving
someone for their own sake. One can imagine various kinds of
other-directed service (e.g. that of a waitress, or a teacher) which
do not involve loving another for their own sake. One might begin to
respond to such objections by claiming that the particular nature of
philosophical service will aim to benefit another insofar as the aim of
guidance will be the delivery of another person's virtue (that is, their
happiness). But this is still not enough to ensure that this benefit is
for that other's own sake. One would need to distinguish between the
intention of an action and its result and ensure that the other person
is an end in view for the sake of which the action is performed.[50] The
intention in this case may be service to the gods and fulfilling one's
demonic nature; this is other directed, but not necessarily caring for
another for that other's own sake. The result of that other-directed
behaviour is to bring out a person's virtue and, if we suppose that this
is for their sake (that they are an end in view), then we might be able
to say that the result of philosophical practice will be caring for
another for that other's own sake.

Second, in what sense does a person guide because of *erōs*? If it is
not in virtue of *erōs* that one performs such guidance then one
cannot give the account of *erōs* an altruistic colouring. It may be a
consequence of seeing the form that one wants to help others, but it
does not follow that it is part of the content of one's desire. One's
desire, after all, was to possess the good *for oneself* forever (206a7). If
one's desire is to possess the good for oneself forever, then caring for
others will not be a function of you as a desiring agent after the good.

---

[49] One might also compare here strategies used to explain the philosopher's return
to the Cave in the *Republic*. Kraut (2000) 730 argues that Plato's concern in the
Republic is 'with a certain pattern of interaction among the parts of a unified whole',
one that 'emphasises the importance of relations between citizens.' So here, I argue,
there is a comparable emphasis on establishing harmonious relations outside the
state of the agent ('. . . so that the whole is bound close together').

[50] Aristotle, *NE* 8.2, where he discusses a wine lover's efforts to benefit his wine, but
not for the wine's own sake. I thank Gabriel Richardson Lear for pointing this out.

One might object that my response claims only that it is a consequence of *erōs*, but not part of its proper function. If so, then we cannot conclude that the account of *erōs* involves care and concern for others. The description of *erōs* as having an intermediary nature does suggest that communicating back from gods to men is not just an incidental consequence of *erōs*, but part of *erōs*' proper nature. That is to say that *erōs* is fulfilled not only in moving away from particular things to the form, but also in moving back down towards particular mortal things again, and communicating back from the divine form. Much will depend here, of course, on how one interprets the nature of this divine communication from gods to men. If care and concern of the sort Diotima shows Socrates can be seen as an instance of this sort of demonic activity, then this, it seems, might not be just a result of *erōs*, but part of its proper nature. But the passage, in fact, just states that demonic activity of this sort is part of the power (*dunamis*) of *erōs* (202e2). This leaves the issue of whether the downward journey is a consequence, or a proper function, of a flourishing *erōs* somewhat open. The downward journey, so to speak, is not a point that Plato dwells on theoretically, but it is clearly one that he dwells on dramatically since Socrates and Diotima—exemplars of the best kind of *erōs*— are evidently very involved in the downward journey (cf. 212b1–c1).

But we should surely like to know why *erōs* moves in both directions, and just what relationship is supposed to hold between contemplation and providing guidance for others. One way to approach this question is to ask why the DHM should want to go back again from gods to men, if contemplation of the form is where his good and happiness reside. What would his aim be in performing such a task, and how would other persons relate to that aim? A plausible suggestion from an earlier part of the account is that human beings cannot engage in continuous contemplative activity. Unlike the divine, we are subject to continuous productive activity (207c5–208b5) and need, we may suppose, to find a way to keep realizing the good for ourselves. One way to do this might be to engage in the kind of philosophical practice that Socrates advocates at the end of his speech (212b5).[51] By guiding others to the contemplation of the divine form, one also practises those rites oneself and can, again, realize the good for oneself. Such practice will not be at odds with

---

[51] Cf. Lowenstam (1985) 94.

one's own happiness; it is a way in which we can continue to honour *nous*, given that we are the kind of beings that we are. It is a way of instantiating the value of the philosophical life in another—albeit less perfect—way. Compare the life of an academic today. Some might argue that teaching students is purely instrumental to research in the sense that it helps one to notice where the troublesome issues are, or that it is instrumental to research insofar as one needs to teach to secure a role at a university to pursue research. But one might take it that meeting with students is a way of manifesting the life of research. It may be less perfectly instantiated when compared to hours of 'pure research' in libraries and so on, but to the extent that it embodies the values of the intellect, it is worth pursuing for its own sake and contributes (non-instrumentally) to a happy scholarly life. If we suppose that philosophical practice—demonic guidance—requires going from gods to men and back again, we may by analogy think that this guidance is a way of manifesting the virtues of *nous*, albeit in a less perfect way. For beautiful bodies and souls arouse the production of *kaloi logoi* and allow one to realize the philosophical life for oneself. The philosophical good—wisdom—is *best* manifested in the encounter with the form, but it can still be realized with other, albeit less perfect, embodiments. Insofar as guiding other persons is a way of realizing this goal in one's life, it will be a manifestation of *nous* and insofar as it embodies noetic activity it provides one with a measure of *eudaimonia* and is to be valued for its own sake. It will also be for the sake of contemplation in the sense that such practices will also be conducive to the guide's (re)attainment of this end.[52]

Such views, one suspects, would need further development to satisfy Vlastos. But the text is not sufficiently determinate to do so,

---

[52] Socrates' own behaviour in the dialogue provides a telling illustration of how a philosopher might embody a valuation of *nous* in everyday life. At the start of the dialogue Socrates is presented as a man with a measure of *eudaimonia* (173d6). He leads Aristodemus to Agathon's symposium, but then urges him to go on alone, stops and contemplates. Although Socrates fails to attend the preliminary proceedings of this symposium, he is in time for the after-dinner conversation. This, we may suppose, is a feature of the occasion that manifests his valuation of the philosophical life (as opposed to the feast, or toasting Agathon's victory). This point does not commit me to the claim that Socrates has completed the ascent (see further below). It just requires the assumption that he values the philosophical life above all else as the happiest life, and that his life instantiates that valuation and in a way that accommodates morally virtuous actions, i.e. attending the symposium with friends to discuss virtue.

and this is to be expected. These arguments should be enough to show that the account is neither incompatible with, nor fails to accommodate, the kind of care and concern we would hope a flourishing individual to exhibit towards his peers, but not enough to meet Vlastos's Aristotelian standard. For Vlastos wanted evidence that 'the ultimate purpose of the creative act is to enrich the lives of others, who are themselves worthy of love for their own sake'. All I have tried to show is not that the purpose of the creative act is to enrich the lives of others (for one's own immortality, or otherwise), but that a consequence of that act is other-directed service, which may well involve caring for others for their own sake, and in a way that does not detract from one's own happiness. But, as I argued in Section 1, Vlastos's standard is inappropriate and there is no need to meet it anyway. The account tells us much about Socrates' thoughts on the nature and goals of human striving and this takes place within the context of a discussion of interpersonal relationships, as we have seen. But in an account of *erōs* one does not expect to be able to meet the criteria Vlastos set for this debate. There may be all sorts of other contexts in which individuals are valued for their own sakes (and I have tried to extrapolate one such context). This, however, is not the central concern of this text. The aim there is to show how philosophical *erōs* can lead to the fulfilment of the desire to possess the good *for oneself* forever, that is, to the kinds of things that are good for rational agents to pursue who are concerned with their own happiness. That fulfilment is precisely what the ascent shows. So Vlastos is right: Socrates does not offer us an account of altruistic love, but that, as I hope to have shown, is a misguided expectation. The flaw in this case is an interpretative one on our part, and not in Socrates' account of *erōs*.

Socrates' account may be revisionary, but it is still anchored in an account of interpersonal relationships and their role in a flourishing life. We have examined the *motivation* of the ascent and seen that although this is predominantly for the sake of the philosopher's own happiness, it involves care and concern for others at certain points. We have also examined the *grounds* of *erōs* and seen that, although the form is the ultimate source of value, insofar as individual bodies and souls embody the beauty of the form they may be valued for their own sakes, *and* for their role in a pursuit of the form. Further, although the *purpose* of the ascent and the focus on the philosopher's own state of happiness is appropriate to an account of *erōs*, I argued that the mediatory nature of *erōs* suggests engagement with others in the role of guide. Contemplation of the form may not require another person, but our natures may require us to keep realizing that activity in our lives and to communicate back from the divine form to the realm of human concerns. And if one is able to see the beauty of the divine form in the world around us more clearly, then that world will be worthy of *erōs* and will surely appear more beautiful as a result. One will also, one imagines, become a better lover (in an interpersonal sense) as a result. For if relationships with others are to play a role in the moral education of the young, as many of the previous speakers had held, then such relationships must be based on an understanding of those things that are genuinely valuable for human life. If lovers are to play such a role in a happy and flourishing life, then they must pursue and know those things that are truly beautiful and conducive to our happiness. This is the kind of seductive pull possessed by those who have put their own souls in order first.

6

'Nothing to do with Human Affairs?': Alcibiades' Response to Socrates

In the last chapter I explored an issue that has been seen to arise from Socrates' account, about the nature of the philosopher's engagement with others. At the end of Chapter 4 I raised a further query about the character of the philosophical life: To what extent is it a distinctively human life? Would Aristophanes' thwarted interjection at the end of Socrates' speech perhaps have been that the ascent to a divine state of wisdom is a hubristic overstepping of our mortal natures (compare his description of an *anabasis* at 190b8 with 211c1)? For in his speech an ascent to the divine led to punishment by the gods. Friendship with the gods resides in recognizing the limits of the human (193b3–4). These two issues are related. For if the godlike philosopher involves himself with other persons and not just the divine form, then we have good reason to suspect that he leads a characteristically human life in, at least, this respect. But since Socrates has taken *erōs* to new intellectual and theological heights, we may want to know more, like Aristophanes (212c5).[1] We are given little opportunity to reflect upon the relationship with the divine form of beauty and the gods, and no time for Aristophanes to air his point. 'Take me to Agathon', we hear a drunken voice bellow in the background. It is Alcibiades, who will provide the answer to this query in his speech about Socrates. Or so I shall argue in this chapter.

---

[1] Aristophanes may also be referring, of course, to Socrates' rebuttal of his claim that *erōs* pursues the *oikeion* (205d10f). But insofar as Socrates' response culminates in the claim that we pursue the happiness characteristic of the divine, these points are intimately connected.

Alcibiades arrives crowned with ivy and violets, drunk and supported by a train of flute girls. He appears as the very embodiment of the Dionysiac forces which, although appropriate to the traditional symposium, have been excluded from this evening's entertainment.[2] Alcibiades offers an encomium of Socrates, though it is also peppered with blame (222a8). Those who focus on Alcibiades' charge of hubris and his use of satyric images argue that his speech undermines that of Socrates by offering us a new and quite different truth about *erōs*, based on the experience of a particular individual who suffered as a consequence of the abstract and distant *erōs* of the philosopher.[3] Alcibiades is appropriately embodied as Dionysus because he is to reintroduce those elements of mortal life denigrated as 'mortal trash' by the distinctively other-worldly philosophical *erōs* depicted by Socrates. Read in this way, Plato leaves the reader with a disturbing vision of philosophical *erōs*, whereby one must choose between the pursuit of an abstract ideal and engagement in human affairs. But others have argued that philosophical *erōs* is positively celebrated in the final speech. The speech is designed to show Socrates as the embodiment of philosophical *erōs* outlined in his own speech, a reading which makes good sense of the praise, in particular.[4] Any interpretation ought to take account of the mixture of insights, by a man who says he will speak nothing but the truth (214e10–215a1, 216a2, 217b2–3, 219c2, 220e4), and of the presentation of those insights by a figure who embodies Dionysus and charges Socrates with hubris.[5] In this chapter, I argue that the mixture of abuse and praise for Socrates, most centrally seen in the description of him as a Satyr, the half-animal, half-divine, lecherous yet wise characters of Greek mythology, is designed to capture both the humanity and the divinity of the philosophical life. The speech of Alcibiades does not serve to undermine the previous account, rather, it is a 'satyric drama' that works dialectically in response to the

---

[2] Bacon (1959) 419; Nussbaum (1979) 162; Rosen (1968) 287.

[3] Gagarin (1977) 36–7; Nussbaum (1979) 131–72.

[4] Bury (1932) lx; Gagarin (1977) 22–37; Dover (1980) 164; Scott (2000*a*); Rowe (1998*a*) 206.

[5] Alcibiades downs eight κοτύλαι (214a1). His drunkenness is apparent in the language of the speech: he is repetitive, garrulous and over-demonstrative (see, for example, the different ways he addresses Socrates and Eryximachus at 213b3–4, and at 214b4–5 with Dickey (1996) 15, 116–17.

supposed objection that philosophical *erōs* has 'nothing to 'do with human affairs'.[6] The pursuit of immortal thoughts takes place very much within the context of a distinctively human character and life.

1. ALCIBIADES' SPEECH:
A SATYRIC DRAMA

Socrates himself characterizes Alcibiades' speech as a 'satyric or Silenic drama' (222d3–4). This clearly refers, at the very least, to the portrayal of Socrates as a satyric character, but satyric drama also means 'satyr play' and reading the speech with this in mind will allow us to appreciate the particular tone of the speech. The claim will not be that Alcibiades' speech is itself a satyric drama in any substantial sense, but that it exploits aspects of the genre of satyric drama, both in its characterization of Socrates, and in its tone. Establishing a case for this reading will lay out the necessary groundwork for the claim that the speech works closely together with that of Socrates, and in a way that does not undermine its central themes.

Although little is known with any certainty about the details of the satyr play, its introduction as the finale of the *tragikē didaskalia* was believed to have been a response to the fact that tragedies had 'nothing to do with Dionysus'.[7] The satyr play, with its cast of lewd and lusty attendants of Dionysus, was the most obviously Bacchic element.[8] Alcibiades' drunken entrance with a train of flute girls, a satyric topos,[9] can be taken to indicate the satyric tone of the speech. Since satyr plays formed the finale at the tragic competitions they often drew on the plot structure of the previous tragedies. Not only were thematic links common practice, but the language of the play often closely resembled that of tragedy, although for humorous purposes it was modified into a more contemporary idiom.[10] We

---

[6] In much the same way as a satyr play was a response to the fact that tragedies had 'nothing to do with Dionysus'.

[7] According to the peripatetic Chamaileon in his monograph on Thespis (fr. 38), and Zenobius 5.40, ed. Wehrl. See Sutton (1980) 163 and Seaford (1984) 12.

[8] Easterling (1997) 37.

[9] Sutton (1980) 128, 158, 161.

[10] Sutton (1980) 142, 161; Easterling (1997) 38.

know of at least twelve such satyr plays, six of which show thematic connections with the previous tragedies.[11] Since we only have one complete satyr play—Euripides' *Cyclops*—and roughly half of Sophocles' *Trackers* (*Ichneutai*), with no preceding tragedy cycle with which to compare either of them, the precise nature of those links remains speculative. But the evidence suggests the themes were revisited in a different spirit by means of a juxtaposition of the heroic and the comic, which generated a humorous incongruity.[12] The satyr play mixed together the *spoudaion* proper to tragedy and the *phaulon* proper to comedy.[13] Lissarrague writes about the satyr play as follows:

The recipe is as follows: take one myth, add satyrs, observe the result. The joke is one of incongruity, which generates a series of surprises... Tragedy poses fundamental questions about the relations between mortals and gods, or it reflects on such serious issues as sacrifice, war, marriage, or law. Satyric drama, by contrast, plays with culture first by distancing it and then reconstructing it through its antitypes, the satyrs. It does not seek to settle a controversy, nor bring man face to face with his fate or the gods. It plays in a different key, with the displacement, distortion and reversal of what constitutes the world and culture of men; it reintroduces distance and reinserts Dionysos in the center of the theater.[14]

The tragic themes were played out 'in a different key'.[15] If Alcibiades' speech is a satyric drama, then we should expect a revisitation of themes from Socrates' speech. The first task, then, is to establish that there is a relationship between the two speeches, and then to examine the nature of this revisitation. For the sake of clarity I will list the numerous points in the speech which directly mirror the portrayal of *erōs* in Socrates' speech.[16]

---

[11] Seaford (1984) 21–4.

[12] Sutton (1980) 160.

[13] On this description of tragedy and comedy, see Aristotle, *Poetics* (2, 1448^{a}2, 17–19; 5, 1148^{a}30–1149^{b}1–20). On the blending of tragedy and comedy in the satyr play, see Horace, *Ars Poetica* 220–50 with Sutton (1980) 123, 162, 193 and Clay (1983) 195.

[14] Lissarrague (1990) 236; cf. Easterling (1997) 41.

[15] Lissarrague (1990) 235 also writes that 'satyr plays were often a means to explore human culture through a fun house mirror'. This accounts for the predominance of satyric characters who appear in a variety of roles as workers or specialists of various sorts, for example, as musicians and pedagogues. See Easterling (1997) 41.

[16] Cf. Bury (1932) lx. Many of these parallels have also been noticed by Maximus of Tyre, *Philosophoumena* xviii 84 B (Hobein); Ficino, *Commentaire sur le Banquet de Platon*, ed. Marcel (Paris, 1956), 242 with Clay (1983) 201.

Description of Eros' nature (S)—Alcibiades' portrayal of Socrates (A)

(1: S) Eros as shoeless (ἀνυπόδητος, 203d1)

(1: A) Socrates as shoeless (ἀνυπόδητος, 220b6)

(2: S) '[Eros] is a schemer after the beautiful and the good' (ἐπίβουλός ἐστι τοῖς καλοῖς καὶ τοῖς ἀγαθοῖς, 203d4–5)

(2: A) 'Socrates is always in love with beautiful young men and is always around them' (Σωκράτης ἐρωτικῶς διάκειται τῶν καλῶν καὶ ἀεὶ περὶ τούτους ἐστί, 216d2–3)

(3: S) '[Eros] always weaving new plans' (ἀεί τινας πλέκων μηχανάς, 203d6)

(3: A) 'you've planned to get a place on the couch next to the most beautiful person' (διεμηχανήσω ὅπως παρὰ τῷ καλλίστῳ τῶν ἔνδον κατακείσῃ, 213c4–5)

(4: S) [Eros] is a lover of wisdom (φρονήσεως ἐπιθυμητής, 203d6)

(4: A) Socrates stood there all day thinking (ἐξ ἑωθινοῦ φροντίζων τι ἔστηκε, 220c7)

(5: S) Eros is a clever sorcerer, trickster, and sophist (δεινὸς γόης καὶ φαρμακεὺς καὶ σοφιστής, 203d8)

(5: A) Socrates' spellbinding *logoi* (κηλεῖ τοὺς ἀνθρώπους, κατέχει, ἐκπλήττει, 215c ff.)

(6: S) Eros is resourceful (πόριμος ... ὅταν εὐπορήσῃ, 203e2)

(6: A) Socrates is resourceful (εὐπόρως καὶ πιθανὸν λόγον ηὗρεν, 223a8)

(7: S) Eros as a *daimōn* (δαίμων μέγας, 202d13)

(7: A) Socrates as a demonic man (τούτῳ τῷ δαιμονίῳ, 219c1).

Highest Mysteries of *erōs* (S)—Alcibiades' portrayal of Socrates (A)

(1: S) The rites of Eros the δαίμων (τελετάς, 203a1)—The Mysteries of *erōs* (τὰ τέλεα καὶ ἐποπτικά, 210–12)

(1: A) Socrates' λόγοι reveal those who are in need of the gods and their mysteries (δηλοῖ τοὺς τῶν θεῶν τε καὶ τελετῶν δεομένους, 215c3–5)

(2: S) The amazing beauty of the form (θαυμαστὸν τὴν φύσιν καλόν, 210e4–5)

(2: A) The amazing and divine beauty inside Socrates (ἔδοξεν οὕτω θεῖα καὶ θαυμαστά, 216e6–217a1)

(3: S) The philosopher searches for educative λόγοι (210c1–4)

(3: A) Socrates' λόγοι are of 'the greatest importance for anyone who wants to become a truly good man' (222a1–6)

(4: S) The philosopher will 'relax this passionate love for one body, despising it and thinking it a small thing' (καταφρον ήσαντα, 210b5)

(4: A) Socrates does not care whether a person is beautiful or rich or famous (καταφρονεῖν, 216d–e, with καταφρονεῖν at 219c4).

These parallels confirm that in the second speech we are revisiting themes from the first, and that the Socrates of Alcibiades' speech is the embodiment of the philosophical *erōs* described in his own speech.[17] Socrates is the shoeless, needy lover who schemes after the good and beautiful things he lacks. His needy nature is also resourceful; he is always weaving new devices, and is a spellbinding magician with *logoi*. He reveals those who are in need of the mysteries of philosophy and possesses the inner beauty of one who knows how to become a truly good man.

This embodiment of philosophical *erōs* is reconstructed in Alcibiades' speech through the images of satyrs and Silenus, images that play out the philosopher's attributes 'in a different key'. The most obvious reconstruction of philosophical *erōs* is through the image of Silenus with which Alcibiades begins and ends his speech.

I declare that [Socrates] is most like those Silenuses that sit in the statuary shops, the ones the craftsmen make, with pipes or *auloi*, and when you open them up by taking them apart, they turn out to have statues of gods inside them. I declare too, that he is like the satyr Marsyas. Now that you are like them in your physical appearance, not even you, Socrates, I imagine, would dispute; but what you are going to hear next is how you resemble them in everything else too (215a6–b6).

The image of the Silenus statues to be 'opened up' by Alcibiades points to a contrast between an accessible appearance and a hidden inner nature. Alcibiades uses this image as part of his claim that nobody really knows Socrates (216c7–d1). It is the incongruity between how Socrates appears—as a lowly, comic character—and his

---

[17] Cf. Bury (1932) lx, Osborne (1994) 96–7, and Rowe (1998a) 206.

beautiful inner nature that generates a humorous collision between the comic and the serious so characteristic of the satyr play.[18]

Socrates' appearance is notoriously ugly (215a5). The satyrs are a fitting figuration of this ugliness, perhaps because they, too, were often portrayed as snub-nosed and with protruding eyes (as well as bearded and goatish).[19] Although Socrates' ugliness was a notoriously comic aspect of the philosopher, Alcibiades is not much interested in his physical appearance here. The contrast he forges between an appearance and a hidden nature is not primarily a contrast between Socrates' physical looks and an inner beauty; the interest lies in the way in which Socrates is like the satyrs 'in everything else' too (215b6). On the one hand, Socrates appears as a lusty satyr who lacks and schemes after the beauty he finds in others (213c, 216d, see also *Charm.* 154c, *Prt.* 309a, *Grg.* 481d). But on a deeper level things are very different. He contains within himself a wondrous and divine inner beauty (καὶ μοι ἔδοξεν οὕτω θεῖα καὶ χρυσᾶ εἶναι καὶ πάγκαλα καὶ θαυμαστά, 216e7–217a), described here in language which echoes the description of the form of beauty (θαυμαστὸν τὴν φύσιν καλόν, 210e, with τὸ θεῖον καλόν at 211e3). This lacking lover is also the very embodiment of the beauty he manifestly lacks on the outside. He is the man with outstanding *sōphrosunē* who disdains (καταφρονεῖν) the physical beauty of the irresistible Alcibiades (219c–d); a man with sufficient endurance to withstand extremes of alcohol and cold weather (220a1–5); a man whose courage on the battlefield at Potidea (219e6–220e7) and Delium (220e7–221c1) should have won him honours in the city had it not been for his disdain (καταφρονεῖν again) of such things (216e1–5 with 220e3–5). Just like the Silenus statues which open up to reveal images of the gods inside, if you open up this apparently *phaulos anēr* there is a *spoudaios anēr* within.

---

[18] On which, Sutton (1980) 162 and Lissarrague (1990) 236. The tension between the serious and the comic was often, but not always, due to the presence of the hero in the world of the satyrs, for example in Euripides' *Cyclops*. In Euripides' *Syleus*, this tension exists in one and the same individual, as it does in the case of Socrates; see Sutton (1980) 161. One should be wary of presuming that the satyric humour was generated primarily through the contrast between the hero and the satyrs, for satyrs themselves embodied an ambiguous position between the *phaulon* and the *spoudaion*.

[19] For satyric looks, see Sutton (1980) 135; on Socrates' satyr-like looks see Xen. *Symp.* 4.19.

The contrast between the *phaulon* and the *spoudaion* is also apparent in Alcibiades' description of Socrates' *logoi*. These *logoi*, too, are
like the Silenus statues which open up: their outer coating is like
'some mischief-making Satyr's skin' (221e3). He talks continually of
pack-asses and blacksmiths, cobblers and tanners, and is always being
ironic and playing with people (εἰρωνευόμενος δὲ καὶ παίζων,
216e4). Moreover, 'he is ignorant of everything and knows nothing'
(ἀγνοεῖ πάντα καὶ οὐδὲν οἶδεν, 216d3). On the one hand, Socrates'
logoi—like his persona—appear to some to be ridiculous, or comic
(221e2: φανεῖεν ἂν πάνυ γελοῖοι τὸ πρῶτον, 221e6–222a1: ὥστε
ἄπειρος καὶ ἀνόητος ἄνθρωπος πᾶς ἂν τῶν λόγων καταγελάσειεν;
see also 213c4). Socrates' *logoi* appear to be those of a *phaulos anēr*,
one who is completely ignorant and goes around exposing his own
need and the needs of others such as Alcibiades (216a4–6). Such *logoi*
expose deficiency in their listeners and make others feel ashamed for
neglecting the things of the greatest importance (216a5, b2). These
are lowly *logoi* inasmuch as they consist in discussion of lowly
characters (pack-asses and blacksmiths, cobblers and tanners), and
because they bring people down, and make himself and others
appear foolish (even his victorious host, as we have seen). But on
the other hand, these *logoi* are also resourceful and persuasive
(223a8). If one really listens, one will find them worthy of serious
attention:

If one were to see [the λόγοι] being opened up, and get inside them—then
first of all one will find that they are the only ones, of the things one hears,
that have intelligence within them; then that they are to the highest degree
divine, contain within them the greatest number of statues of virtue, and
have the greatest reach—or rather, that they extend to everything that it is
appropriate for the man who means to be a person of quality to consider
(222a1–6).

These very same *logoi* that cause ridicule should not dismissed as
foolish nonsense. They reveal 'all that is necessary for a good and
beautiful man to know' (222a5–6; see also 216a4, 217a1–2), perhaps
those very rites of *erōs* of which Socrates says he tries to persuade
others, as he himself has been persuaded by Diotima (212b1–7). This
same man who goes around talking of pack-asses and cobblers, and
claims that he is ignorant of everything—a *phaulos anēr* who is a

fitting subject for comedy and laughter—is also a *spoudaios anēr* and one who is worthy of serious attention. We may laugh, but we should always be aware of the serious and beautiful undertone.

It is not only the incongruity between an apparent baseness and an inner beauty that generates the characteristically satyric humour of this speech, but also the way in which this dual nature effects a confusing and deceptive role reversal. The incongruity between how Socrates appears (as a lover) and his hidden nature (which makes him an object of desire for others) generates a comic *mise en scène* as the beautiful young Alcibiades chases after the ugly, older Socrates. When his inner beauty is unmasked, Socrates transforms himself, like the artful trickster of the satyr play, from lacking lover into beautiful beloved. Alcibiades blames Socrates for this deception which he exposes so that others will not also be deceived (222b4–5).[20] Trickery and deception were prominent elements in many satyr plays. Trickster characters, such as Autolycus, Odysseus, Sisyphus, and Hermes—the most notorious mythological tricksters—all appeared in satyr plays. The portrayal of Socrates as a deceiver who transforms himself from lover into beloved can be seen as playing on this satyric topos.[21]

In a narrative break that illustrates the modification of serious themes characteristic of the satyr play, Alcibiades goes on to reveal the details of his attempted seduction of Socrates as if he were revealing the highest mysteries. Alcibiades mimics the transition between the lower and the higher mysteries from Socrates' speech with a break in his narrative between those aspects of his account that can be told to anyone (217e2–3), and those he can reveal only to the

---

[20] It is this confusion of traditional pederastic roles, I take it, which made Alcibiades suffer, and caused its admission to others, which he hopes will forestall any potential relationship between Agathon and Socrates (222d1).

[21] Sutton writes that 'the presence of this character type seems sufficiently predominant that he, if anybody, can be identified as the satyric hero'; cf. Sutton (1980) 169, 150. Another prominent character in satyr plays was the magician, who often appeared with magical objects such as musical instruments. See, for example, Aeschylus' *Circe*, and Sutton (1980) 151. When Alcibiades likens Socrates' skill with *logoi* to the flute-playing skills of Marsyas which bewitch and enchant their listeners, like the magical song of the Sirens (215b3–216c3), he can be seen as drawing on this satyric topos. Alcibiades is also showing that Socrates manifests Eros' nature as 'a clever magician and sorcerer' (203d).

initiated (218b3–4, compare with 209e5–210a3). Since Alcibiades
was implicated in the profanation of the Mysteries which, incidentally, was supposed to have taken place at a symposium, Plato gives
this moment of parody a particular poignancy.[22] It is not the Eleusinian Mysteries that Alcibiades is making fun of to his detriment
here, but those of erōs.

The details of Alcibiades' attempted seduction of Socrates play
with Socrates' aetiological myth about erōs. Penia was described as
scheming 'because of her lack' to have a child from the resourceful
Poros who lies asleep in the garden of Zeus (cf. ἐπιβουλεύουσα,
203b7). She lay down beside Poros and conceived Eros (cf.
κατακλίνεταί, 203c1). Here it is Alcibiades who schemes after Socrates (ἐπιβουλεύων, 217c8; ἐβούλετο, d1; ἐπιβουλεύσας, 2) as a way of
remedying his lack. He lies down beside the sleeping Socrates, as
Penia lay down with the slumbering Poros (κατακλινείς, 219b7).
Socrates' ample inner beauty reverses the traditional pattern of
seduction, and makes him an object of desire for others who lack
such beauty themselves (222b1–2). It is the beautiful and young
Alcibiades who ends up admiring (ἀγάμενον) this man's inner
beauty—his σωφροσύνη and courage (219d4–5). Socrates becomes
'more of a beloved himself instead of a lover' (222b2–3) and Alcibiades is left confused at having to pose as the lover of this ugly old
man, 'as if I were an ἐραστής, plotting to have his way with his
παιδικά' (217c7–8).

Alcibiades sets up a 'mock trial' where we are invited to judge
Socrates' apparent hubris.

This man so much got the better of me, looked down on me, laughed at my
beauty, treated it criminally—and it was just in that respect that I thought I
was something, gentlemen of the jury; for it is up to you to judge Socrates'
arrogance... What state of mind do you think I was in after that: on the one
hand thinking I'd been humiliated, on the other loving this man for his
nature, his self-control, his courage, because I'd come across a person with
the sort of wisdom and capacity for endurance I thought I'd never encounter
(219c–d).

---

[22] Cf. Nussbaum (1979) 132.

It is an ironic twist to this scene that the hubris often associated with sexual assault,[23] and attributed to the behaviour of the lusty satyr, is here the result of Socrates' *sōphrosunē* and sexual abstinence. This character trait was identified in popular Greek culture with the very opposite of hubris (cf. *Phdr.* 237e–8a). Judged by Alcibiades' perceptions of beauty, Socrates' rejection of his advances may well appear unfair. But Socrates asks Alcibiades to rethink his criteria for beauty, and adds that if he really sees in him an inner beauty of the kind he describes, then Alcibiades' outer beauty is not an appropriate bargaining chip (218e5–219a1). With his inner beauty as an object of desire, Socrates drives a much harder bargain. The humorous collision between the perception of Socrates' lowly outer appearance and the admirable qualities that arouse Alcibiades' desire, provides a good illustration of the strategy of revisiting serious themes in a different spirit. Socrates may appear to be a lowly, hubristic, character, but he embodies the sentiment of the correct lover in the ascent who disdains the beauty of the body and thinks it a small thing (210b5–6).[24] His rejection is not hubris, but ultimately unmasked as temperance and worthy of admiration (219d4–5).

The serio-comic manner in which Alcibiades depicts the philosopher's virtue is also apparent in his description of Socrates' courage at Delium. He recalls the army's retreat from Delium, when he was there as a cavalryman and Socrates was there as a hoplite (220e7–221c1). In the retreat, Socrates and Laches got away safely because of Socrates' composure and acute look-out skills. He stood his ground without fear and effectively dodged the enemy. So we are told from a man with insight into the event. But he appeared quite differently. The perceptive scouring of the battlefield for the enemy is described—with a direct quotation from Aristophanic comedy—as though Socrates were on the look-out for beautiful young men, as he goes 'swaggering and casting his eyes this way and that' (221b3–4 with *Clouds* 362). Again we are invited to perceive the virtues of this man, from a perspective where Socrates appears as lowly and base,

---

[23] See, for example, Lys. 1.2, Dem. 19. 209 with Fisher (1992) 104–11. See also Gagarin (1977) 25, who cites Thuc. 8.74.3, and Macdowell (1976) 17 for the association of *hubris* with lust. A satyr play of Sophocles carries the title *Hubris*; On this issue, see Gagarin (1977) 31 n. 39.

[24] Cf. Bury (1932) lx; Dover (1980) 164; Scott (2000a); Rowe (1998a) 205.

but is, in fact, virtuous: he may swagger around, but he is, nonetheless, a resourceful soldier.

Whilst on this campaign Socrates stood for many long hours in thought and again aroused the suspicion of his fellow soldiers (215a2, 221d2). We are invited to imagine him, in front of a group of uncomprehending soldiers, who came out to stare at him (220c6). Alcibiades invites us to perceive Socrates' contemplation, as they perceived it, as strange and out of place in this context. The description of Socrates contemplating, desirous of the wisdom that eluded him, recalls the description of Eros the eager seeker after wisdom ([Eros] φρονήσεως ἐπιθυμητής, 203d6–7; [Socrates] ἐξ ἑωθινοῦ φροντίζων τι ἔστηκε, 220c7). Socrates may appear odd, but he is engaged in the pursuit of wisdom. The soldiers further thought that Socrates was disdaining them (καταφρονεῖν again, 220c1) by walking barefoot across the ice, when they found it difficult to cross with shoes. But Socrates is not disdaining the *soldiers,* any more than he was disdaining Alcibiades. Socrates exhibits the barefoot, hardy nature of Eros ([Eros] ἀνυπόδητος, 203d1; [Socrates] ἀνυπόδητος, 220b6) and embodies the sentiment of the correct lover of his own speech who disdains the body (καταφρονεῖν) and thinks it a small thing (210b5). We may laugh at his eccentricity, or resent his apparently base disdain, but we should take a second look and catch his beauty: courage and temperance.

The serio-comic manner in which Alcibiades explores the virtues of the philosopher is characteristic of the way in which satyric dramas explored serious themes in a different, humorous, spirit.[25] We are invited to laugh at the man who wanders around in a state of ignorance talking of pack-asses and cobblers, the man who pursues the beauty of the young and yet causes confusion by rejecting their advances, the man who appears eccentric on campaign contemplating, and disdainful in his temperance, but this does not serve to undermine Socrates' character and life. Rather, it returns always to the philosopher's virtue. And this is what we might expect from the satyric genre. Satyric humour was not designed to lampoon its subjects, or simply to render the serious characters ridiculous, but

---

[25] Alcibiades' drunkenness is appropriate here. He speech combines sincerity (214e10–215a1, 216a2, 217b2–3, 219c2, 220e4) and comedy (215a).

to 'explore and translate into contemporary idiom the moral issues implicit in the [Homeric] prototype', in much the same way as Alcibiades does here.[26] Indeed notice that when Alcibiades revisits previous themes he explores these in a familiar context of social and civic life. We witness the philosophical character engaged in relationships, on campaign, and in conversation with others. This generates the humorous incongruity at various points, for when placed in this context the philosopher is much misunderstood.

It also has a point which the ample resonances between Alcibiades' description of Socrates and the highest mysteries invite us to explore. Socrates is honouring the rites of philosophical *erōs* and this practice takes place within a distinctively human life. Socrates does not disdain human affairs, but engages actively with them, albeit in his own way. This is what is misunderstood by people. Socrates wants a relationship with Alcibiades, but in a way that embodies his valuation of wisdom: he rejects his advances *and* pursues a different kind of relationship, just as the DHM disdains the body in favour of the soul (210b5). His disdain is not a hubristic rejection of human relationships, but a revision of their role and nature. It is the mark of one who is not a self-serving Pausanian lover, but an educator concerned with the possibility of Alcibiades' own development. Socrates wants to engage Alcibiades, as he puts it here, in a joint search for the good things he desires (219a5–b2). Alcibiades must become a subject of *erōs* himself, rather than an object of male attention and a passive recipient of the wisdom of others. The same theme emerges in other episodes. Socrates appears to be lost in reflection on campaign but he also engages in effective action on the battlefield. He seems to be disdaining the soldiers, but his courageous defence of his peers tells otherwise. Socrates is shown to embody a host of social and civic virtues: he is temperate, wise, courageous, and pious, if we suppose, as I have suggested, that philosophical practice is itself an act of piety and service to the gods (See Chapter 5, Section 3). Honouring the rites of philosophical *erōs*, it is suggested, does not require disdain for mortal life.

---

[26] Sutton (1980) 123 commenting on the *Cyclops*. In this play the humour does not ridicule the central theme of the *Odyssey* story: we still witness retribution for the violation of the laws of hospitality. See also Lissarrague (1990) 236.

Although Socrates' behaviour appears strange to his peers, the resonances between the two speeches invite us to go back and explain this behaviour. Once we do so we can understand what Alcibiades does not, that philosophical *erōs* is a revisionary approach to human affairs, but not a rejection of them as such. Whether or not Socrates has completed the ascent (the evidence suggests he has not), we can at least conclude that the pursuit of its divine heights does not require hubris (contra Aristophanes, perhaps). Nor does it require one to choose between the pursuit of an abstract ideal and a life of involvement in human affairs (contra Nussbaum). Socrates' revisionary behaviour informs a distinctively human life. That, I submit, is the point of 'translating the issues implicit in the prototype' into contemporary idiom.[27]

2. SATYRS AND PHILOSOPHERS

So far, then, I have argued that the satyric revisitation of themes from Socrates' speech does not undermine that account of philosophical *erōs*. Rather, it enriches our appreciation of philosophical *erōs* by showing how it informs a human life, and it does so by showing the philosopher engaged in the world of human affairs and interacting with others. This is often portrayed in a comic light, as we have seen,

[27] In order to use Alcibiades' speech to respond to the charge that once the ascent has been made the philosopher becomes 'godlike' and disengaged from the world, one would need evidence from Alcibiades' speech to suggest that Socrates has *completed* the ascent. The most suggestive claims are that Socrates contains a divine and wondrous inner beauty (described in language which echoes the description of the form (216e6–217a with 210e4), and that Socrates' *logoi* alone have *nous* and are most divine (222a1–3). But since Socrates says he knows nothing but 'erotic matters' (177d), and embodies the characteristics of *erōs* as a seeker after wisdom, as we have seen, it is difficult to suppose that he has achieved a godlike state of understanding. One way to interpret his wisdom, which is perfectly compatible with the description of *erōs*, is to see Socrates, not as knowing the form of beauty, but as knowing how to get there (that is, the practices outlined in the ascent). In this respect he embodies both the aporetic and the euporetic aspects of *erōs*. Making this distinction does weaken my claim here. Socrates can be used as a model of philosophical *erōs* but not as someone who has completed the ascent. But see Ch. 5, sect. 3 for an argument against the claim that the completion of the ascent requires disengagement.

generated in part by the way in which the philosopher's complex behaviour is misunderstood by others. In such descriptions, Plato seems to be allowing himself a comic treatment of Socrates—one perhaps, to rival Aristophanes, but which serves not to challenge the depiction of philosophical *erōs*, but to underline its distinctive nature. And this brings me to the reason why philosophical *erōs* warrants a satyric exploration: the serio-comic nature of the philosopher.[28] It is here that we see the philosopher as a complex mixture of the human and the divine.

On the one hand, Socrates is the *phaulos anēr* who is ugly, hardy, and barefoot, always exposing his own deficiencies and those of others (216a4–6), and desirous of the beauty and wisdom he lacks. On the other, he is a *spoudaios anēr*, the resourceful educator who knows all that is necessary to remedy those deficiencies (222a1–6) and to that extent he is beautiful and amazing (216e6). This ambiguous nature that mediates between a lowly ugliness and ignorance, and a divine beauty and wisdom makes the comparison with the satyrs most appropriate. As Seaford explains, 'the satyr is an ambiguous creature, cruder than man and yet somehow wiser, combining mischief with wisdom and animality with divinity.[29] The satyrs, half-human and half-animal in appearance, manifested a bestial nature, but, on the other hand, they had a privileged relationship with the divine which showed itself in the divine insights which Midas sought, for example, by catching a Silen in his garden.[30] Silenus, according to some stories, was, in fact, the pedagogue of Dionysus, as Socrates was to this 'Dionysus' character, Alcibiades.[31] The semi-divine Marsyas was associated with the wisdom and sexual abstinence which are central to Socrates' portrayal here (cf. 222a1–6, 219c–d).[32] The satyrs themselves were demonic beings and the

---

[28] On the serio-comic nature of Socrates, see Rowe (1998*a*) 214; Clay (1983) 189, 198.

[29] Seaford (1984) 6–7, Lissarrague (1990) 234.

[30] Hdt. 8. 158; cf. Seaford (1984) 7.

[31] Seaford (1984) 40.

[32] Zanker (1995) 38. Marsyas was also a creature of the wild whose flute-playing was both associated with ugliness and distortion, and sublime enchantment. Just as Socrates' 'auletic λόγοι' are both base and beautiful (215c1–5). On the ambiguity of both Marsyas and the *aulos*, see Wilson (1999) 72, 78, 85.

intimate companions of gods.[33] Since Socrates manifests a similarly ambiguous position in between the lowly and the divine, the satyrs are appropriate models for comparison (221d5). This mixture of the lowly and the divine, the *phaulon* and the *spoudaion*, in Socrates' nature makes it fitting that Alcibiades employs the very genre whose essence it is to blend together those two categories.

This serio-comic mixture is designed to embody insights into the nature of philosophical *erōs*. Socrates manifests the complex nature, inherited from Penia and Poros, of the lacking but resourceful Eros— that demonic being who mediates between ugliness and beauty, ignorance and wisdom, poverty and nobility, the human and the divine (201e–202c, 203d–204a). Eros is the offspring of the lowly character Penia, who came begging, uninvited, to the feast of the gods. As a lowly character, she is a fitting subject for comedy. But the divine Poros is a highbrow character who partakes of the happy life of the gods. As the offspring of this mixed parentage, Eros is placed between the lowly and the divine, the needy and the resourceful, *aporia* and *euporia*. Eros is aware of all that he lacks, and yet able to remedy those deficiencies (204b4–6), just as Socrates is aware of his deficiencies (216d3), and yet 'resourceful in finding something persuasive to say' (καὶ νῦν ὡς εὐπόρως καὶ πιθανὸν λόγον ηὗρεν, 223a9).[34]

To the extent that Socrates is a mixture of the *phaulos* and the *spoudaios* he is a fitting subject for both comedy and tragedy. One might resist the idea that the exposure of deficiency is comic, but it is a feature of many so-called elenctic dialogues, in particular. In the *Charmides*, for example, in response to the *aporia* about the nature of temperance, Socrates says that the inquiry has exposed as useless

---

[33] Seaford (1984) 32 cites the following: Silenus θεοῦ μὲν ἀφανεστέρος τὴν φύσιν, ἀνθρώπου δὲ κρείττων, ἐπεὶ καὶ ἀθάνατος ἦν (Theopomp. 115 *FGH* 75).

[34] Alcibiades explores both a character who engages in elenctic practice and advocates the awareness of lack, and *also* a creative, euporetic character. Thus I disagree with Vlastos (1991a) 33 that the Socrates of Alcibiades' speech is that of the elenctic dialogues exclusively (Cf. Brickhouse and Smith (1994) 105). This is a rather dubious category, but I take it that their point is that the Socrates of such dialogues does not propound the sort of positive doctrine we see in dialogues such as the *Phaedo* and the *Republic*. But this picture of Socrates is difficult to square with Alcibiades' description of Socrates as the man who knows all that is necessary for a good and beautiful man to know (222a5–6).

the definition which they presented earlier, and in so doing it has 'made fun' of the truth (ἀλλὰ τοσοῦτον κατεγέλασεν αὐτῆς, 175d–e). In response to the *aporia* about the definition of courage in the *Laches*, Socrates suggests that they search for the best possible teacher 'and if anyone laughs at us (εἰ δέ τις ἡμῶν καταγελάσεται) because we think it worth while to spend our time in school at our age, I think we should confront him with the following phrase, "Modesty is not a good mate for a needy man" ' (201a–b). In the *Lysis*, when the inquiry reaches *aporia*, Socrates says that 'we have made fools of ourselves' (καταγέλαστοι γεγόναμεν, 223a), since they have not been able to find out what a friend is when they are friends with each other. In the *Protagoras*, Socrates says that if the discussion had a voice it would mock them, and chide both Protagoras and Socrates for being ridiculous (ὥσπερ ἄνθρωπος κατηγορεῖν τε καὶ καταγελᾶν, 361a–b).[35] The characters involved in the inquiry are lowly characters—fitting for ridicule—because they do not know the things of the greatest importance. But philosophers are not just eccentric people who expose their deficiencies, and seem to need instruction beyond their years, but also men who are resourceful, and to that extent beautiful, good, and *spoudaioi*. Philosophers are those who are in between lack and possession, ignorance and wisdom, the *phaulon* and the *spoudaion*, the mortal and the divine. They are not too puffed up with pride to think themselves to be in possession of the goods of the gods, nor are they like the ignorant. They are very much aware of their human limitations, and yet resourceful in pursuit of a divine ideal. As such they warrant a genre that combines the comic and the tragic in its presentation of the humanity and the divinity of the philosophical life.

Perhaps this is the reason why the final words of the dialogue are devoted to an argument to convince Agathon and Aristophanes that the man with knowledge is able to write both tragedy and comedy (223d1–5). As many commentators have noted, a natural way to imagine the force of this argument is to suppose that it reflects Plato's view of the demanding requirements for a genuine *technē*, and in so doing it highlights the value of philosophy.[36] But there may be a

---

[35] Cf. *Tht.* 174d1, where the philosopher ἀπορῶν οὖν γελοῖος φαίνεται.

[36] See Kahn (1996) 109, who compares this argument to the one made more explicitly in the *Ion*. Cf. Bury (1932) and Rowe (1998a). Waterfield (1994), and Clay,

further reason that links this final argument more directly to the expressed subject of the dialogue. If *eros'* true nature is in between the lowly and the divine, and the *spoudaion* is a fitting subject for tragedy and the *phaulon* for comedy, then *one with knowledge of erōs*, in particular, must know how to combine the two.[37] And these two interlocutors are particularly appropriate here. For recall that Aristophanes emphasized the lowly nature of *erōs* and its needy nature. He highlighted the particularly *human* character of *erōs* and expressed concern that *erōs* stay in its proper (mortal) place and avoid a hubristic ascent to the divine (190c8). Agathon, by contrast, claimed that Eros was a great god and lovers in a divine state of abundance (195a5, 197a1). Socrates' account has explained that *erōs* is in between a state of lack and possession, the mortal and the divine. Since *erōs* has this nature, one who understands it must know that it is not just a deficient state fitting for Aristophanic portrayal, nor just an abundant state of communion with the divine, fitting for a priestess or tragedian to portray. The true nature of *erōs* is a needy, yet productive aspiration towards a divine state and is best captured by a combination of the low and the high, the mortal and the divine, the comic and the tragic. The answer to Aristophanes' thwarted interjection, then, is embedded in both the form and the content of Alcibiades' speech. Eros has a compound nature, straddled between the mortal and the divine. The gods will not punish those

(1983) further argue that this is Plato's way of highlighting his own skill in combining comedy and tragedy in this dialogue. Lesher (in correspondence) has argued that although there are comic and tragic elements in the dialogue as a whole, the deeper tragic–comic dynamic that underlines the dialogue is the following: 'The person who responds to the urge to know the highest truths will inevitably seem ridiculous to the average person (who lacks the capacity for genuine intellectual engagement), and risk both personal animosity and physical harm. Both in general, and in the specific case of Socrates, the philosopher is both a comic and a tragic figure.' My reading is compatible with these suggestions, though the specific sense of tragedy and comedy I outline here connects it specifically to *aporia* and *euporia*, and thereby links the final argument to the dialogue's central theme: *erōs*.

[37] Cf. Clay (1983). For the relationship between the σπουδαῖον and tragedy in the Platonic dialogues, see *Laws* 817c. In the *Republic* it is said that the same person cannot write both tragedy and comedy since this would contravene the 'one man one job' principle believed to promote unity (396–7). There is little danger in this text that this would fragment an individual; rather, it would be a proper expression of the complex nature we embody as lovers.

who are aware of, and yet try to transcend their mortal limitations, for this is what it is to be the distinctively human, desiring, beings that we are.

3. DEFENDING SOCRATES AS EDUCATOR

If Alcibiades' speech captures the true nature of philosophical *erōs*, we might be left wondering why it is delivered by a notoriously wayward associate of its stellar practitioner. The use of Alcibiades to praise Socrates, and the emphasis on his educational conversations cannot help but recall the charge that Socrates corrupted the youth.[38] The praise of Socrates can be seen as an extended version of that section of the defence speech which presents the services of the accused to the city.[39] The fact that such praise is delivered by Alcibiades provides a rich opportunity to address a remaining and pressing objection to my account: If Socrates was not a distant and uncaring companion, but engaged in human affairs, in part, as a concerned and resourceful educator, then what went wrong in this case? Within the larger context of the dialogue defending Socrates as educator is an important part of showing that philosophical *erōs* is beneficial and praiseworthy.

The inclusion of Alcibiades is particularly pertinent to the theme of the dialogue, and not just because of his association with Socrates. Alcibiades was notorious for his wayward *erōs*.[40] Plutarch reports that he carried a shield depicting a thunder-bearing Eros in place of the usual ancestral emblem (*Alc.* 16.1–2) and there are ample reports of his overbearing sexual appetites. In a dialogue concerned with the correct form *erōs* should take, the inclusion of Alcibiades must be of particular significance. These associations are recalled when

---

[38] See Bury (1932) lx, Robin (1933) x–xi, xcviii–ci, Dover (1980) 164, and Rowe (1998a) 206.

[39] This might explain why many of Socrates' civic virtues are highlighted (220d5–e2). Gribble (1999) 113, 116 provides evidence that the encomium is capable of supporting an ἀπολογία.

[40] Cf. παρανομία κατὰ τὸ σῶμα (Thuc. 15.4); περὶ ἔρωτας ὑβρίσματα (Plut. *Alc.* 16) with Wohl (1999) 366.

Alcibiades enters as the embodiment of drunken and lewd behaviour: he threatens violence (213d2), rejects Eryximachus' plea for justice (214c), and shows an overbearing attachment to Socrates (213d1–5). Alcibiades was also famed for his overbearing desire for honour.[41] This character trait is recalled in the dialogue when Alcibiades explains that it is his desire for honour from the crowd which draws him away from the path of philosophy (216b5). He fails to stay with Socrates for fear that he will grow old beside him and so he stops up his ears to reject the siren song of philosophical conversation (216a5–b1). Within the larger context of praise of Socrates as a great educator, the recollection of Alcibiades' wayward desires can be seen as playing a role in the exoneration of Socrates. In Socrates' own speech the central contrast between the desiring agents of the lower and higher mysteries is that between the love of honour and the love of wisdom; the misguided *erōs* of the former type is ultimately responsible for their failure to produce genuine virtue (cf. 208c3, 210a–212a). Given Alcibiades' own admissions here, it seems reasonable to assume that the love of honour is at least partly responsible for his failure to benefit from Socratic *erōs*. Alcibiades failed to evince the necessary commitment to the philosophical life because he was so enraptured by the values perpetuated by city, and embodied here by Agathon and his peers. Alcibiades' misguided *erōs* was not fostered by Socrates.

But we should still like to know why the relationship with Socrates failed. After all, Alcibiades was a particularly promising associate, a talented man of the city who was clearly attracted by what Socrates had to offer. Why did philosophical *erōs* fail to get a firm hold on Alcibiades? The ample resonances between the speech of Alcibiades and Socrates invite us to compare Alcibiades' description of his

---

[41] See Isoc. 16. 32–4, Xen. *Mem.* 1.2.12–14, Thuc. 5.43, 6.15, Plut. *Alc.* 2.1, 16. 3–4; Gribble (1999) 57. These characteristics of Alcibiades figured prominently in post-Peloponnesian war rhetoric. The desire for honour was cited by Thucydides as a reason for the disastrous Sicilian expedition that cost Athens the war (6.24); Alcibiades figures prominently in this explanation. According to Thucydides, Pericles' political heirs ignored his war strategy and acted κατὰ τὰς ἰδίας φιλοτιμίας καὶ ἴδια κέρδη 'as a result, many mistakes were made, but especially the Sicilian expedition' (2. 65. 7). It becomes increasingly clear that Thucydides has Alcibiades in mind. He later adds that a cause of war was φιλοτιμία· ἀρχὴ ἤδιὰ πλεονεξίαν καὶ φιλοτιμίαν (3. 82. 8). See further, Wohl (1999) 367.

interaction with Socrates with the account of philosophical *erōs* for some answers. Let us turn back to the detail. Alcibiades clearly perceives something valuable about Socrates and desires to reap the benefits of that beauty for himself (219d4–5). This recalls the behaviour of Socrates' associates at the start of the dialogue. His appearance of happiness and inner beauty confronts Alcibiades, Apollodorus, Aristodemus, and even Agathon, with something they lack themselves and desire to embody in their own lives. Alcibiades explains that the perception of Socrates' beauty makes him feel ashamed for neglecting the things of the greatest importance; in the presence of Socrates, he desires to improve himself (216a5). Socrates' associates find him (psychically) attractive and in associating with him they hope to reap the benefits of that beauty for themselves. In light of the account of philosophical *erōs*, we can now appreciate that these associates have made a promising start in their attachment to a beautiful soul. As the ascent showed, if we are to become beautiful ourselves and achieve the happiness we crave, we need to be drawn towards the right kind of beauty (cf. 210c1), and to use that attraction as an occasion for reflection upon the sorts of things that are responsible for the creation of beautiful souls. So what went wrong?

Since Alcibiades reveals the details of his attempted seduction of Socrates as if he were revealing the highest mysteries (cf. 218b3–4 with 209e5–210a3), perhaps this episode provides the answer. Alcibiades invites Socrates over so that he can reap the benefits of this man's company. He schemes after Socrates (ἐπιβουλεύων, 217c8; ἐβούλετο, d1; ἐπιβουλεύσας, d2) as a way of remedying his lack, and lies down beside the sleeping Socrates (κατακλινείς, 219b7). Such details, as we have seen, recall Socrates' aetiological myth about *erōs*. Penia was described as scheming 'because of her lack' to have a child from the resourceful Poros (ἐπιβουλεύουσα, 203b7); she lay down beside Poros and conceived Eros (κατακλίνεταί, 203c1). Now the story also explained that wisdom is one of the most beautiful things (204b2–3) and, we learn later, the proper object of *eros*' pursuit (212a3–6). Although this is evidently what Alcibiades desires from Socrates (it is his soul that is the basis for the attraction here, and not his body, 219d4–5), he fails to pursue that wisdom in the appropriate manner. Alcibiades chases *Socrates* instead and becomes the lover of this man, 'as if I were an ἐραστής, plotting to have his way with his παιδικά' (217c7–8). Alcibiades desires to exchange his physical charms for those of Socrates' soul. This is the opposite step to that of the correct lover of the ascent (here embodied by Socrates), who disdains the body in favour of the soul (210b5–6). On perceiving the beauty of soul one should use this as an occasion for exploring the basis of the beauty of soul (210c3–4). It is only if one engages in such reflection that one can come to understand the real nature of psychic beauty and so begin to embody that beauty in one's own life. If Alcibiades thinks that wisdom is the sort of thing that can be exchanged for the physical charms of his body then he has not understood what wisdom is, or how one should go about getting it.

Socrates' reaction here suggests that Alcibiades' profanation of the Mysteries of philosophy was to misidentify its real object.[42] His idolatrous attachment to Socrates prevents Alcibiades from making genuine progress towards wisdom and virtue. The transformative potential of *erōs* is thwarted by the manner of Alcibiades' engagement with Socrates, just as it is for the others. It is not only Alcibiades who attaches himself to Socrates and wants to 'do whatever Socrates told [him] to do' (217a1); Aristodemus, too, desires to 'do whatever Socrates commands' (174b1). Aristodemus follows him around 'as usual' (223d10) and fails to say a single word (at least any worthy of remembrance) at this symposium. Apollodorus repeats Socrates' conversations (174–5). And Agathon attempts to 'lay hold of' *Socrates'* wisdom (175d1, 219a1). Apollodorus, Agathon, and Alcibiades all make a similar mistake. The transformative benefits of an erotic relationship with Socrates are thwarted by their fixation upon Socrates as an individual and the repository of all that can make them happy.[43]

Socrates' rejection of such associations is not due to a lack of concern on his part, quite the contrary: he urges a relationship of shared aspiration towards happiness. Socrates wants to be an occa-

---

[42] Alcibiades' revelation of the Mysteries of philosophy brings to mind his involvement in the profanation of the Eleusinian Mysteries, the ominous event before the departure of the Sicilian expedition. Cf. Nussbaum (1979) 132 and O. Murray (1990a) 149–61. As Rowe (1998a) 206 argues, Plato's contribution to this post-war debate is that all might not have turned out as it did if only Alcibiades had not profaned the Mysteries of philosophy and become a lover of wisdom.

[43] I am here in agreement with Nussbaum (1986) 168.

sion for a *joint* search into the nature of beauty (219b1 for his response to Alcibiades, 174d3–4 for Aristodemus, 194–5, for the elenchus with Agathon). Socrates' point is that we need to reflect on our erotic attachments in a way that is conducive to the acquisition of good things and happiness. The beauty instantiated by others should urge us to realize our own. To see individual persons, like Socrates, as the repository of all that can make us happy is not only a heavy burden for them to carry, but it is also an abrogation of our own sense of freedom and the possibility of our own self-realization. Other persons can awaken you to a sense of possibility—as Socrates evidently does—but we should not be looking to other persons to make us complete, like Aristophanes' lovers. If the nature and manner of their pursuit of Socrates is responsible for the failure of Socrates' associates to be improved by him, then the mistake is ultimately exposed as a misunderstanding of the nature and role of interpersonal relationships in a flourishing life.

Now I do not intend to deny that Alcibiades' speech also shows us the difficulties of engaging in the type of challenging relationship offered by Socrates.[44] A partner who will readily confront one with deficiencies and continue to urge progress towards self-improvement will be hard work. Regular bouts of appraisal in the public sphere may well seem quite tempting. But happiness, Socrates urges, is not to be found that way. The goods that will bring us happiness are those of our own soul. None of Socrates associates seems particularly happy. Apollodorus says that he is wretched, though better off for knowing he is in such a state, and Alcibiades is groping in the dark— 'Take me to Agathon'—he bellows; the pun suggests he cannot find his way to the good. The awesome responsibility of self-creation is what Alcibaides, Apollodorus, and Agathon are awakened to in their perception of Socrates' beauty, but ultimately rejecting in their fixation upon him as an individual. Plato, too, is playing out this drama, as are those of us who spend out time interpreting Socrates. Plato seems fixated upon the figure of Socrates and he is presented to us, especially in this text, as an intensely desirable object of attraction. But, like Alcibiades and his peers, we never get quite enough from

---

[44] See Lear (1998) 148–67 on Alcibiades' struggle from a psychoanalytic perspective. I would like to thank Jethro Bennett for sharing his insights on this issue.

Socrates, or Plato. Perhaps 'the communicator disappears, makes himself serve only to help the other become'.[45] This is a seductive strategy and invites us to wonder whether, and in what sense, we will take the bait.

I have argued that Alcibiades' speech functions dialectically in the dialogue and answers the supposed objection that philosophical *erōs* has 'nothing to do with human affairs'. To the extent that we are persuaded by its answer, we will also be persuaded that this reading is a response both to (what I have taken to be) Aristophanes' concern about *erōs* overstepping the limits of the human and to those critics who have read the speech as a challenge to the preceding account of *erōs*. Philosophical *erōs* does not require a hubristic disdain of human affairs. One need not choose between the pursuit of divine wisdom and engagement with others. Rather, the choice is between a life in pursuit of wisdom and virtue, which informs a human life in a variety of beneficial ways, and a life in pursuit of honour. We know where Alcibiades' choice led him.

In reading Alcibiades' speech we have seen that although Alcibiades may not be willing to embark on the philosophical life, the speech nonetheless contains insights into its nature. This can be seen as another indication that the views presented by non-philosophers in this dialogue contribute towards an increased understanding of the topic. This is a theme I have tried to bring out with reference to earlier parts of the dialogue, too, and it is now time to turn back to those speeches and substantiate that claim.

[45] Kierkegaard, *Philosophical Fragments*.

7

Shadow Lovers:
The Symposiasts and Socrates

Having read Socrates' speech in its entirety, and met two objections to that account, we are now in a position to return to the relationship between Socrates and his predecessors, broached in the first chapter. In particular, we are now in a position to substantiate the claim that Socrates' speech is continuous with that of his predecessors and completes and resolves some of the issues raised previously. Now Socrates' account is clearly polemical in tone. For *if* we are persuaded that it is only in philosophical *erōs* that one can achieve the benefits previously claimed for *erōs*, then we must also be persuaded that there is something amiss in the previous accounts of the role of *erōs* in a flourishing life. There have already been indications that the Socrates character occupies a privileged place in the dialogue. As we have seen, the dialogue is framed by portraits of Socrates, and he is emphasized from the outset as occupying a special place in this rhetorical contest (172b1, 175e7–10). Most significant, as we have seen, is the extended critique before Socrates' own speech (198b1–199b5). If Socrates' account is continuous with those of his peers, then, it must be so in a way that accommodate these factors. In the first part of the chapter I show the various ways in which Socrates' account is continuous with the same themes as his predecessors, and resolves many of the puzzles that emerged from their speeches. In the second, I argue that the contrast between the symposiasts and Socrates exemplifies the contrast between different kinds of *erōs*, now familiar from the lower and higher mysteries of Socrates' speech. In this dialogue Plato not only explains why, but also shows that, it is only in philosophical *erōs* that one can be truly productive. Understanding the speeches in light of this contrast will also provide a further reason for thinking that the previous speeches are for the sake of our philosophical education, in much the same way as the account of the lower mysteries was presented as a propaideutic for Socrates' instruction into the higher. The philosophy of the *Symposium* is extended throughout the dialogue, and those of us who wish to read it philosophically will have good reason to consider the work as a whole.

1. SOCRATES' SPEECH:
CONTINUITY AND RESOLUTION

Let us review Socrates' speech in order to clarify how issues raised by the previous speakers are employed in that account. As we have seen, Socrates professes to 'speak the truth' and that is construed, at least in part, in terms of first explaining the character of *erōs* and then its effects (199cf–d.). Since Agathon had made an attempt at this sort of procedure, his account is a promising place to start an inquiry into *eros*' nature (199c, cf. 201e). As we have also seen, Agathon claimed that *eros*' nature is beautiful and that *erōs* pursues beauty (197b). On reflection, he also is shown to believe that *erōs* lacks what it desires (200e1–5). These opinions are inconsistent. For if *erōs* desires beauty, and lacks what it desires, then *erōs* cannot possess beauty. Either *erōs* does not, in fact, pursue beauty, or *erōs* lacks the beauty it desires. Both Agathon and Socrates preserve the view that *erōs* pursues beauty. This is a dominant view in all the speeches and, perhaps, one that was the subject of repeated elenchi between Socrates and Diotima (for which see 201e3–7, 206b5–6, 207a5–6). This leads to the preliminary conclusion that *eros*' nature is such that it lacks the beauty it pursues (202d1–3). This clarification of *eros*' relationship to beauty is extended throughout a large portion of Socrates' account and the resolution of the confusion between the status of lover and beloved that emerged from Agathon's speech aided the formulation of a viable account of *erōs*' nature (see esp. 204c6 with Chapter 1, Section 5).

Only when a viable definition of *erōs* is reached does Socrates proceed to build up his account and move on to the aims and activity of *erōs*. Socrates considers what follows from this proposed definition: If *eros'* nature is intermediate, then what use is *erōs* for human beings (204c6–7)? What does *erōs* aim to achieve in this deficient, yet resourceful, state (204d1–206a12)? The needy nature of *erōs* was a central feature of Aristophanes' account. Because *erōs* had a needy nature Aristophanes inferred that *erōs* was after the pursuit of the whole: the *oikeion*. Although Socrates does not engage Aristophanes in an elenchus, he explicitly refers to this view and uses it to argue towards a clarification of the aim of *erōs* (205d10–206a1). The claim that *erōs* pursues the *oikeion* as such is rejected when a further premiss is introduced: that we are happy to relinquish diseased limbs (e3–5). If we want only to possess *healthy* limbs (implicit), then there must be a connection between our desires and our good. Unless the *oikeion* and the *agathon* are the same (more on this later), we will not aim to replenish a lack of the *oikeion* as such, but the good (206a1). For it is by the possession of good things that we are made happy, and we all want *that* (205a1–7; *eudaimonia* was said to be the result of *erōs* correctly employed in almost all the speeches: 180b7, 188d8, 193d5, 194e6, 195a5, 205a1). Though it is true that *erōs* pursues what it lacks, Aristophanes had given the wrong account of what it is that we are lacking. Notice, too, that when this view is subjected to critical modification it is modified on the basis of a view he also holds, namely that *erōs* has a connection to *eudaimonia* (193d5).

So much for the aim of *erōs*, but what about his activity? Phaedrus and Agathon had claimed that good things (e.g. the virtues) arise from the love of beautiful things (178d1–2, 196e4–5), but their accounts left the relationship between *eros'* characteristic pursuit of beauty and this goal unclear. Socrates considers this next in the account (206b1 ff.). The desire for good things manifests itself in the pursuit of beauty (206b1), because it is in the pursuit of beauty that we can be productive of the good and beautiful things we value (206c1f–2.), as Phaedrus and Agathon had also held (178d1–4, 197b8–9). And we now have an answer to why the pursuit of beauty is typically creative rather than possessive. Desiring agents are not in the abundant state Agathon envisaged; we are needy creatures subject to flux and change who need productive work. Unlike the divine, human beings cannot possess things in any straightforward way (207d5–208b5). Production is the mortal approximation to a state of divine possession (208b5). So, *erōs* manifests itself in creativity as the mortal way in which we can possess good things. We pursue beauty because beauty arouses us to realize ourselves in certain ways and to make manifest whatever good we take to be central to our happiness. If the desired good end is honour, then desiring agents will pursue beautiful cities and souls in which they can realize themselves as honourable lawmakers, poets, educators, and craftsmen (209a1–e4), all activities cited in the previous accounts (182a7, 186d5, 197a–b). Phaedrus and Agathon were right that some desiring agents manifest this productive tendency in a love of honour (178c5, 197a3–6 with 208c5–e3), but wrong to think that this holds for all desiring agents. The love of honour characterizes those of the lesser mysteries, among whom are Admetus and Achilles and Patroklus (208d3), examples mentioned in Phaedrus' speech (179b5–7, e1–5).

Many speakers cited virtue as the proper outcome of *erōs* (179d1–2, 184d7, 185b5, 188d4–9, 196d4–e6), and *eudaimonia*, as we have seen (180b7, 188d8, 193d5, 194e6, 195a5, 205a1). But there was little, or no, consensus about the nature of the virtuous and happy life. For Phaedrus and Agathon there was some connection between honour and virtue (178c5, 197a3–6), but this was construed as the virtues of the battlefield by the former, and as poetic wisdom by the latter. For Pausanias, virtue had an intimate connection to some kind of wisdom (184d7–e1). In the lower and higher mysteries, Socrates clarified the relationship between virtue, honour, wisdom, and *eudaimonia*. Although all human beings are pregnant with 'wisdom and the rest of virtue' (209a3–4, a direct echo of Pausanias' turn of phrase, 184d7–e1), manifesting this in the pursuit of honour does not deliver the happiness we crave. Virtue must be a real end, and not procured for the sake of honour, for it to be the sort of good that will satisfy our desire for happiness. After all, one wants to be honoured for virtue (it is the good poets who are envied: 209d1–4). This is the real end of all desire. Honour is not a real end, but sought as a mark of 'immortal virtue'—for the cults and shrines established for one's virtue (209d6–e4). The activity of contemplating the beautiful is not procured for the sake of any further end. This is a final good, and the true end of human aspiration. Genuine virtue and happiness are to be found in the goods of the soul.

If such virtue is, in fact, the real end of the desire for good things and happiness, then we need an account of how this can be achieved. This is the method of the ascent to the form of beauty, described by Socrates in the higher mysteries of *erōs* (210a1–212a7). Pausanias had already suggested that there was a connection between virtue and wisdom (184d7–e1). This was borne out by his characterization of a proper relationship as one that fosters *wisdom* and virtue (184c5–d1), and is focused upon the soul and not the body (180d1, 183d8). Socrates' account employs both of these suggestions. To be able to produce genuine virtue is to know and love the cause of all beauty: Pausanias was right to claim that *erōs* can only achieve wisdom and virtue if it is focused on the soul and not the body (210c1–2). And we now have an explanation. The love of soul is important because it encourages one to turn to other bearers of beauty—those things that are responsible for the creation of beautiful souls—and so to continue searching into the nature of beauty (210c5–6). For if one is interested in the beauty of soul one will be interested in the kinds of things that are responsible for the creation of beautiful souls: laws, practices, and knowledge. This expansive encounter with different kinds of beauty encourages reflection upon the nature of beauty in a wide variety of cases. And if one is to produce something beautiful oneself (*kaloi logoi* about virtue, or genuine wisdom), then one must understand the cause of all beauty in the world: the form.

So, we now have an account of the nature of virtue and an account of a method that can lead to this end. If a relationship is to lead to the virtue they praise, it must be one that leads to the form. This is the *technē* mentioned by Eryximachus as required for the production of virtue (188d). Notice, too, how Socrates has revised the nature and role of an erotic relationship. A proper relationship will have no part of the slavish *erōs* discussed by Pausanias (183a1–2 with 210d2–4), nor will it share the element of exchange endorsed by him (184c4–5, and compare 175d). On Socrates' account, one does not exchange wisdom for physical beauty, but leads and turns another towards the appropriate beautiful media (cf. 210a6, 7, 210c7, 211c1, and the use of τετραμμένος, 210d4) in whose presence they can realize the resources of their own soul. Eros, as Socrates puts it, is a 'co-worker' with our nature (212b3).[1]

---

[1] One can see the notion of pregnancy here as an important part of forging a new educational mode. Cf. Burnyeat (1977), who argues that the notion of psychic pregnancy forges part of a contrast with sophistic models of education in

In the contemplation of the form of beauty a desiring agent will no longer see an individual as the ultimate source of value—so that he is ready 'to stop eating and drinking and just gaze at them and be with them' (211d5–e1), like Aristophanes' copulating lovers. But, as Aristophanes suggested, he will at last find a *paidika* in accordance with his *nous* (cf. 193c7–8): the form of beauty. This union issues in the creativity praised by Agathon (196d7–e2 with 212a4), but this time not for the sake of fame, as Phaedrus and Agathon claimed (197a3–6), but for its own sake. If what we want is a good whose possession delivers *eudaimonia* (205a1–3 with 180b7, 188d8, 193d5, 194e6, 195a5, 205a1), this is found, above all, in the life of contemplation (211d1–3 with 212a1–5). This is the best human life (211d1–3), and a godlike life, which issues in a friendship between gods and men, as Eryximachus had claimed (188c1–d1 with 212a6). The ascent to the divine form will not arouse the enmity of the divine, as Aristophanes' thwarted interjection would perhaps have questioned (212c5). For this is the fullest expression of our nature, and *erōs* is to be praised as the best 'co-worker' with human nature (212b5). Desiring the good and desiring the *oikeion* are, in fact, one and the same thing: human nature is, at best, an imitation of the divine. As Alcibiades' speech goes on to make plain, the attempt to imitate the divine best expresses a complex nature straddled between the lowly and the resourceful, the mortal and the divine, humanity and divinity. And this nature does not disdain his human side, or his fellow man. Alcibiades' speech works dialectically as a response to the supposed objection that philosophical *erōs* is hubristic and that it has 'nothing to do with human affairs'.

From the above we can see that Socrates' speech is continuous with many of the same themes as his predecessors, the most central of which are that *erōs* pursues beauty, and that this pursuit can lead to virtue and happiness.[2] It also employs many of the specific

---

the *Theaetetus*. One can see this borne out not only by the language of guidance in the ascent, but also by the use of αὐτόν at 210a8, which reads in Rowe's translation as follows: 'and then he realises for himself that the beauty…' Rowe (1998a)194, argues tentatively that αὐτόν serves 'to mark the difference between the "leader" and an ordinary teacher—the lover/pupil comes to see what is the case *"for himself"*' (emphasis in original). The DHM must realize things 'for himself' because he is developing his own soul.

[2] For Socrates' positive use of the previous speeches compare Grube (1935) 96, Markus (1971) 133–4, and Brentlinger (1970) 21 and Reeve (1992) 91. Although they all see the previous speeches as providing material for Socrates' more developed account, they do not

ideas expressed previously. Consider, for example, the following: that *erōs* desires what it lacks (191a5–6); that *erōs* is of beauty (197b8); that *erōs* for the soul is more valuable than *erōs* for the body (184a1); that good things arise from the love of beautiful things (197b8–9); that *erōs* is related to virtue (178c5–6, 179a8, 180b7–8, 188d5–6), the good (188d5), and happiness (180b7, 188d8); that *erōs* must be governed by knowledge (188d1–2; cf. 184d1–e1); that it has some relationship to *phronēsis* (182b7–c2, 184d1), *epistēmē* (187c4–5), *sophia* (196d5–6), and that *erōs* brings together the human and the divine (188d8–9). As we have seen, the speakers have different conceptions of what constitutes *eudaimonia* or wisdom, for example. It is partly because of such differing, and often inconsistent, accounts of virtue, or *erōs*' relationship to beauty and wisdom, that many of the previous views appear in a modified form. For example, Phaedrus was right that *erōs* aims at virtue, though wrong that the pursuit of virtue is the only, or even the best, way to achieve this. Pausanias was right that there is an intimate relationship between beauty and wisdom, though wrong about the slavish transmission of wisdom and virtue. Eryximachus, though right that expertise is essential to the proper activity of *erōs*, mistakenly identified this with the medical art, and music, prophecy, and astronomy. Aristophanes was right that *erōs* pursues what it lacks, but wrong that this is the *oikeion*. And Agathon was right that *erōs* has an intimate relationship to beauty, though wrong about the details of this relationship. But the point is that there is no sharp separation between the things said by the previous speakers—what they say about *erōs* in a muddled or incomplete form—and Socrates' account. Furthermore, many of the puzzles and inconsistencies have been clarified by Socrates' account and put on a more plausible rational foundation.[3]

explore which claims are so used, and how, in any detail. Some readers (e.g. Nussbaum 1986, Clay 1975, and Halperin 1985), view Aristophanes' speech, in particular, as somehow important for Socrates. Stokes (1986), as we have seen, integrates that of Agathon in some detail. Halperin, for example, argues that Plato has prepared the reader for Diotima's theory of *erōs* 'by embedding her premises symbolically in Aristophanes' myth' thus providing 'the non-philosophical reader with a basis in ordinary human experience for initiation into the mysteries of Platonic erotics' (1985: 169). It is unclear to me why Plato should make use of only two such speeches.

[3] Someone might object that the speakers have such different conceptions of what constitutes virtue or wisdom, for example, that it makes little sense to talk of continuity between the speeches. I thank Christopher Rowe for this objection. One

If it is the case that the speeches raise significant issues and questions in need of resolution for a philosophical account, then we have gone some way towards elucidating their role in the dialogue. The benefit of having puzzled our way into some of the central ideas and issues that an account of *erōs* needs to address is that we can better appreciate the resolutions of Socrates' account. In this respect, at least, there is a structural similarity between Plato's procedure here and Aristotle's endoxic method.[4] There are also differences. There is little indication that the previous views are employed because they are seen to be authoritative and so can ground the truthfulness of an account of *erōs*.[5] There is no explicit statement to the effect that a good theory of *erōs* must respect and preserve ordinary, or reputable, views about *erōs*, for example. Nor is Socrates' account littered with 'We all believe that P' statements that serve as authoritative grounds for his arguments.[6] Further, if it is only accidentally that the precious speakers 'hit upon the truth' (cf. 198d7–e6), their news cannot be employed because they are seen to be authori-

option here might be to reduce the continuity to verbal echoes, where this is neutral on the question of whether the speakers have the same beliefs. But I hesitate to drive a wedge between what one might term 'verbal continuity' and 'belief continuity' for the following reason. However revisionary the results of Socratic dialectic may turn out to be, Socrates and his interlocutors must mean something similar when they employ the concepts they use, otherwise how would any inquiry get off the ground at all. If Socrates is referring to something entirely different from, say, Agathon when he argues that *erōs* is not, in fact, in possession of the beauty it pursues, then how could he argue with Agathon about the nature of the *kalon*, or *erōs*? Socrates engages both forcefully and productively with this speaker, at least, in a way that suggests that they are both referring to the same phenomena, albeit with differing degrees of clarity. I thank C. D. C. Reeve for help in meeting this objection. There is also evidence from other dialogues that Plato considered the important thing to be what the speakers are referring to by the words they use, and not what is in the heads of individual speakers, or even what is determined by the meaning of their words (e.g. *Cratylus*). Insofar as the speakers are referring, albeit dimly, to the same thing, there is continuity between their beliefs. For further discussion of this issue, see Sheffield (2006).

[4] And note that we have reason to suppose that the things said by the speakers are not just things that struck Plato as possibly plausible things to say about *erōs*, but are views which are related, albeit loosely, to broad intellectual undercurrents operative in the fifth century. See Ch. 1, sect. 2, and below, Ch. 7, sect. 2.

[5] This would bring the status of the previous accounts closer to that of Aristotelian endoxa, On this role for endoxa in Aristotle, see Barnes (1980), Burnyeat (1986), Owen (1986), and Nussbaum (1986). I thank Ben Morison and Hendrik Lorenz for helpful discussion of this issue. For further discussion of this issue, see Sheffield (2006).

[6] Note, too, that within the dramatic framework of the account Socrates has already learnt his account from Diotima before he encountered the views of the symposiasts. But for a cautious reading of Diotima's presence in the dialogue, see Ch. 2, sect. 5. At any

tative. required for knowledge proper. But we need not suppose that they justify or ground the truthfulness of Socrates' account in order to appreciate their philosophical role. For by making us aware of where the difficulties lie, and the kinds of phenomena that a proper account needs to explain, the previous accounts nonetheless play a significant role in the development of a philosophical understanding of the topic. Our understanding emerges ultimately from engagement with issues and questions raised in all the speeches. This is surely what their inclusion in an account professing to 'speak the truth' makes plain. The shared wreath of wisdom given by Alcibiades to Socrates *and* the symposiasts' greatest representative is richly deserved (213e1–5).[7]

2. SHADOW LOVERS

Insofar as Socrates' speech completes and resolves those of his predecessors it can be seen as critical and agonistic, and in a way that vindicates philosophical reflection and reasoning as superior to other approaches.[8] But insofar as we can see ways in which Socrates' speech employs previous views we emphasize the cumulative and teleological character of the dialogue. Socrates and the symposiasts,

rate, my concern is with Plato's composition of the dialogue and why he constructs such continuity between the accounts. Socrates' visit to Diotima does nothing to underlie that fact, though it might well be relevant to an interpretation of how such continuity is to be explained.

[7] One might wonder what grounds Plato's confidence in the ability of non-philosophers to prompt readers to reflect in a constructive and useful way about the topic in hand. When Aristotle considers the opinions of his predecessors he defends this on the grounds that they are wise and have spent much time on these matters and so there must be something in what they say. Man, after all, is naturally inclined towards the truth (*Rhetoric* 1355o15). There are reasons to think that epistemological optimism is in play in the *Symposium*, too. All human beings, after all, are said to be pregnant with wisdom and virtue, albeit to varying degrees (206c1–3 with 209a3; see above for a discussion of this image). Perhaps the idea that the human soul is naturally inclined towards the truth, is enough to ensure that those who are intellectually inclined will tend in the right direction. For a discussion of intellectual pregnancy see Sheffield (2001*a*).

[8] Since the speeches reflect the broader intellectual currents flowing through 5th- and 4th-cent. thought—sophistic reasoning, poetry, medical science, and so on, we can see how this works well as an attempt to vindicate Plato's philosophical project. I thank Jim Lesher for putting this to me. For a discussion of the agonistic dimension to Plato's dialogues generally, see Nightingale (1995). It may also be worth noting in this connection that through these speeches we are offered a *tour de force* of the traditional wisdom of the various Greek Muses. Of the nine muses traditionally

after all, are aiming at the same thing, namely, an account of *erōs* as a great benefactor to mankind. But, much like the desiring agents of the lower mysteries, the symposiasts manifest this desire in the pursuit of honour—the appearance of wisdom that will generate the most applause—and so they engage in the kind of epideictic rhetorical display designed to manifest that desired end. This stands in contrast to Socrates' conception of this end: to speak the truth (199a7). This distinction embodies an important and now familiar distinction from Socrates' own account: between the desiring agents of the lower mysteries (DLM) and those of the higher (DHM). Exploring the parallels between the DLM and the symposiasts promises to enrich our understanding of their relationship to Socrates' speech.

Let us recall the basics. The DLM were quite a special group of people: lawmakers and poets and craftsmen—'so many as are said to be inventive' (209a5) and they are honoured as such by the *dēmos*. Many of the symposiasts celebrated *erōs* through these very practices, as we have seen.[9] The symposiasts make creative use of poetry (Phaedrus, Aristophanes, and Agathon, in particular), law (Pausan-

included in the list, Plato manages to cover at least six (for the Muses, see Hesiod, *Theogony* 75–9). Calliope was traditionally responsible for heroic poetry, the inspiration for Phaedrus' epic allusions, and for his praise of the traditional heroic virtues. Pausanias' knowledge of local Greek history relates his speech to historiography and hence to Clio. Urania inspired astronomical expertise, explicitly invoked by Eryximachus, along with Polyhymnia (187d7–e1). Thalia is associated with comedy, also invoked, though not by name, by Aristophanes (189b6–7), and Melpomene with tragedy, the muse of Agathon. Of these nine Muses, only Euterpe, responsible for the music of the flute, Erato, responsible for lyric poetry and hymns, and Terpsichore, responsible for lyre, lyric, and dance, are left out. But if we include the flute girl who enters with Alcibiades (212d7), and the lyric poetry drawn on by many of the symposiasts in their speeches (see below), then it appears that Plato has created a remarkably inclusive invocation of traditional Greek wisdom against which to pit his philosopher. I do not intend to suggest that Agathon's speech is actually a tragedy, any more than Pausanias' speech is actually a piece of historical writing, but rather that they exploit features which are the particular provenances of their respective muses, and in so doing serve as an inclusive backdrop for a contest with philosophy.

[9] Pausanias' speech praises the practices of Eros which are lawful (182a7), Eryximachus praises Eros as a fine craftsman (186d5), and Agathon praises his poetic practices (197a–b). See also Rowe (1998*a*) 190, who argues that the reference to the poets is meant as 'an ironic compliment to Aristophanes and Agathon', and the reference to the craftsmen is meant to recall Eryximachus who is indirectly 'compared to the great inventors of the past (δημιουργός, 'craftsman' used by him of the doctor in his praise of Eros at 186d5)'.

ias), and crafts (Eryximachus). Perhaps not all of them are as inventive as others: Phaedrus, for example, may not be a poet himself, but
his use of epic traditions and the way in which he weaves them into
his speech displays a degree of inventiveness. Other speakers are more
inventive in terms of the content of their speech: Aristophanes, for
example, creates a magical tale to account for the origin of the sexes.
But either in terms of the content or the style of their speeches, and to
varying degrees perhaps, they can all be classed as 'inventive', like the
DLM (209a5). They are, after all, the intellectual elite of the day,
gathered at this symposium to celebrate the recent achievements of
one of their members.

The symposiasts also share a broad conception of *eudaimonia* with
the DLM. The DLM privileged the soul over the body and were
concerned to use a love relationship to inculcate virtue (209c). The
symposiasts showed a predominant concern for *erōs* for the soul over
the body (endorsed most clearly by Pausanias), and they, too, displayed a concern for the educative dimension to a proper relationship and the importance of cultivating virtue, as we have seen. This
is, after all, a symposium of partners who enjoy the goods of the soul:
they have dismissed the flute girls, are drinking lightly, and are
enjoying the pleasures of conversation (176e4–10). Further, the symposiasts are gathered together to celebrate a life in pursuit of honour:
Agathon's victorious, theatrical, life. As we have seen, the pursuit of
this goal is responsible for the kinds of activities that these symposiasts engage in: both Agathon's theatrical exploits and the giving of
encomia are more concerned with receiving applause from the crowd
than they are with wisdom (cf. 198d7–e6; 194b6–7). The love of
honour characterized the life of the DLM who engaged in the kinds
of activities (law-making, poetry, and educative pederasty) productive of honour.

The parallels between the symposiasts and the DLM suggest that
the symposiasts are exemplifications of the DLM. The DLM, after all,
were expected to be familiar to Socrates in his role play with Diotima
(209e5); in other words, they are supposed to be familiar to Agathon
and his peers as types of characters that they would recognize. If so,
then we can appreciate the relationship between Socrates and his
peers in the dialogue in terms of the contrast between the DLM and
the DHM. As we have seen, neither the DLM nor the symposiasts

adopted a method that leads to knowledge. They immediately produce speeches about *erōs* and its relationship to virtue even though
they fail to understand some of the central concepts they employ in
those speeches. They set themselves up as educators before *seeking
out* such discourses, as Socrates does with Diotima.[10] As the elenchus
of Agathon demonstrated, they delivered their insights prematurely
and they are, consequently, underdeveloped. Both the DLM and the
symposiasts are right that *erōs* is of great benefit for the cultivation of
virtue, but they fail to understand how a love relationship should be
conducted so as to lead to that end. To bring genuine virtue to light
one must understand the nature of the *kalon*, and that is to know the
form. The love relationships they advocate will issue only in shadow
virtue. Just as the DLM failed to reach the true end of *erōs* because
they aimed at honour, so the symposiasts fail to reach the end of a
proper encomium—the truth—because they aim at honour. This
goal does not encourage the proper development of their insights
in a way that would lead to the production of something of genuine
value. This much was indicated earlier in the exchange between
Socrates and Agathon (194a5–d1). The previous speakers are ultimately exposed as shadow lovers, who produce accounts that reflect,
but do not fully instantiate, the beauty of a philosophical account, in
much the same way as the DLM produced an image of the virtue
possessed by the DHM. By presenting an account that resolves and
completes these of his predecessors, Socrates not only explains why,
but also *shows* that, it is only in philosophical creativity that one can
produce something of genuine value.

If the relationship between Socrates and his peers exhibits the
relationship between the lower and higher mysteries of *erōs*, then
there is a crucial implication. Their speeches, we may suppose, are
given 'for the sake of' Socrates' speech. For the account of the lower
mysteries was offered to Socrates *for the sake of* his understanding of

---

[10] There is a shift of emphasis in the higher mysteries to the DHM as the *educated*
party rather than as the *educator*, which was the role assumed by the DLM, who went
around in search of a beautiful boy to act as a recipient of his pregnancy (209b–c). The
activity of the DHM shows that one needs knowledge before one can deliver true virtue.
Since the DLM does not have knowledge, he does not have virtue (cf. 212a3–5),
in which case, we may infer, he has no business setting himself up as an educator of
anyone else. The shift in the ascent to the lover as the educated party can be seen as part
of the polemic with the DLM.

the higher (210a6–7). So, if the symposiasts are illustrative examples of the DLM, then we may also suppose that we will have been instructed by the previous speeches as a propaideutic for Socrates' speech. They are a necessary part of our philosophical education, just as hearing the account of the lower mysteries was for Socrates. Socrates did not describe a process where he went through numerous accounts of *erōs* in the way that we have done, but he does say that he visited Diotima on many occasions (201e3–7, 206b5–6, 207a5–6). Perhaps he went through the details of the lower mysteries in more detail, as we have been through the speeches in some detail. But the point is that the similarities between the symposiasts and the DLM, coupled with the fact that exposure to the latter is explicitly said to be for the sake of understanding the highest mysteries, strongly suggests that exposure to these speeches is necessary preparatory training for Socrates' speech. In other words, this confirms that they play an important role in coming to a philosophical understanding of *erōs*: they are designed as part of our philosophical education, just as they were for Socrates.[11]

This need not imply that the other speeches have *only* instrumental value, however. Clearly when judged by other criteria—their rhetorical prowess, for example—Socrates' speech may not come out best, but in relation to the philosophical standards Socrates sets in this dialogue they need not have only instrumental value either. Understanding the relationship between Socrates and his predecessors depends on how one construes the 'for the sake of' relationship in this case. The clearest example of such a relationship is that between the pursuit of beautiful particulars and the Form, which is said to be 'that for the sake of which all previous toils are for' (210e6).

---

[11] In the Eleusinian Mysteries, whose language Plato draws on here, one could only be initiated into the Higher Mysteries after having gone through the lesser mysteries. For ancient mystery cults generally, see Burkert (1987); for the Eleusinian Mysteries, in particular, see Mylonas (1961). For Plato's use of Mystery terminology, see Lloyd (1992) on the use of such terminology in the *Meno*. Lloyd argues that it is the obscurities of what Plato describes as the lesser mysteries that prompt the reader to make progress: 'it is the very obscurities that provide its point, namely that we stand in need of initiation' (181). This is compatible with my reading of the *Symposium* inasmuch as I have argued that the other speeches, although often insightful, raise difficulties and puzzles which prompt the sort of reflection both demonstrated and described in Socrates' speech.

Lesser beautiful objects are pursued for the sake of the form because the form is the ultimate source of their value. But other beautiful objects share in the character of the form (211b3–5) and to the extent that they participate in its nature they embody a quality worth valuing for its own sake. The ascent does not imply that other beautiful objects are not really beautiful; they are beautiful, albeit not in the same unqualified manner of the form. Indeed, if they were not beautiful, then they could not be part of an ascent to the most beautiful object. If beautiful bodies and souls partake of the beautiful character of the form, then they will be worthy of *erōs*. Similarly here, insofar as the previous accounts embody insights ('hit upon the truth') they partake of the beauty of a philosophical understanding. They do not do so perfectly, or completely, or in every respect. They are also defective, impartial, and muddled in some respects, as we have seen. But the point is that insofar as they are insightful and raise the right sorts ideas and issues, they are to be valued, and for their own sakes. They *also* point beyond themselves in the sense that they make apparent gaps and puzzles to be resolved in the next speech. Insofar as they perform that role they will aid our further understanding and are to be valued for their role in Socrates' account. But the salient point is that there is no sharp separation between what makes itself apparent to the previous speakers and Socrates' account. Socrates' speech is the ultimate source of their value—*for a philosophical understanding*—in the sense that this is what explains the insights in those speeches, which 'participate', so to speak, in its truth. But Socrates is able to develop and complete the previous accounts because they too embody insights into *erōs'* nature and goals. If this is the case, then we can see the philosophical portion of this text as extended throughout a much larger portion of the dialogue, in much the same way as beauty is extended throughout the world of its participants.

One might raise the following objections to this account. First, it might be objected that my reading assumes that a philosophical perspective is the only source of value from which the other speeches are to be measured. This is not so. A non-philosophical reading of the dialogue clearly requires no external source of value of the sort outlined above. They will set for themselves the standards of their own merit when judged by other criteria. Second, it might be objected that I am committed to taking Socrates' speech as functioning within the dialogue as a piece of knowledge, for it is only by doing so that I can make the comparison between Socrates and the DHM. This is difficult to square with his admission at the start of the dialogue that his wisdom is as debatable as a dream (175e4).[12] In the *Meno* this dreamlike state characterizes the state of true opinion, it is without an explanatory *logos* which would render it stable and secure (85c9–10 with 97e5–98a8). If Socrates is in a dreamlike state of true opinion then he will not yet be knowledgeable, and his speech cannot be seen as functioning within the dialogue as a piece of knowledge. In terms of the DHM's ascent, he would have to be located somewhere before the leap to the form, when knowledge proper takes place. But Socrates does say that he is an expert (*deinos*) on erotic matters (198d1), and that he knows about erotic matters (177d8). One way to combine the latter claims with the former would be to suppose that knowledge of erotic matters is knowing how *erōs* is best satisfied (in the method of the ascent). Claiming that one knows how to become virtuous is not the same as claiming that one has achieved this (i.e. that one has knowledge of the form of beauty).[13] This is, perhaps, the kind of substantive knowledge that he disclaims when Agathon attempts to 'lay hold' of some concrete bit of wisdom from Socrates (175d1). If Socrates does have such knowledge, then he will be able to deliver a speech which explains why philosophical activity is the best and most productive form of *erōs*. And he does not need knowledge of the form of beauty to deliver that. But nothing commits me to the claim that Socrates' speech is a full exposition of the truth, anyway. If we suppose just that Socrates' speech aims for, and pursues, this goal (199b3), we might agree that insofar as it does so it achieves greater clarity and explanatory force than the previous accounts. And that is enough to understand the sense in which the other speeches are for the sake of Socrates' speech—from a philosophical perspective, at least. They are part of an emerging (if not complete and perfected) understanding of the nature and goals of *erōs*.

---

[12] I thank Robert Wardy for putting this objection to me.

[13] Compare Socrates in the *Republic* who can provide an account of an ascent to the form of the good, but disclaims knowledge of the form of the good.

Viewing the symposiasts as exemplifications of the DLM also explains why Plato does not simply present some of the salient ideas, the problems generated by them, and then go on to offer the beacon of philosophical resolution. Plato was an author who appears to have been deeply concerned with the life and character of the philosopher and others, as Alcibiades' rich portrait of Socrates illustrates. The embodiment of the opinions in characters serves to remind us that these beliefs are components of lives. For what is at stake in this dialogue is the nature of human happiness and 'the life worth living' (211d1–3). By offering us speeches long enough to reveal the characters of those delivering them we are invited to reflect upon the way in which certain beliefs are expressed in certain types of speeches, characters, and ultimately, ways of life.[14] These are men who believe that honour is the central goal around which one's life should be organized. That goal is enacted in their self-presentation and rhetorical prowess. They are not just describing how one's desires should be moulded as part of a good life but embodying it by their discursive practices and this banquet of celebration.[15] We, the readers, are invited to consider what sort of person we may become by directing our *erōs* in these ways. Are we aroused by the legal pedantry of Pausanias, the pompous polymathy of Eryximachus, or the rhetorical brilliance of the youthful and confident Agathon? Is it the philosophical distinctions of Socrates that engage us and, if so, will we stay the (rather arduous) course? By presenting these speeches in such detail Plato shows us the sorts of productions and

---

[14] Cf. David O'Connor on Plato's use of character in the *Republic* (forthcoming); 'Plato characterizes fully human beings. First to the reader's sight are arguers and arguments, so the logical dimension of character becomes most immediately visible. But these men are not mere talking heads or disembodied minds. They have about them the smell of mortality, with their individual histories, personalities and commitments. It is not just a question of what arguments are made, but of what sort of man would make a particular argument, or accept it, or long for it.'

[15] The Greek for 'speaker' is a homonym for 'lover' and Socrates seems to play on this at 198d7 where it is unclear whether he is referring to himself as a speaker, or as a lover. This pun might be taken to suggest that the speeches are embodiments of a certain type of *erōs*. Just as Agathon shows himself as an honour-lover by the production of theatrical displays, so the symposiasts, by privileging rhetorical performance over the truth (198df.), will likewise be shown to desire the same goal. Their speeches embody an *erōs* for honour, just as Socrates' will embody an *erōs* for wisdom.

characters that are produced as a result of a certain kind of *erōs*. This is not just argued out theoretically, but presented dramatically in the dialogue at large. As Nehamas has recently argued:

Some philosophers want to find answers to general and important questions, including questions about ethics and the nature of the good life, without believing that their answers have much to do with the kind of person they themselves turn out to be. Others believe that general views, when organised in the right manner and adhered to in everyday life, create the sort of person—perhaps really good, perhaps simply unforgettable and, to that extent, admirable. In the case of pure theory, the only issue that matters is whether the answers to one's questions are or are not correct. In the case of a theory that affects lives, the truth of one's views are still an issue, but what also matters is the kind of person, the sort of self, one manages to construct as a result of accepting them.[16]

The distance between the narrative frame and the events depicted in the dialogue serves to remind us of the very lives that were constructed by the participants and just what is at stake in this discussion. Agathon and Aristophanes were at the height of their fame, Alcibiades fresh with ambition and confidence, and Socrates busy playing gadfly to the Athenians. But there is tragedy to come. Alcibiades introduces into the dialogue the very drunken sympotic disorder thought to have been responsible for the mutilation of the Herms, a dishonourable event in which Eryximachus and Pausanias were also implicated.[17] A love of honour had driven the disastrous Sicilian expedition and Athens had fallen. If such men were after good things and happiness, how many of them achieved it in their pursuit of honour? By the time Plato had written the dialogue we know that Socrates had also met a bad end. But we know, too, that he was not a lover of honour. His life did not revolve around the pursuit of fame in the theatre or on the battlefield, but was structured around an activity of the soul—the pursuit of wisdom. To the extent that Socrates engaged in such activity, he will have achieved a measure of *eudaimonia*. And if his *eudaimonia* resides in a certain activity of the soul in pursuit of wisdom and true virtue (as his speech has argued),

[16] Nehamas (1998) 2. Cf. Rosen (1968) xxi.
[17] Cf. Thuc. 6.28.1, Plut. *Alc.* 18.4, 19.1, Andocides, 1.34.61, with O. Murray (1990*b*) 152–3 and Wohl (1999).

then whether he was defamed, accused, and put to death, will not, one suspects, have affected his *eudaimonia* at all. Socrates' virtue has also stood the test of time and the *Symposium* itself continues to make that manifest. Apollodorus, Plato, and we the readers, are all continuing to make his life a vivid and enduring production. But Socrates' *eudaimonia* is not dependent upon such practice. If *eudaimonia* resides in a perfection of the soul, then the opinions of men and the vicissitudes of time can do little to affect that. We bear witness to the productive effects of Socrates' beauty, and continue to make his *eudaimonia* manifest, but this is not for his sake, but as a way of inspiring our own. We also bear witness to the productive effects of Plato's life. The dialogue itself is an inspiring and beautiful production. But again, since its author was a philosopher, one suspects that its attractions will be for our sake. Its beauty serves to inspire the very transformative effects towards which Plato urges us in the dialogue. It will be a telling feature of our own lives just where we believe the *kalon* best resides and how we respond to its call.

Conclusion

Let us go back to the question posed by Hephaestus at the start of this book. Imagine again the copulating lovers puzzled by Hephaestus' question: 'What is it that you human beings *really* want from each other?' Socrates, like those lovers, avoids sexual reductionism, and claims more from the intensity and eagerness with which we pursue the objects of our desire. 'We want to be happy and flourish as human beings' is the answer Socrates would give to Hephaestus. More specifically, what we want is to possess the good things that will make us happy, and we think that somehow our lovers play a role in the attainment of that end. Socrates has argued that total and sustained union with another person cannot alone lead to fulfilment. This does not mean that other persons cannot be treated as ends in themselves, as we have seen. It is just that they must also be seen as parts of a happy life, and, in a certain context, experienced together with other valuable things that are productive of good things and happiness. Other persons, Socrates might say, can be our guides and our muses, their beauty an occasion for us to be productive of our own, but they are not the sole repository of all that is valuable in life. Nor are they to be used as a substitute for the creation of a life for oneself. Instead of turning our gaze toward another, we need to experience value wherever it arises, and come to understand the source of that value so that we can create a valuable life for ourselves. For, human beings are needy creatures whose happiness is not a given state of the soul. We have been endowed with potential, and with *erōs*, whose task it is to respond to value and awaken a desire to realize that potential in ourselves. Various kinds of creative endeavour, from childbearing to philosophy, are ways in which we try to procure our good and in so doing to create a life we deem to be worth living. And that is what our lovers should be enabling. If lovers are to play a role in the attainment of that end, then they should themselves be clear about the relationship between our desires and their real end, and the value of different productive activities in achieving it. Their concern with our happiness must be grounded in an understanding of those things that are good for us to value and desire. Only so can they guide us towards the pursuit of genuine value and, ultimately, our happiness.

One might reject Socrates' claims that cultivating the goods of the soul is the best route to happiness, and that the form of beauty is the proper object of such a pursuit. But this is not to reject the account as such. Nor is it to suppose that Socrates has changed the subject. We might agree that our lives are better when our desires, sexual and otherwise, are placed within the larger context of a happy life, and evaluated on the basis of some conception we hold of where our happiness resides. And we might also agree that if our lovers are to play such a role in our lives, then their siren song had better lead to genuine goods and happiness. Part of Socrates' point is that if our lovers are to make a positive contribution to a happy life then they had better have some understanding of the sorts of things in which our well-being resides. This, at any rate, is what justified the kinds of relationships with which all the speakers at this symposium are concerned. If such relationships are to be effective, they must be informed by an understanding of the sorts of things that are good to value and desire, and which will lead to genuine happiness. That is why philosophers make the best lovers.

When seen within this context Socrates' account is revisionary, but it is not a rejection of the role of interpersonal love in our lives. Our lovers can awaken us to a sense of potential and promise in ourselves—in much the same way as Socrates did for Apollodorus and Alcibiades—but failing to cultivate that is an opportunity for genuine happiness missed. What Socrates might say to the copulating lovers, then, is that they have experienced an awakening of this possibility, and they should seize that sense and expand their horizons to reap the rewards. With their gaze fixed only on each other, that sense of possibility and excitement will soon dim and they won't find anything either *oikeion* or *agathon* after all.

Appendix
Socratic Psychology or Tripartition in the Symposium?

It is not altogether clear how the psychological theory of the *Symposium* should be seen in light of other Platonic dialogues such as the *Meno* and the *Republic*. Recent scholarship seems divided on the issue of whether and, if so, in what sense, the theory of *erōs* in the *Symposium* assumes, or is compatible with, (*a*) what is referred to as 'Socratic' psychology, that appears in the *Meno*, for example, or (*b*) the psychological theory of the *Republic*. The Socratic view is often characterized by the claim that all desires are rational desires, and the psychological theory of the *Republic* by the inclusion of non-rational motivation in the soul and its division into parts (leaving aside, for the moment, the issue of how those parts are conceived). Price, Irwin, and Rowe all agree that the *Symposium* contains what they refer to as the 'Socratic conception of desire', or 'Socratic psychology'.[1] Socrates claims that all *erōs* is for the good (205e7–206a1), and that happiness is the ultimate aim of all *erōs* (205a1–3). For Price, although Plato may not be

---

[1] Price (1997) 254–5: 'A remarkable aspect of the *Symposium* is its loyalty to the Socratic psychology of the *Lysis* ... It serves Socrates' present purpose, which is to say nothing against erotic desire, that he gives no hint of any divergence or conflict of the kind that serves in the *Republic* to distinguish rational and irrational desires ... We must take the background assumption to be Socratic: happiness is the ultimate goal of all desire, animal as well as human.' Irwin (1995) 303: 'The conversation between Socrates and Diotima in the *Symposium* begins with the sexual aspect of *erōs*, as desire for the beautiful (204d). But this description is soon supplemented or replaced by two others: *erōs* as desire for the good and for happiness (204e), and *erōs*, as the desire to 'give birth in beauty' (206b7). Plato uses '*erōs*' not in its usual restricted sense, but to refer to the generalized desire for the good from which more specific desires are to be derived (205a–d). In doing this, Plato implies that he can explain a more specific love of persons, and in particular a more specific love of beauty, by appeal to this more general desire ... the *Symposium* thus eliminates the common conception of *erōs* in favour of the Socratic conception of desire.' But Irwin adds later that '[the *Symposium*] neither endorses nor rejects the division of the soul, since he neither affirms nor denies psychological *eudaemonism*'. Rowe, C. J. 'The *Symposium* as a Socratic Dialogue' (2006) sees 'Socratic style psychology' as 'a central feature of the *Symposium*'. And he raises a puzzle. In the *Symposium* 'we find an allegedly "middle" dialogue that nevertheless contains at its core a psychology that (*a*) belongs to the "Socratic" dialogues (as normally so called) and (*b*) is actually and deliberately

actually committed to a Socratic theory of desire any more (his metaphysical commitments in the *Symposium* suggest distance from his Socratic heritage), it serves the purposes of eulogy that Socrates 'makes no distinction between good and bad love'.[2] All desire, on such a view of the *Symposium*, is rational in the sense that it is based on considerations about the good. There is no evidence of non-rational motivation of the sort that appears in the discussions of the *Republic*, and so some reason to take it that the soul is a unitary and exclusively rational entity. For Hobbs and Nehamas, however, the connection between Socrates' account of *erōs* and the tripartite theory of the soul in the *Republic* is a strong one. For Socrates divides different lovers into those concerned with physical production and those concerned with the production of fame and philosophy (esp. 208–12).[3] It is not quite

(in its pure form), *rejected* in other "middle" dialogues, notably the *Republic* and the *Phaedrus*. Socratic psychology on the one hand; Platonic forms on the other. How are we to explain the mix?'

[2] Price (1995) 9: 'By retaining a Socratic psychology Plato can combine what Socrates contrasts: Socrates will tell the truth as he sees it, but in Plato's eyes that will be a half truth too approving of love by half. It is striking that Socrates makes no distinction between good and bad love such as was drawn by Pausanias.... As we shall see, Socrates remains free of moral error in Plato, for his vision of love is blind to those aspects that are not proper objects of eulogy. A Socratic conception of love is an expression of innocence.'

[3] Hobbs (2000) 251: 'I believe that Diotima's speech assumes, if not precisely the tripartite psychology of the *Republic*, then at least something very close to it. Having claimed that personal immortality is impossible for humankind, she argues that humans can and do pursue three different kinds of substitute immortality; in ascending order of importance these are biological offspring, fame for noble deeds, and the creation of artistic, legislative, educative and philosophical works. Such aims undeniably overlap with those of appetite, *thumos*, and reason.' Nehamas (2004): 'The two lower kinds of lovers—those who reproduce themselves physically and those who are made famous by their accomplishments—correspond to the two parts of Plato's divided tripartite soul, which makes in that way a clear if indirect appearance in the *Symposium*. The lowest class are ruled by the soul's appetitive part. Plato does in fact say that they are "pregnant in body" and contrasts them with those pregnant in soul. But that does not make the body an independent entity with its own desires. All human desire is, as it also is in the *Phaedo*... ultimately due to the soul, but some of them occur only when the soul is embodied. These desires are clearly very common to every human being (which is another way of saying that Plato does not leave them behind). Others, though, are not as widely shared—better, they are not as strong in all as they are in some. One such class of desires emerges in the "lesser mysteries" of the *Symposium*. And Plato's emphasis on the love of honour (*philotimia*, 208c3), the desire for glory (*kleos*, 208c5, 209d3) and the craving for fame (*doxa*, 208d8) and memory (208d5, 209d3) makes the connection between this sort of *erōs* and the *thumoeides* part of the soul, which thirsts for *time* and *doxa* (cf. *Rep.* 580d–583a), unmistakeable.'

clear to me whether the position is that the *Symposium* is compatible with tripartition, or whether it is the stronger view that the text assumes it. Nehamas sometimes indicates the latter; for he uses the idea that the soul has parts to argue for an inclusivist reading of the philosopher's ascent.[4] In the following I offer no more than a few cautionary remarks designed to bring out the difficulties of deciding the issue one way or another.

There are at least three relevant claims that Socrates makes about the nature of *erōs*. First, Socrates claims that 'the whole of desire for good things and for happiness is the supreme and treacherous *erōs* to be found in everyone' (205d1–3; trans. Rowe). Second, he claims that everyone always desires to possess good things (205b1, 206a11–12 with 206b1).[5] And third, that 'there is nothing else that people desire except the good' (205e7–206a1). We need to consider the scope and implications of these claims. The second claim might be taken to mean only that at any given time it will be the case that everyone has a desire for the good, and not that this is the only desire that they have. But a stronger sense of the claim whereby it means that everyone always has a desire for the good and *only* for the good gains some force from the second claim that 'there is nothing else that people desire except the good' (205e7–206a1). If everyone always desires the good, and there are no desires other than those for the good, then this is very suggestive of a 'Socratic' psychological picture. All desires (at least those under consideration here) will be rational ones in the sense that they are all and only desires for what the agent perceives to be good (whether or not she is mistaken).[6]

The idea that all *erōs* springs from, or consists in, a belief as to what is good was highlighted in the earlier account of the nature of *erōs*. Eros is, by nature, 'a schemer after the beautiful and the good' (203d4). The nature of a

---

[4] 'And since each part of the soul, as we know from the *Republic*, has its own appropriate pleasure, so each part of the soul, the *Symposium* implies, has its own appropriate *erōs*, directed at objects whose beauty each different part of the soul appreciates. For that reason, just as the pleasures of the soul differ in immense degree but are still for all that pleasures, so every object of *erōs*, however humble in comparison to the beauty of the Form, is still beautiful and, however, dimly, reflects the Form's light.'

[5] Note that 'always' is applied both to the possessing of good things, and to the desiring of good things: it is said that we always *desire* the good, and that we desire [*to possess*] the good always (205a6–7: πάντας τἀγαθὰ βούλεσθαι αὑτοῖς εἶναι ἀεί, 'everyone wants to possess good things always'; 205b1: πάντες τῶν αὐτῶν ἐρῶσι καὶ ἀεί, 'everyone desires good things and always desires them.' At 206a9 ἀεί seems to qualify εἶναι with τὸ ἀγαθὸν as the subject of εἶναι indicating that everyone desires that the good 'always' belongs to them.

[6] On this characterization of what it is to have a rational desire, see Penner (1990) 49.

desiring agent is such that it is moved towards something characterized as *kalon* or *agathon* in some respect, and the object in question is desired under that description (201a8–10, b6–7, c4–5, 202d1–3, 203d4). Now, if it is the nature of all *erōs* to be based on, or to consist in, a belief as to what is good, then we must surely agree with Price, Irwin, and Rowe that this is strikingly similar to 'Socratic'-sounding claims made in other dialogues.[7]

Whether such a reading is enough to rule out the psychological theory of the *Republic* though, depends on how one interprets the details of that theory, and the scope of this one in the *Symposium*. According to a prevalent view, part of the novelty of the psychological theory of the *Republic* is that it introduces desires for simple, unqualified, objects such as for 'drink itself' (438a1–5, cf. 439a9–b1) which do not involve considerations about the good. It is the presence of such desires that pull 'like a beast' (439b4) away from the commands of reason, that forms part of Socrates' argument for the division of the soul in *Republic* 4.[8] If the Socrates of the *Symposium* is arguing that all desires are rational ones, then he is ruling out 'brute' desires of the *Republic*'s kind. All *erōs* (contra Pausanias) is 'heavenly' by nature and directed towards good things. This is not, of course, to say that we will not have to struggle against error as to the sorts of things that are such as to satisfy desire. But the struggle, if there is to be one, will be between our beliefs about what sorts of things are good and such as to satisfy *erōs*, and not one between desires. This explains why Socrates' account in the *Symposium* is heavy on the epistemology (e.g. 'the ascent').

Although this reading has some force, there are considerations that make it difficult to rule out a more complex psychological picture. First, the claim that there is nothing else that human beings desire except the good is not incompatible with the *Republic*. After all, Socrates claims there that 'This [the good] every soul pursues and does all its actions for its sake' (505d11). This need not (and, on the standard view, is not) taken to imply that every desire—even those of the lower parts—is for the good. In light of the considerations of Book 4, one might rather take it that even when an agent is driven by a lower desire, it is reason that decides which desire to follow on the basis on an overall judgement about the good of the agent. This kind of overall judgement is the particular provenance of the rational part, though

---

[7] Compare, for example, *Protagoras* 358c6–d2, *Meno* 78b1–2, *Gorgias* 468b1–2.

[8] See, for example, Kahn (1987) 85 and Irwin (1995) 209 and 214–15 on the grounds for dividing the rational and the appetitive part. Kahn argues that 'in order to establish the distinction between reason and appetite Plato must here define, for the first time, the notion of desire that is essentially *independent of* any judgement concerning what is good.' For a discussion of desires in the *Republic* see Lorenz (2004).

in this instance its role will be somewhat stunted (441e4, 442c5). In this way one can see that the good enters into *all* the soul's pursuits, *and* that the soul is dominated by a non-rational desire. This is not uncontroversial. But such a view accommodates the claim that we all desire the good and the possibility of non-rational motivations in the soul. Hence, if one argued that Socrates' claim in the *Symposium* is restricted in some such way, then it would be perfectly compatible with the psychological theory of the *Republic*. If the claim that 'there is nothing else that human beings desire except the good' is restricted to saying that when a human being desires it will employ the resources of the good-directed rational part, then one leaves room for the possibility of non-rational desires with no concern for the good. One might draw on the fact that it is *anthrōpoi* rather than *epithumiai* or some other desire term which is the subject of the relevant claim in the *Symposium* (205e7–206a1); it is not said that each and every *desire* is for the good.

The scope of Socrates' claims in the *Symposium* is not clear. Is Socrates referring to all desires when he claims that there is nothing else that people desire except the good? Or is he referring to a specific kind of desire (e.g. rational desire) which is always, and only, for the good? All that is, in fact, implied by the first claim that 'the whole of the desire for good things and for happiness' is *erōs* is that whenever one has a desire for good things, this is a case of *erōs*. This leaves it open whether one can also desire things that are not for the good (e.g. drink as such). The point is just that such desires will not count as cases of *erōs*. If that is the point, then this leaves room for the sort of non-rational motivation characteristic of the psychology in the *Republic*. In the claims highlighted above Socrates nowhere states that each and every desire (ἐπιθυμία) is for the good; he says only that *erōs* is for the good, and that the *epithumia* for good things is *erōs*. There is some terminological slippage in his account between different desire terms. Socrates does not stick to *erān* and cognate words exclusively when describing the operations of *erōs*. But that just shows that all *erōs* is a case of desire, and just because all *erōs* is a case of desire (for good things) that does not imply that all desire is a case of *erōs* and so after the good. Evidence of the latter claim, broader and stronger than the first, is needed to argue for a clearly 'Socratic' account and incompatibility with the *Republic*. And this we do not have.

Restricting the scope of *erōs* in this way makes good sense of the distinctive nature of *erōs*' characteristic activity. Recall that *erōs* involves pregnancies and beautiful media and so on (206b1–d5). Are we really to suppose that all desires, even those like hunger and thirst, express themselves in such a way? But it makes less sense, perhaps, of two further features of the account. First, Socrates ascribes *erōs* to animals in the *Symposium*. If he meant only to discuss rational desire, why did he include creatures explicitly excluded from *logismos* (207b6–c1)?⁹ Second, he includes sexual desire as a species of *erōs* for the good (205d6). If even our sexual desires are counted as cases of desire for the good, as well as non-rational animal behaviour, then why not include thirst, or any other *epithumia* one cares to consider? Such cases do not sound as if Socrates is talking exclusively about a certain kind of rational desire for the good. A natural response here is to say that even in such cases, those desires we share with animals (e.g. sexual ones) still involve the perception of some *kalon* or *agathon* feature of the object in question; they need not be construed as 'blind drives'. Such cases of *erōs* will not involve a rational grasp of the *kalon* (indeed most cases of *erōs* will not involve that), but there will be some cognitive grasp of the value of the object of pursuit in such cases if they are to count as cases of *erōs*. Some lower-grade cognitive endowment will be sufficient for animals to perceive a thing as *kalon* and to take steps to procure that desired thing. Socrates does not specify just what cognitive endowment animals do have, but some cognition, such as *doxa* perhaps, might inform their erotic experiences. In the *Timaeus* animals are said to have *doxa* (77a–c). If we broaden our conception of what counts as a rational desire in some such way, then one can accommodate such cases within a 'Socratic' picture.

But if we do so it would seem that we are also closing the gap with the *Republic*. For one might broaden the range of desires with a concern for the good in the *Republic* and so bring the two psychological theories together. One might argue (with Carone, for example) that even the lower parts of the soul in the *Republic* have a concern with what they take to be their own distinctive good.¹⁰ They will not exhibit this concern in the same way as reason: the rational part is the only part with a prioritized and inclusive conception of the good, whereby considerations about the value of the object ground the desire, and take into account the overall good of the agent.¹¹ But if it is the case that they can still, in some sense, be said to concern themselves with (what they take to be) the good, then even lower drives can be seen to exhibit certain characteristic features of 'Socratic' psychology. And if so, then the presence of those characteristics in the *Symposium* does little to decide the issue one way or the other. We need

---

⁹ For other passages where Plato excludes animals from *logismos*, or *logos*, cf. *Rep.* 441a–b, *Laws* 963e with Ch. 2, sect. 2.

¹⁰ For just such a reading see Carone (2001), who argues (against the standard view of the *Republic*) that even the desires of the lower parts aim for the good, albeit in some limited sense. In light of the parallel between city and soul she cites the perceived good of the oligarch and the democrat in Book 8: the good for the oligarch is wealth (562b3–4); the good for the democrat, freedom (562b9–10).

¹¹ On this see Cooper (1999*b*) 135.

more detailed information than we get in the *Symposium* about the nature and manner of the pursuit of the good in each case to drive a wedge between that account and the *Republic.*

I turn next to the arguments in favour of tripartite psychology in the *Symposium.* Those who argue in favour of tripartition in the *Symposium* do so because of Socrates' later division of different desiring agents. As we have seen, the desire for *eudaimonia* manifests itself in creative activity in the presence of beauty because this is the distinctively mortal way in which it can achieve a share of divine happiness. It is the account of the creative activities of different desiring agents as they strive to achieve this aim that is apparently suggestive of tripartition. It begins with the following distinctions. First, Socrates claims that there are some human begins who are pregnant in their body and some who are pregnant in their soul more than in their body (206c1–3 with 209a1–2). So, when human beings engage in the kind of productive activity required to achieve a share of *eudaimonia,* they do so in a way fitting to their nature (i.e. in accordance with whether they are more pregnant in body or soul). Those who are more pregnant in body produce physical offspring (208e3), whilst those more pregnant in soul produce psychic offspring of various kinds (e.g. poems, laws, or philosophical *logoi,* 209d1–210d5). Second, he divides his account of the productive activities of different desiring agents into the so-called lower and higher mysteries of *erōs.* This distinction is one based on differing conceptions of what will secure good things and happiness: those of the lower mysteries are honour lovers (208c3), and those of the higher mysteries are lovers of wisdom (210a–212a). Now, Hobbs and Nehamas take it that those who engage in productive activity of a physical nature manifest the tendencies of the appetitive part of the soul familiar from the *Republic.* Those who engage in productive activities of a psychic kind for the sake of honour manifest the drives of the *thumoeidēs.* And those who pursue wisdom manifest the drives of the *logistikon.* Such aims, argues Hobbs, 'undeniably overlap with those of appetite, *thumos,* and reason.' Nehamas agrees with this view: 'The two lower kinds of lovers—those who reproduce themselves physically and those who are made famous by their accomplishments—correspond to the two parts of Plato's divided tripartite soul, which makes in that way a clear if indirect appearance in the *Symposium.*'[12]

There are numerous difficulties with this view. It is questionable whether we can, in fact, determine three distinct aims of this sort in the *Symposium*'s account. For those who engage in productive activities of a physical kind are included amongst the *honour* lovers and make their appearance accordingly

---

[12] See above, n. 3.

in the lower mysteries of *erōs* which is characterized by this tendency. The love of honour is definitive of the lower mysteries and dealt with from its start (208c3) and continues until the start of the higher mysteries (209e4). Those who are pregnant in their body and turn towards women are mentioned at 208e1, the clear implication being that they are being considered as members of this group. One should not be surprised at the inclusion of those who are pregnant in their body and beget physical offspring amongst the honour lovers (209a2–3). In the *Laws* the desire to be remembered by one's descendants is cited as a reason for marriage and the production of offspring (721b–d; cf. *Rep.* 618b, for the fame which derives from one's ancestors). Also included in the lower mysteries as honour lovers are those who manifest the sorts of concerns more characteristic of the *Republic*'s *thumoeidēs*: those who desire fame by arranging cities and households and writing poems and laws and so on (209a1–e4).[13] So, it seems to be the case that the production of children and the production of poems and laws and such like are both being considered as different ways in which one can secure honour. If that is the case, then there is little evidence for separating out the 'body-lovers' as definitively appetitive in nature.

It is not as if Socrates could not have availed himself of a more *Republic*-style tripartite distinction at this point in his account. Earlier it was claimed that examples of the desire for good things and happiness range from the love of money-making and the love of sports to the love of wisdom (205d4–5). The love of money is characteristic of the appetitive part in the *Republic*, so why didn't Socrates employ that specification of aims to different desiring agents here, if he was concerned to demarcate three distinct aims and corresponding parts of the soul? Those associated with the body here are concerned not with the gratification of the appetites through the having and spending of money, but with 'immortality and memory' through the production of bodily offspring which they believe will provide them with '*eudaimonia* for all time to come' (208e4). Honour and wisdom, the two goals mentioned in the text, are presented as different ways in which the desiring agents in question conceive of a good central to their conception of a flourishing life. Even the 'body-lovers' exhibit a concern with '*eudaimonia* for all time to come' (208e4).

The picture that emerges, then, seems rather to be the following. All desiring agents seek good things and happiness (206a11–12). There are those who specify the good central to a flourishing life as honour (208c3), and those who believe wisdom to be central to a good and happy life

---

[13] Such types are also said to desire 'immortal virtue' (208d7), an 'immortal memory of their virtue' (d5–6), and *kleos* (208c5), all of which, I take it, are various ways of describing their definitive desire for honour (208c3).

(210a1–212a6). People try to secure this good for themselves by engaging in productive activities of various kinds, and these will be determined not just by a conception of the good in each case, but also by the tendencies predominant in their nature. Those more pregnant in body will try to secure fame through the production of children, providing for themselves 'immortality, memory and happiness, as they believe, for all time to come' (208e3–5). Those more pregnant in soul can secure either fame, or wisdom through the production of psychic offspring of various kinds. Socrates' account, in short, functions with two natural tendencies in human beings, those of a physical and those of a psychic kind (206c1–3 with 209a–6), and two specifications of a good central to *eudaimonia* in each case (honour and wisdom). So, although there are three productive activities mentioned: the production of children, poems and laws etc., and philosophical *logoi*/true virtue, these do not fit neatly into the three distinct aims characteristic of tripartition in the *Republic*.

This is a confusing picture for anyone who wants clear evidence of tripartition in the *Symposium*. But the fact that Socrates' account treats those with predominantly physical tendencies who produce children alongside those who try to secure fame through poetry and law-making, does not provide evidence against a tripartite psychological undercurrent either. It may be the case simply that Socrates has other distinctions he wishes to foreground in this context such as, for example, an epistemological distinction between those who are concerned with appearances and those who concern themselves with truth and reality. From this perspective both those with appetitive tendencies and those with *thumos* tendencies can be considered to belong to the same class, in a way that is perfectly compatible with other more complex psychological distinctions. In the *Republic* those who are dominated by one of the lower parts of the soul (e.g. money lovers, or honour lovers) are sometimes classed together in this way. In Book 9, for example, money lovers and honour lovers are treated alike as those who enslave their reason and are concerned with becoming, as opposed to being; they do not have knowledge of the truth (583b, 585b–587c). The point, I take it, is that those who indulge the lower parts of the soul share some similar traits—from an epistemological point of view. They are both those who fail to develop their reason properly and are concerned with appearances, rather than the truth. There are good reasons for thinking that the epistemological viewpoint is the operative contrast in the *Symposium*. This is borne out by the contrast made at the end of Socrates' account between productive activities grounded in the truth and productive activities grounded in images (212a4–6). A clear contrast between the desiring agents of the lower and higher mysteries is that the former fail to engage in the right kind of method that leads to the form, as we have seen. Consequently their productive activities produce only images of the virtue produced by the philosopher (212a4–6). This contrast is one grounded in different epistemological states, rather than in a psychological structure. But since the *Republic* provides evidence that this sort of contrast is compatible with other operative contrasts (e.g. the psychological divisions of Book 4), the presence of a twofold classification of desiring agents in the *Symposium* does not rule out tripartition. The operative epistemological distinctions may be simply a matter of emphasis, rather than indicative of specific psychological commitments. They do, however, dilute the strongest piece of evidence in favour of the tripartite undercurrent.

So far, then, although we cannot rule out the psychological divisions of the *Republic*, the evidence in favour of tripartition is weak. And even if it were the case that the aims of the desiring agents in the *Symposium* correspond to the aims of the three parts of the soul in the *Republic* that would still not be enough to show any more than compatibility with such a theory. Even if it were the case that we could determine three distinct kinds of motive operative in the account, this in itself does not get us to a division of the soul. The claim that there are three kinds of motive in human life is present in the *Apology* (29d7–e3), and the *Phaedo* also discusses three kinds of character (82c2–8). Neither of these texts function with a tripartite psychology. So even if we could determine three distinct kinds of motive and corresponding psychological tendencies, we would still need to establish that each individual has all of these psychological tendencies within him.[14] It could, of course, be the case that Socrates lays out the forms or kinds of motivation in the *Phaedo* and the *Symposium* which receive greater articulation and grounding in a tripartite psychological structure in the *Republic*. But that would be a different, and certainly weaker, claim.

I turn finally to considering the possibility of psychic conflict in the *Symposium*. As is well known, in the *Republic* Plato grounds different forms of motivation in the divided soul, in part, to account for cases of psychic conflict. Socrates assumes that if a desire for something conflicts with a simultaneous aversion to the same object, then the aversion belongs to a different soul part (440a5–6). Although we have no such principle in the *Symposium*, we can consider whether there is evidence of the sort of psychic conflict that plays a role in the division of the soul in the *Republic*, and perhaps consider this to be indirect evidence of such a veiw. Is there any evidence of conflict of a kind that can't be dealt with without supposing a

[14] On the specific claims that lead to tripartition in the *Republic*, see Lorenz (2004) 84 n. 3.

division of the soul? Of if there are cases of conflicting desires mentioned in the text can they be understood along 'Socratic' lines? Although there is no discussion of conflict of desires in the mainstream of Socrates' account, it might be thought that there is, in fact, rich evidence of psychological conflict provided by the case of Alcibiades. Perhaps, it could be argued, his confessional autobiography provides evidence of the very phenomenon that plays such a central role in the division of the soul in the *Republic*. If so, then perhaps we need to assume a divided soul, after all, in order to understand such conflict. Or, we might suppose just that Plato is signposting a problem that remains to be dealt with when he comes to deal with the nature of the soul in more detail.

Let us examine this case. When Alcibiades recounts the details of his interaction with Socrates he explains how, though he is moved by the power of his words and the goodness of the man himself, he fails to do what he advocates. Instead, he indulges a desire for honour (216a2–c3). He is both attracted to the path of Socratic wisdom and to the honour from the crowd. Here, again, we have the two familiar goals from the lower and higher mysteries, and now they appear to belong to one and the same individual. Let us examine the details. Alcibiades describes himself as follows:

What's more, even now I'm conscious that if I were prepared to listen to him, I wouldn't be able to resist, and the same things would happen to me. For he forces me to admit that although there's much that I lack myself, it's myself I neglect and do the Athenian's business. So I forcibly stop up my ears and I'm off, as if I were running away from the Sirens, to prevent my sitting there and growing old beside him. He's the only person in the world towards whom I have experienced what one wouldn't suppose I had in me—feeling ashamed towards someone, no matter who; it's only towards him that I feel it. For I'm conscious that I'm not capable of arguing against doing what he tells me to do, and that whenever I leave him, I'm giving in to my desire for the honour that comes from ordinary people. In any case I'm off and away from him like a runaway slave, and when I see him I'm ashamed because of what's been agreed between us. Often, I'd happily see him gone from this world; but then, if that were to happen, I'm well aware that my grief would be much greater, and so I just don't know what to do with this man (216a2–c3; trans. Rowe).

Alcibiades is evidently experiencing some kind of conflict. But exactly what sort of conflict is this? On the one hand Alcibiades wants to listen to Socrates and to change his ways, on the other he desires honour from the crowd. Alcibiades has both tendencies within himself, but it is evidently honour that wins out; for Alcibiades 'stops up his ears' and runs away from Socrates.

But when he comes into contact with Socrates he experiences shame at his actions. Now, notice that the conflict here does not seem to be one where Alcibiades experiences a desire for Socrates' wisdom and aversion for it at the same time. It seems rather to be the case that when he is in the presence of Socrates he is enamoured of his words and desires to improve himself, but *whenever he leaves him* he gives in to a desire to please the crowd. The desire for honour occurs at a later time, when he no longer experiences the desire to improve himself. So, there are two competing motivational tendencies here—for honour and wisdom—and they do reside within one and the same individual—Alcibiades—but they do not occur at the same time in relation to the same object. Alcibiades' conflict seems to be between a desire for one perceived good at one time (wisdom) and a desire for another perceived good at a later time (honour). This, then, does not provide evidence of the kind of psychological conflict that motivates the division of the soul in the *Republic*.

Alcibiades does not appear to be exhibiting the marks of *akrasia*. In Davidson's classic formulation: 'In doing x an agent acts incontinently if and only if (*a*) the agent does x intentionally; (*b*) the agent believes there is an alternative action y open to him; (*c*) the agent judges that, all things considered, it would be better to do y than x.'[15] It is the presence of this phenomenon that threatens the 'Socratic' claim that we all desire and act in light of some perceived good. But there is little evidence that Alcibiades judges that all things considered it would be better to stay with Socrates (the better course of action) and instead indulges a desire for honour (the worse course of action). Rather, when he is with Socrates he believes at this time that the best course of action is not to do the Athenian's business, but to improve his soul. But *whenever he leaves* Socrates he is persuaded—by the Athenians, presumably—that the life of honour is the best course of action and so he chooses a different course of action which appears to him, at that time, to be the better one. We do not witness in this case a man who chooses the worse option when *at the same time* he is persuaded of the fact that it is the worse option. This is borne out further by the fact that it is only when he sees Socrates that he feels shame, the implication being that when he gives in to his desire for honour he is not feeling shame, and so there is no conflict at this time. Contrast the classic case of Leontius in the *Republic*. Leontius sees some corpses and 'he had a desire to look at them but at the same time he was revolted and turned away' (439e–440a). It is this simultaneous desire for and aversion to the same object that motivates the division of the soul in the *Republic*. And the case of Alcibiades provides no evidence of that.

[15] Davidson (1980) 21–2.

Behaviour of this kind need not be explained in terms of psychological divisions, then, but in epistemological terms familiar from the so-called 'Socratic' dialogues. Alcibiades exhibits what one might term 'weakness of belief'.[16] Although he is persuaded by Socrates, his beliefs do not remain long enough to motivate consistent action over time. Without the secure grounding of knowledge one will lead an unstable existence and be subject to the whims of appearances and the clamour of the crowd.

None of the passages considered, then, assume, or require, a division of the soul, and the evidence in favour of this psychological thesis is weak. Although the evidence for the 'Socratic' picture is stronger, there is no evidence to rule out tripartition either. The picture that emerges from the *Symposium* is underdetermined in many ways. It may be the case simply that Socratic desire is the only item on the evening's agenda, and not that it is the only item on the cards.[17]

---

[16] I borrow the phrase from a paper delivered by Myles Burnyeat at Bristol (2000).

[17] Cf. Kahn (1996) 264: 'In dialogues before the *Republic* Plato offers no general account of moral psychology. On the contrary, his discussion of desire is systematically *limited* to rational desire for the good, since that is the fundamental thought underlying the Socratic paradox.'

References

ADAMS, R. (1999), *Finite and Infinite Goods: A Framework for Ethics* (Oxford).

ALLEN, R. E. (1970), *Plato's Euthyphro and the Earlier Theory of Forms* (London).

ANNAS, J. (1982), 'Plato's Myths of Judgment', *Phronesis*, 27: 119–39.

—— (1999), *Platonic Ethics Old and New* (Ithaca, NY, and London).

—— and ROWE, C. J. (2002), *New Perspectives on Plato, Modern and Ancient* (Washington: Center for Hellenic Studies Colloquia).

ARCHER HIND, R. D. (1894), *A Commentary on Plato's Phaedo* (Cambridge).

ARMSTRONG, J. (2004), 'After the Ascent: Plato on Becoming like God', *Oxford Studies in Ancient Philosophy*, 26 (Summer).

ASMIS, E. (1992), 'Plato on Poetic Creativity', in Kraut (1992) 338–65.

BACON, H. (1959), 'Socrates Crowned', *Virginia Quarterly Review*, 35: 415–30.

BALME, D. M. (1987), 'Teleology and Necessity', in Gotthelf and Lennox (1987) 275–87.

BARNES, J. (1981), 'Aristotle and the Methods of Ethics', *Rev. Int. Phil.*, 34: 490–511.

—— (1984) (ed.), *The Complete Works of Aristotle: The Revised Oxford Translation.* (2 vols.; Princeton).

BENSON, H. (1990), 'The Priority of Definition and the Socratic Elenchus', *Oxford Studies in Ancient Philosophy*, 8: 19–65.

BLONDELL, R. (2002), *The Play of Character in Plato's Dialogues* (Cambridge).

BLUCK, R. S. (1964), *Plato's Meno* (Cambridge).

BOARDMAN, J. (1990), '*Symposion* Furniture', in O. Murray (1990*a*) 122–35.

BOLTON, R. (1993), 'Aristotle's Account of the Socratic Elenchus', *Oxford Studies in Ancient Philosophy*, 11: 121–52.

BOWIE, A. M. (1997), 'Thinking with Drinking: Wine and the Symposium in Aristophanes', *Journal of Hellenic Studies*, 107: 1–21.

BREMMER, J. M. (1990), 'Adolescents, *Symposion*, and Pederasty', in O. Murray (1990*a*) 135–49.

BRENTLINGER, J. (1970), *Plato's Symposium* (Amherst, Mass.).

BRICKHOUSE, T., and SMITH, N. (1994), *Plato's Socrates* (New York).

BRISSON, L. (1999), *Platon*, Banquet (Paris).

BROWN, R. (1987), *Analyzing Love* (Cambridge).

BURKERT, W. (1985), *Greek Religion: Archaic and Classical*, trans. J. Raffan (Oxford).

—— (1987), *Ancient Mystery Cults* (Cambridge, Mass.).

BURNET, J. (1991), *Platonis Opera*, vol. ii (Oxford Classical Texts; Oxford).

BURNYEAT, M. F. (1977), 'Socratic Midwifery, Platonic Inspiration', *Bulletin of the Institute of Classical Studies*, 24: 7–16; repr. in H. H. Benson (ed.), *Essays on the Philosophy of Socrates* (New York, 1992), 53–65.

—— (1986), 'Good Repute', *London Review of Books* (Nov) 8 (19): 11.

—— (1992), 'Gregory Vlastos', *Phronesis*, 137–9.

—— (1999), 'Couches, Song and Civic Tradition', *The Tanner Lectures on Human Values*, 20 (Cambridge, Mass.).

—— (2000), 'Plato on why Mathematics is Good for the Soul', in T. Smiley (ed.), *Mathematics and Necessity: Essays in the History of Philosophy* (Oxford), 1–81.

BURY, R. G. (1932), *The Symposium of Plato* (Cambridge).

BUXTON, R. (1999) (ed.), *From Myth to Reason? Studies in the Development of Greek Thought* (Oxford).

CALAME, C. (1999), *The Poetic of Eros in Ancient Greece* (Princeton).

CARONE, G. R. (2001), '*Akrasia* in the *Republic*: Does Plato Change his Mind?', *Oxford Studies in Ancient Philosophy*, 20: 107–49.

CASTAGNOLI, LUCA, (2001), 'L'elenchos di Agatone: Una rilettura di Platone, Simposio, 199c3–201c9', *Dianoia*, 6: 39–84.

CHEN, L. (1992), *Aquiring Knowledge of the Ideas: A Study of Plato's Methods in the Phaedo, the Symposium and the Central Books of the Republic* (Stuttgart).

CLAY, D. (1975), 'Platonic Studies and the Study of Plato', *Arion*, 2/1: 174–5.

—— (1983), 'The Tragic and Comic Poet of the *Symposium*', in J. P. Anton and A. Preus (eds.), *Essays in Ancient Greek Philosophy* (Albany, NY), ii. 186–203.

COLE, T. (1991), *The Origins of Rhetoric in Ancient Greece* (London).

COOPER, J. (1987), 'Hypothetical Necessity and Natural Teleology', in Gotthelf and Lennox (1987) 243–75.

—— (1999*a*) (ed.), *Reason and Emotion* (Princeton).

—— (1999*b*), 'Plato's Theory of Human Motivation', in Cooper (1999*a*) 118–38.

CORNFORD, F. M. (1950), 'The Doctrine of Eros in Plato's *Symposium*', in *The Unwritten Philosophy and Other Essays* (Cambridge), 68–80; repr. in Vlastos (1971) 119–31.

CROMBIE, I. (1962), *An Examination of Plato's Doctrines*, vol. i (New York).

DAVIDSON, D. (1980), 'How is Weakness of the Will Possible?', in Davidson, *Essays on Action and Events* (Oxford) 21–48

DAY, J. (1994) (ed.) *Plato's Meno in Focus* (London).

DENNISTON, J. D. (1952), *Greek Prose Style* (Oxford).

DICKEY, E. (1996), *Greek Forms of Address from Herodotus to Lucian* (Oxford).

DIELS, H., and KRANZ, W. (1951), *Die Fragmente der Vorsokratiker*, 6th edn. (Berlin).

—— SCHUBERT, W., and HEIBERG, J. L. (1905), *Berliner Klassikertexte*, vol. ii (Berlin).

DILLON, J. (1969), 'Ennead III.5: Plotinus' Exegesis of the *Symposium* Myth', *Agōn*, 3: 24–44.

DIRLMEIER, F. (1935), 'ΘΕΟΦΙΛΙΑ—ΦΙΛΟΘΕΙΑ', *Philologus*, 90: 57–77.

DOVER, K. J. (1966), 'Aristophanes' Speech in Plato's *Symposium*', *Journal of Hellenic Studies*, 66: 41–50.

DOVER, K. J. (1968), *Aristophanes Clouds* (Oxford).

—— (1978), *Greek Homosexuality* (London).

—— (1980), *Plato: Symposium* (Cambridge).

EASTERLING, P. (1997), 'A Show for Dionysus', in Easterling (ed.), *The Cambridge Companion to Greek Tragedy* (Cambridge), 36–54.

EDELSTEIN, L. (1945), 'The Role of Eryximachus in Plato's *Symposium*', *Transactions of the American Philological Association*, 76: 83–103.

FEHR, B. (1990), 'Entertainers at the *Symposion*: The *Akletoi* in the Archaic Period', in O. Murray (1990*a*) 185–96.

FERRARI, G. (1992), 'Platonic Love', in Kraut (1992) 248–77.

FINE, G. (1992), 'Inquiry in the *Meno*', in Kraut (1992) 200–27.

—— (2000), (ed.), *Oxford Readings in Philosophy: Plato* (2 vols.; Oxford).

FISHER, N. R. E. (1992), *Hybris: A Study in the Values of Honour and Shame in Ancient Greece* (Warminster).

FOUCAULT, M. (1985), *The Use of Pleasure: The History of Sexuality*, vol. ii (London).

FREDE, D. (1993), 'Out of the Cave: What Socrates Learnt from Diotima', in R. Rosen and J. Farrell (eds.), *Nomodeiktes: Greek Studies in honor of Martin Ostwald* (Ann Arbor), 397–422.

FREDE, M. (1996), 'The Literary Form of the Sophist', in C. Gill and M. McCabe (eds.), *Form and Argument in Late Plato* (Oxford), 135–51.

GAGARIN, M. (1977), 'Socrates' *Hubris* and Alcibiades' Failure', *Phoenix*, 31: 22–37.

GILL, C. (1990), 'Platonic Love and Individuality', in A. Loizou and H. Lesser (eds.), *Polis and Politics: Essays in Greek Moral and Political Philosophy* (Aldershot), 69–88.

—— (1996), *Personality in Greek Epic, Tragedy and Philosophy* (Oxford).

GOTTHELF, A., and LENNOX, J. G. (1987), (eds.), *Philosophical Issues in Aristotle's Biology* (Cambridge).

GREEN, P. (1979), 'Socrates, Strepsiades and the Abuse of Intellectualism', *Greek Roman and Byzantine Studies*, 20: 15–25.

GRIBBLE, D. (1999), *Alcibiades and Athens* (Oxford).

GRUBE, G. M. A. (1935), *Plato's Thought* (London).

GUTHRIE, W. (1962), *A History of Greek Philosophy* (Cambridge).

—— (1975), *A History of Greek Philosophy*, vol. iv: *Plato, the Man and his Dialogues* (Cambridge).

HACKFORTH, R. (1950), 'Immortality in Plato's *Symposium*', *Classical Review*, 64: 43–5.

HALPERIN, D. (1985), 'Platonic Eros and what Men Call Love', *Ancient Philosophy*, 5: 161–204.

—— (1986), 'Plato and Erotic Reciprocity', *Classical Antiquity*, 5: 60–80.

—— (1990*a*), 'Why is Diotima a Woman? Platonic Eros and the Figuration of Gender', in D. Halperin, J. Winkler, and F. Zeittin (eds.), *Before Sexuality: The Construction of Erotic Experience in the Ancient World* (Princeton), 257–308.

—— (1990*b*), 'Why is Diotima a Woman?', in Halperin (ed.), *One Hundred Years of Homosexuality and Other Essays on Greek Love* (New York), 113–51.

—— (1992), 'Plato and the Erotics of Narrativity', *Oxford Studies in Ancient Philosophy*, suppl. vol., 93–129.

HENDERSON, J. (2000), 'The Life and Soul of the Party: Plato, *Symposium*', in A. Sharrock and H. Morales (eds.), *Intratextuality* (Oxford), 287–325.

HICKS, R. D. (1993), *Aristotle de Anima*, Books I and II (Oxford).

HOBBS, A. (2000), *Plato and the Hero* (Cambridge).

HUNTER, R. (2004), *Plato's Symposium* (Oxford).

HUSSEY, E. (1991), 'Heraclitus on Living and Dying', *Monist* 74: 517–30.

IRWIN, T. (1977), *Plato's Moral Theory* (Oxford).

—— (1985), *Aristotle: Nicomachean Ethics* (Indianapolis).

—— (1995), *Plato's Ethics* (Oxford).

ISENBERG, M. (1940), *The Order of the Discourses in Plato's Symposium* (Chicago).

JANAWAY, C. (1995), *Images of Excellence* (Oxford).

JOWETT, B. (1928), *Plato: The Four Socratic Dialogues* (Oxford).

KAHN, C. (1985), 'The Place of the Prime Mover in Aristotle's Teleology', in A. Gotthelf (ed.), *Aristotle on Nature and Living Things: Philosophical and Historical Studies presented to D. Balme on his Seventieth Birthday* (Pittsburgh and Bristol), 183–207.

KAHN, C. (1987), 'Plato's Theory of Desire', *Review of Metaphysics*, 41: 77–103.

—— (1996), *Plato and the Socratic Dialogue: The Philosophical Use of a Literary Form* (Cambridge).

KENNEDY, A. (1963), *The Art of Persuasion in Greece* (Princeton).

KIDD, I. (1995), 'Some Philosophical Demons', *Bulletin of the Institute of Classical Studies*, 40: 217–24.

KOSMAN, L. A. (1976), 'Platonic Love', in W. H. Werkmeister, *Facets of Plato's Philosophy* (Assen), 53–69.

KRAUT, R. (1973), 'Egoism, Love and Political Office', *Philosophical Review*, 82: 346–9.

—— (1976), 'Aristotle on Choosing Virtue for Itself', *Archiv fur Philosophie*, 58: 223–39.

—— (1992), *The Cambridge Companion to Plato* (Cambridge).

—— (2000), 'Return to the Cave: *Republic* 519–521', in Fine (ed.), *Oxford Readings in Philosophy: Plato* (2 vols.; Oxford) 717–36.

LEAR, J. (1998), *Open Minded: Working out the Logic of the Soul* (Harvard).

LESHER, J. H. (1987), 'Professor Vlastos on Socrates' Disavowal of Knowledge', *Journal of the History of Philosophy*, 25: 275–88.

——, NAILS, D., and SHEFFIELD, F. (2006), *Plato's Symposium: Issues in Interpretation and Reception* (Harvard).

LISSARRAGUE, F. (1990), 'Why Satyrs are Good to Represent', in J. Winkler and F. Zeitlin (eds.), *Nothing to do with Dionysus? Athenian Drama in its Social Context* (Princeton), 228–36.

LLOYD, G. (1966), *Polarity and Analogy* (Cambridge).

—— (1992), 'The *Meno* and the Mysteries of Mathematics', *Phronesis*, 37.

LORENZ, H. (2004), 'Desire and Reason in Plato's *Republic*', *Oxford Studies in Ancient Philosophy*, 27 (Winter).

LOWENSTAM, S. (1985), 'Paradoxes in Plato's *Symposium*', *Ramus*, 14: 85–104.

LUCE, J. V. (1952), 'Immortality in Plato's *Symposium*: A Reply', *Classical Review*, 66: 131–41.

LUDWIG, P. W. (2002), *Eros and Polis* (Cambridge).

McCABE, M. (1988), 'The Virtues of Socratic Ignorance', *Classical Quarterly*, 38: 331–50.

—— (1993), 'Persistent Fallacies', *Proceedings of the Aristotelian Society*, 93: 73–93.

—— (1994), *Plato's Individuals* (Princeton).

MACDOWELL, D. M. (1976), '*Hybris* in Athens', *Greece and Rome*, 23: 14–31.

McPHERRAN, M. (1985), 'Socratic Piety in the *Euthyphro*', *Journal of the History of Philosophy*, 23: 283–309.

MARKUS, R. A. (1971), 'The Dialectic of Eros in Plato's *Symposium*', in Vlastos (1971) 132–43.

MATHEWS, G. (1999), *Socratic Perplexity* (Oxford).

MENN, S. (1995), *Plato on God as Nous* (Journal of the History of Philosophy Monograph Series; Carbondale, Ill.).

MORAVSCIK, J. (1971), 'Reason and Eros in the "Ascent" Passage of the *Symposium*', in J. P. Anton and G. I. Kustas (eds.), *Essays in Ancient Greek Philosophy* (Albany, NY), 285–303.

MORRISON, J. S. (1964), 'Four Notes on Plato's *Symposium*', *Classical Quarterly*, 14: 42–55.

MURRAY, O. (1990*a*) (ed.), *Sympotica: A Symposium on the Symposion* (Oxford).

—— (1990*b*), 'The Affair of the Mysteries: Democracy and the Drinking Group', in Murray (1990*a*) 149–61.

MURRAY, P. (1999), 'What is a *Muthos* for Plato', in Buxton (1999) 251–63.

MYLONAS, G. E. (1961), *Eleusis and the Eleusinian Mysteries* (Princeton).

NAGY, G. (1974), *Comparative Studies in Greek and Indic Meter* (Cambridge, Mass.).

NAKHNIKIAN, G. (1994), 'The First Socratic Paradox', in Day (1994) 129–52.

NEHAMAS, A. (1994), 'Meno's Paradox and Socrates as Teacher', in Day (1994) 221–49.

—— (1998), *The Art of Living* (Princeton).

—— (1999*a*), *The Virtues of Authenticity* (Princeton).

—— (1996*b*), 'What Did Socrates Teach and to Whom Did He Teach It?', in Nehamas (ed.), *The Art of Living* (Princeton) 59–63.

—— (1996*c*), 'Eristic, Antilogic, Sophistic, Dialectic: Plato's Demarcation of Philosophy from Sophistry', in Nehamas (ed.), *The Art of Living* (Princeton) 108–22.

—— (2004), 'Only in the Contemplation of Beauty is Life Worth Living (Plato, *Symposium* 211d)', part of the Gray Lectures, Cambridge (unpub.).

NEHAMAS, A., and WOODRUFF, P. (1989), *Plato: Symposium* (Indianapolis).

NIGHTINGALE, A. W. (1993), 'The Folly of Praise: Plato's Critique of Encomiastic Discourse in the *Lysis* and the *Symposium*', *Classical Quarterly*, 43: 112–30.

—— (1995), *Genres in Dialogue: Plato and the Construct of Philosophy* (Cambridge).

NUSSBAUM, M. (1979), 'The Speech of Alcibiades: A Reading of Plato's *Symposium*', *Philosophy and Literature*, 3: 131–72.

—— (1986), 'The Speech of Alcibiades: A Reading of Plato's *Symposium*', in *The Fragility of Goodness* (Cambridge), 165–95.

NYGREN, A. (1982), *Agape and Eros* (London).

O'BRIEN, M. J. (1984), 'Becoming Immortal in Plato's *Symposium*', in D. Gerber (ed.), *Greek Poetry and Philosophy: Studies in Honor of Leonard Woodbury* (Chico, Calif.), 185–205.

O'CONNOR, D. (forthcoming), 'Rewriting the Poets in Plato's Characters', in G. Ferrari (ed.), *The Cambridge Companion to Plato's* Republic.

OSBORNE, C. (1994), *Eros Unveiled* (Oxford).

OWEN, G. E. L. (1986), 'Tithenai ta Phainomena', in M. Nussbaum (ed.), *Logic, Science and Dialectic: Collected Paper in Greek Philosophy* (1986) 239–52.

PARFIT, D. (1984), *Reasons and Persons* (Oxford).

PATTERSON, R. (1991), 'The Ascent Passage in Plato's *Symposium*', *Proceedings of the Boston Area Colloquim in Ancient Philosophy*, 7: 193–214.

PECK, A. L. (1953), *Aristotle: Generation of Animals* (Cambridge, Mass.).

PELLIZER, E. (1990), 'Outlines of a Morphology of Sympotic Entertainment', in O. Murray (1990a) 177–85.

PENDER, E. (1992), 'Spiritual Pregnancy in Plato's *Symposium*', *Classical Quarterly*, 42: 72–86.

PENNER, T. (1971), 'Thought and Desire in Plato', in Vlastos (1971), 96–119.

—— (1990), 'Plato and Davidson: Parts of the Soul and Weakness of Will', *Canadian Journal of Philosophy* Suppl. vol. 16: 35–74.

PRICE, A. W. (1989 (1997)), *Love and Friendship in Plato and Aristotle* (Oxford); 2nd edn., 1997.

—— (1995), *Mental Conflict* (London).

PRIOR, W. (1998), 'The Priority of Definition', *Phronesis*, 43: 97–113.

—— (2001), 'Eudaimonism and Virtue', *Journal of Value Inquiry*, 35: 325–42.

RABINOWITZ, W. G. (1958), 'Platonic Piety: An Essay towards the Solution of an Enigma', *Phronesis*, 3: 108–20.

REEVE, C. D. C. (1992), 'Telling the truth about love: Plato's Symposium', *Proceedings of the Boston Area Colloquium in Ancient Philosophy*, 8: 89–114.

RICHARDSON, LEAR, G. (2004), *Happy Lives and the Highest Good: An Essay on Aristotle's Nicomachean Ethics* (Princeton).

ROBIN, L. (1929), *Platon: Le Banquet* (Paris).

—— (1933), *Platon: Phèdre* (Paris).

ROBINSON, R. (1953), *Plato's Earlier Dialectic* (Oxford).

ROSEN, S. (1968), *Plato's Symposium* (New Haven).

ROSLER, W. (1990), '*Mnemosyne* in the *Symposion*', in O. Murray (1990a) 230–8.

ROWE, C. J. (1986), *Plato: Phaedrus* (Warminster).

—— (1998a), *Plato: Symposium* (Warminster).

—— (1998b), 'Socrates and Diotima: *Eros*, Creativity and Immortality', *Proceedings of the Boston Area Colloquium in Ancient Philosophy*, 14.

—— (1998c), 'On Plato, Homer and Archaelogy', *Arion* (Winter), 140–52.

—— (1999), 'Myth, History, and Dialectic in Plato's *Republic* and *Timaeus-Critias*', in Buxton (1999) 263–79.

—— (2006), 'The *Symposium* as a Socratic Dialogue', in Lesher, Nails, and Sheffield (eds.), *Plato's Symposium: Issues in Interpretation and Reception* (Harvard).

Scott, D. (1995), *Recollection and Experience* (Cambridge).

—— (2000*a*), 'Socrates and Alcibiades in Plato's *Symposium*', *Hermathena*, 168 (Summer).

—— (2000*b*), 'Aristotle on Posthumous Fortune', *Oxford Studies in Ancient Philosophy*, 18 (Summer).

—— (2006), *Plato's* Meno (Cambridge).

Seaford, R. (1984), *Euripides: Cyclops* (Oxford).

Sedley, D. (1982), 'The Stoic Criterion of Identity', *Phronesis*, 27: 255–76.

—— (1999), 'The Ideal of Godlikeness', in Fine (1999) 309–28.

Sheffield, F. (2001*a*), 'Psychic Pregnancy and Platonic Epistemology', *Oxford Studies in Ancient Philosophy*, 20: 1–35.

—— (2001*b*), 'Alcibiades' Speech: A Satyric Drama', *Greece and Rome*, 48: 193–209.

—— 'The Role of Earlier Speeches in Plato's *Symposium*: Plato's Endoxic Method?', in Lesher, Nails, and Sheffield (eds.), *Plato's Symposium: Issues in Interpretation and Reception* (Harvard).

Shorey, P. (1933), *What Plato Said* (Chicago).

Sier, D. (1997), *Die Rede der Diotima: Untersuchungen zum platonischen Symposion* (Stuttgart).

Slater, W. J. (1991), (ed.), *Dining in a Classical Context* (Ann Arbor).

Sorabji, R. (1993), *Animal Minds, Human Morals* (London).

Stehle, E. (1997), *Performance and Gender in Ancient Greece* (Princeton).

Stokes, M. (1986), *Plato's Socratic Conversations* (London).

Sutton, D. (1980), *The Greek Satyr Play* (Meisenheim am Glan).

Taylor, A. E. (1908), *Plato* (London).

—— (1926), *Plato: The Man and his Works* (London).

Tecusan, M. (1990), '*Logos sympotikos*, Patterns of the Irrational in Philosophical Drinking', in O. Murray (1990*a*) 238–63.

Thornton, B. (1997), *Eros: The Myth of Ancient Greek Sexuality* (Colorado).

Vander Waerdt, P. A. (1994), 'Socrates in the Clouds', in Vander Waerdt (ed.), *The Socratic Movement* (Cornell), 48–87.

Vermeule, E. (1979), *Aspects of Death in Early Greek Art and Poetry* (Berkeley).

Vickers, M. (1990), 'Attic *Symposia* after the Persian Wars', in O. Murray (1990*a*) 105–22.

Vlastos, G. (1962), 'Justice and Equality', in R. B. Brandt (ed.), *Social Justice* (Englewood Cliffs)

—— (1971) (ed.), *Plato, Volume ii: Ethics, Politics and Philosophy of Art and Religion; A Collection of Critical Essays edited by Gregory Vlastos* (New York).

VLASTOS, G. (1981), 'The Individual as an Object of Love', in Vlastos (ed.), *Platonic Studies* (Princeton), 1–34.

—— (1983), 'The Socratic Elenchus', *Oxford Studies in Ancient Philosophy*, 1: 27–58.

—— (1985), 'Socrates' Disavowal of Knowledge', *Philosophical Quarterly*, 35: 1–31.

—— (1991*a*), 'Socratic Piety', in Vlastos (ed.), *Socrates: Ironist and Moral Philosopher* (Cambridge) 157–79.

—— (1991*b*), 'Elenchus and Mathematics', in Vlastos (1991*a*) 107–32.

—— (1994), *Socratic Studies*, ed. M. F. Burnyeat (Cambridge).

WARDY, R. (2002), 'The Unity of Opposites in Plato's *Symposium*', *Oxford Studies in Ancient Philosophy* 23 (Winter).

WARNER, M. (1979), 'Love, Self and Plato's *Symposium*', *Philosophical Quarterly*, 29: 329–39.

WATERFIELD, R. (1994), *Plato: The Symposium* (Oxford).

WHITE, F. C. (2004), 'Virtue in Plato's *Symposium*', *Classical Quarterly*, 54: 366–78.

WHITE, F. C. (1989), 'Love and Beauty in Plato's *Symposium*', *Journal of Hellenic Studies*, 109: 149–58.

WIGGINS, D. (1982), 'Heraclitus' Conceptions of Fire, Flux and Material Persistence', in M. Schofield and M. Nussbaum (eds.), *Language and Logos: Studies in Ancient Greek Philosophy presented to G. E. Owen* (Cambridge), 1–33.

WILLET, R. F. (1970), 'Blind Wealth and Aristophanes', an inaugural lecture (Birmingham).

WILLIAMS, B. (1998), *Plato* (Great Philosophers Series; London).

WILSON, P. (1999), 'The *Aulos* in Athens', in R. Osborne and S. Goldhill (eds.), *Performance Culture and Athenian Democracy* (Cambridge), 58–95.

WOHL, V. (1999), 'The Eros of Alcibiades', *Classical Antiquity*, 18/2: 349–85.

WOODFIELD, A. (1976), *Teleology* (Cambridge).

WOODRUFF, P. (1982), *Plato: Hippias Major* (Oxford).

ZANKER, P. (1995), *The Mask of Socrates: The Image of the Intellectual in Antiquity* (Berkeley).

General Index

Index of Passages